FUGITIVE POSES

The Abraham Lincoln Lecture Series

This series aims to reflect the principles
that Abraham Lincoln championed:
education, justice, tolerance,
and union.

GERALD VIZENOR

Fugitive Poses

Native American Indian Scenes
of Absence and Presence

University of Nebraska Press

Lincoln and London

♾ The paper in this book meets the minimum
requirements of American National Standard for
Information Sciences – Permanence of Paper
for Printed Library Materials, ANSI z39.48-1984.

The lectures based on this book were sponsored by
the University of Nebraska Press, the Native
American Studies program, the Center for
Great Plains Studies, the College of Arts and
Sciences, the Athletic Department, and
the Department of Anthropology at
the University of Nebraska–Lincoln.

Library of Congress Cataloging in Publication Data
Vizenor, Gerald Robert, 1934–
Fugitive poses : Native American Indian scenes of
absence and presence / Gerald Vizenor.
p. cm.
Includes bibliographical references and index.
ISBN 0-8032-4664-1 (alkaline paper)
1. American literature – Indian authors –
History and criticism. 2. Indians in
literature. I. Title.
PS153.I52V59 1998 810.9'897–dc21
97-18262 CIP

If one were only an Indian, instantly alert, and on a racing horse, leaning against the wind, kept on quivering jerkily over the quivering ground, until one shed one's spurs, for there needed no spurs, threw away the reins, for there needed no reins, and hardly saw that the land before one was smoothly shorn heath when horse's neck and head would be already gone.

FRANZ KAFKA, "The Wish to Be a Red Indian"

If I do not deny my origins, it is because it is ultimately better to be nothing at all than a pretense of something.

E. M. CIORAN, *The Trouble with Being Born*

The written page is no mirror. To write means to confront an unknown face. . . . The book closes always on a lost face.

EDMOND JABÈS, *The Little Book of Unsuspected Subversion*

A society requires antecedents. Where these are not naturally at hand, where a community is new or reassembled after a long interval of dispersal or subjection, a necessary past tense to the grammar of being is created by intellectual and emotional fiat.

GEORGE STEINER, *In Bluebeard's Castle*

In general, the writer seems to be subjected to a state of inactivity because he is the master of the imaginary, and those who follow him into the realm of the imaginary lose sight of the problems of their true lives. But the danger he represents is much more serious. The truth is that he ruins action, not because he deals with what is unreal but because he makes *all* of reality available to us. Unreality begins with the whole.

MAURICE BLANCHOT, *The Work of Fire*

Clarity and concision hamper the storyteller, for he makes his living from unpredictable leaps of transformation and an inexhaustible supply of breath.

ELIAS CANETTI, *The Agony of Flies*

Mammadaty was my grandfather, whom I never knew. Yet he came to be imagined posthumously in the going on of the blood, having invested the shadow of his presence in an object or a word, in his name above all. He enters into my dreams; he persists in his name.

N. SCOTT MOMADAY, *The Names*

CONTENTS

FUGITIVE POSES

Tragic Wisdom

Native American Indians are the storiers of presence, the chroniclers in the histories of this continent. There are no other secure stories that tease the creation of a native presence, that actuate the sovenance and totemic observance of nature. Native stories are the traces of natural reason, not the spoils of surveillance. Native stories are communicative, autonomous creations, and the traces of a "second nature" in these essays of *Fugitive Poses.*

The Chinese Monkey King, and the stories of the *anishinaabe* trickster *naanabozho*, are evocations on the presence, conversions, and censure of natives; these stories are an introduction to five essays on academic surveillance, simulations, resistance, natural reason, survivance, and the *transmotion* of native sovereignty.[1]

The People's Republic of China convenes an elusive tolerance of the "educative function" in creative narratives; likewise, the insincere, and moralistic versions of native stories in translation might be tolerated, but *naanabozho*, the carnal, raucous, priapean *holosexual* trickster in *anishinaabe* stories, would never survive communistic censure.

The Chinese Monkey King, in *The Journey to the West*, is the cousin of *naanabozho*, the native trickster; the natural stories of their provenance are stone, water, and survivance. The mind monkey and native trickster are the clever teasers of creation, totemic conversion, and even their own continuance in literature.[2]

The Monkey King stories have outlasted colonial treasons, the warlords, many missions, reversions, revolutions, and communistic censure. The oral stories of *naanabozho*, the tricky cousin in the east, were expurgated as educative moral lessons in the translations of missionaries; moreover, these stories, once liberative, were abated as mimetic evidence in social science studies. The causal

1

translations of these stories cocked the arcane trickster to be a heroic enactment and a tragic representation of native culture, rather than a creature of creative and liberative stories, a mind trickster.

The Monkey King is performative literature, in the sense that the action is created, and the conversion is a tease, but not mimetic, or heroic, or a representation of the real world. Chinese drama is the "*expression* of emotion and thought, rather than *representation* or *imitation* of life," observes James J. Y. Liu in *Essentials of Chinese Literary Art*. "In other words, it does not seek to create an illusion of reality, but rather seeks to express human experience in terms of imaginary characters and situations. Chinese dramatists do not attempt to disguise the fact that what is being presented is not reality but only a play, but, paradoxically, the frank admission that the play is *not* real often underlines, rather than destroys, its basic affinity with reality."[3]

The Monkey King might have been the native trickster in this literary critique. Clearly, *naanabozho* is a creation, not the case or cause of documents or histories. The mind monkey and trickster stories are liberative; the cousins of the stone were never mimetic, representations of the real, or the tragic notions of closure; rather, the stories tease creation, the seasons, and survivance.

The Chinese Cultural Revolution caused the "relentless persecution of most of the prominent writers of the previous decades," notes Bonnie McDougall in *Popular Chinese Literature and Performing Arts in the People's Republic of China*. Later, in response to the new sense of tragedy in a socialist culture, "scar literature" was published. "The systematic destruction of an existing culture, even if undertaken to clear the way for the growth of a new one, is perhaps always a new loss for the whole of humanity." The Communist Party removed some writers, recruited others, and at the same time created scapegoats; in this way, "the fear of public attack and punishment has proved a very effective control device."[4]

Merle Goldman concludes in *Literary Dissent in Communist China* that, in spite of the Cultural Revolution and the persecution of revolutionary writers, the "struggle will persist. One day it may be shown that China's writers, under overwhelming pressures, kept alive a sense of freedom and an appreciation for human and artistic values. In the West, where writers have been free to say what they please, composing a poem or writing a literary criticism is not a rebellious act, but in Communist China it can be an act of courage and fortitude."[5]

For instance, Feng Jicai, an artist and author, "began secretly to write fiction during the Cultural Revolution," writes Susan Wilf Chen in the introduction to *Chrysanthemums and Other Stories*. Feng "recalls that it was the 'intensity of the horror' of the Cultural Revolution that moved him to begin to write. He made a conscious decision to try to re-create the experience in fiction for his descendants. He believes that 'in a sense catastrophe is fortunate for a writer of fiction,' because it provides inspiration and reveals the inner thoughts of all kinds of people who would normally remain a mystery."

Feng mentions a "place by the Hai River in Tianjin called Guajiasi, where a few swimmers drown every summer; their bodies are fished out and laid on the banks until their relatives come to claim them. But during the Cultural Revolution people committed suicide there practically every day; they were dragged out of the river with grappling hooks and laid out in rows on the banks." Some of the women had "drowned themselves with their babies strapped to their waists."

Yang Hansheng, then vice chairman of the China Federation of Literary and Art Circles, declared that "our literary and art workers should adhere to the slogan of literature and art in the service of the people and of socialism," but he observed that "some writers and artists have shown themselves apathetic by their manifest lack of interest in writing about revolutionary history," and "by their fondness for love stories and the fabrication of bizarre, preposterous plots; or by concentrating on depressing, negative things."[6]

Griever: An American Monkey King in China, my second novel, was published a few years after the notice by cadre Yang Hansheng. Griever de Hocus, the native trickster and mind monkey, is a teacher at Zhou Enlai University.

Tianjin is partitioned in memories of lost relatives, colonial concessions, shadow capitalism, and painted faces from classical operas.

Griever considered the old street names on colonial maps, Marechal Foch, Saint Louis, Gaston Kahn, and then located the cathedral where the Lazarist Sisters of Saint Vincent de Paul had opened an orphanage.

John Hersey wrote that in their eagerness to win souls the sisters

3

paid "a cash premium for each child brought in to them; and, what was worse, they were said to have paid to have sick and dying children carried to them, so they could baptize them in articulo mortis. In 1870, rumors were circulated that after conducting their mystic rites the nuns extracted the babies' eyes and hearts for purposes of witchery. Four men were arrested and beheaded. One man, under torture, confessed that he stole children and sold them to the verger of the cathedral."

"The city went wild," wrote Hersey, who was born in Tianjin, the son of missionaries. "The mob stripped the sisters naked, one by one, and in full sight of the surviving nuns ripped their bodies open, cut their breasts off, gouged their eyes out, and, finally, impaled them on long spears, hoisted them in the air, and threw them into the burning chapel of the orphanage."[7]

The Tianjin University library had received a literary favor, an extensive collection of several thousand novels, short stories, and other publications in English by American authors. The books were shelved in a security area, and neither the authors nor the titles were listed in the card catalog. My students were curious, but they had been warned, and were wise not to enter that secured area of the library.[8]

I had been invited as a visiting professor to teach the same language and literature that was otherwise proscribed at the library; so, to evade the obvious contradictions, the university administration executed an elaborate procedure of providing daily photocopies of a few pages of a novel for each student in my class, the actual number of pages my students could read in one class session. Obviously, in this way, the censors were prepared to monitor every word on each page.

The only photocopier was located in an interior room behind three locked doors. Daily, two university cadre carried out the cause of that secured copier in routine silence; one cadre unlocked each door, click, click, click, and then the other loaded the machine. Many days that fall semester my students waited in an unheated classroom for the late arrival of a few *warm* pages of *The Red Pony* by John Steinbeck.

These students were natives of institutive communism, at the crease of two revolutions: the ruins of ancient traditions and the salvation of electronic machines. They were eager and, generous with their humor, teased the words—but never the nation—and read out loud the hue of emotion in another culture, the liberative action of the novel; there, the transmotion of survivance seemed to pass over the contradictions of a proscriptive education in the People's Republic of China.

"Chance was in the garden" is the second sentence of *Being There* by Jerzy Kosinski. Pages of that novel, the next on our list, were delivered warm, a few pages at a time, day by day. Chance, the name of the trickster character, was born in a mansion, the son of servants, and as his presence was not documented, he had no civil history. Naturally, he learned to be a gardener and was socialized by television. Chance assumed the name Chauncey Gardiner.

The President of the United States once visited the mansion and was not aware that the man he asked about the "bad season" of the stock market was a mere servant. Chance told the visitor that there are seasons in a garden. "There are spring and summer, but there are also fall and winter. And then spring and summer again. As long as the roots are not severed, all is well and all will be well." The President thought his market metaphors were "refreshing and optimistic." Yes, and like "nature, our economic system remains, in the long run, stable and rational, and that's why we must not fear to be at its mercy." Surely, these cozy garden metaphors of capitalism would not be expurgated by the censors.

Chance was naive, and so was my chance as a teacher in the People's Republic of China. Daily pages of the novel continued to be delivered, and then one morning we were told that the photocopier was broken. The cadre would not estimate how long it might take to repair the machine. Copier parts, so we reasoned, must be ordered from a great distance. Later that week, however, the cadre made copies of several documents for a senior administrator. The contradiction, of course, was carried out with manners and cultural silence. We were never told that the censor and thus the photocopier could not get past page ninety of *Being There*.

Chance, who had no political history, was considered the perfect candidate for the vice presidency. The trickster was hounded by the media, politicians, and spies, but there were no documents in his name. Chance, who had learned the manners of the mansion, carried on conversations with measured metaphors of the garden. He was cautious, but not suspicious of others. Seductively, a man with silky gray hair gestured to the naive candidate at a diplomatic event. Then the "man gazed into Chance's eyes and impatiently slid his hand under Chance's arm. With his surprisingly strong forearm he pressed Chance to him. 'It's time for us,' he whispered. 'Let's go upstairs.'" The man "kissed his neck and cheeks, then sniffed and mussed his hair. Chance wondered what he had said or done to prompt such affection." He could not remember any similar scene on television. Then, a few pages later the novel is more carnal and erotic. Chance could not understand why the man had removed his clothes; the man reached out and "without a word raised and pressed the sole of Chance's shoe against his hardened organ."[9]

The photocopier was declared "broken" on the words "hardened organ." That was the end of the warm pages delivered daily to the classroom. So, to elude the censors that semester, my students read short stories that had been published by the Foreign Languages Press in Beijing, the imprimatur of the People's Republic of China. The Chinese authors wrote with great courage, and some of the stories in that anthology were revolutionary; insinuations of a *wounded* literature that were not the educative cause of communistic histories. Chance, the metaphorist of the garden, and the creative tease of these stories in translation were elusory.

BEARHEART COVENANT

Saint Louis Bearheart warns readers: "The bear is in me now. Not since the darkness at the federal boarding school and the writing of this book, the heirship chronicles on the wicked road to the fourth world, has the blood and deep voice of the bear moved in me with such power. Listen, ha ha ha haaaa."

"To read *Bearheart* is to take risks, for no preconceived notion of identity is safe, no dearly held belief inviolable," observes Louis Owens, the novelist, in his afterword to *Bearheart: The Heirship Chronicles.*[10]

Richard Nixon announced his resignation of the presidency that summer, at the very first sentences of my novel, then titled "Cedarfair Circus." Patricia Hearst was indicted that same summer in connection with the robbery of a San Francisco bank. Hearst, who was associated with her abductors, the Symbionese Liberation Army, was convicted two years later. Jimmy Carter was a presidential candidate; Paul Robeson died in Philadelphia; Saul Bellow was awarded the Nobel Prize in literature, and my first novel was with an agent in New York City.

Introduction

The literary agent reported that two copies of the manuscript were lost by publishers. My editor at the *Minneapolis Tribune* sent the novel to one of his associates, a major publisher, and that, the third copy of my manuscript, was lost by association. David Wilk, owner of Truck Press, published *Darkness in Saint Louis Bearheart* two years later. The first typesetters of the original manuscript refused to continue after a few chapters because, in their view, the novel was "too obscene and violent."[11]

My first public discussion of the novel was not by invitation; rather, it was a serious obligation to a friend, who had assigned the book in a literature course at a community college. The students were furious with their instructor and with me, the author of a trickster novel. The students were the new censors, and they read novels as representations of the real; however, in this instance, the native *real* was an *indian* simulation, a fugitive pose that my novel evaded and deconstructed. My first response to the students that morning was a rhetorical question: show me the real violence in trickster stories, and is there anything in *Bearheart* that is not true, that you have not already paid good money to see as entertainment in movie theaters, that you have not already seen on television or read in newspapers?

Bears masturbate, but humans are the censors of that common, totemic pleasure in stories. The bear is a native totem, the trace of creation, sovenance, and stories; a creative expression, not the mere representations of the real. Bears are hunted to extinction, and that is a real act of violence. Stories of bears are heroic ventures; humans are the perpetrators of violence, the creators of aesthetic tragedy, an imitation of horror, torture, and pain as passive entertainment. The humans, never the bears, are the demonic storiers of this perverse, chemical civilization, and, at the same time, humans are the censors of totemic bears. Storiers might evade the real but never the pieties of censors. How could trickster stories represent more violence than the real furies of terminal creeds, more savagery and persecution than the historical documents of modernism and civilization?

Chinese cuisine once featured bear paw and other curious tastes as status meals on special occasions.[12] The bear on the menu is a document of devastation, and not a connection to totemic bears in trickster stories. The cuisine bear is manneristic, not totemic, not a human on the menu; the human as the bear is totemic, the bear as the erotic human might be censured as literature.

Saint Louis Bearheart, the old man and author of the novel, has worked in the heirship division of the Bureau of Indian Affairs. There, he entered the names of dead natives, the official heirs to the land of treaties. The records were secure, but the land could not be inherited because it was held in trust by the Secretary of the Interior. Bearheart entered the names and wrote a novel at the same time. *The darkness moves in ursine shivers, moves in the muw.*

> *Where did you come from old man?*
> *Listen ha ha ha haaaa.*
> *You got nuts ideas about skins, she says.*
> *Trickster liberation, says the bear.*
> *Weird skins, man.*
> *Bears see memories, not our bodies.*
> *Whose speech are you in now?*
> *Mouth on the bear.*
> *She moans and shudders.*
> *Bearheart, ha ha ha haaaa.*
> *What is your book about?*
> *Sex and violence.*
> *Show me the hairship documents.*

Bearheart: The Heirship Chronicles, the new edition, was published twelve years later. Terry Cochran, then a senior editor at the University of Minnesota Press, reported that the contract printer protested the content of my novel and refused to continue production of the new edition. The company lost several other contracts because of that decision; the righteous cause to censor seemed to be more important than economic incentives in the case of the trickster novel *Bearheart*. The manners of censors are terminal creeds.[13]

"To teach *Bearheart* is even more dangerous, as I discovered several years ago when I learned that three students in my American Indian fiction course had reported me to the dean," noted Owens. "The three students, all mixedblood women raised in southern California, had known how to respond to the familiar tragedies of Indians," but "*Bearheart*, with its wild humor, upset them. Not only was there sexual violence in the novel, but even transsexual Indians. Indians in the novel were capable of cowardice as well as courage, of greed and lust as well as generosity and stoicism." *Bearheart* "is a trickster narrative, a postapocalyptic allegory of mixedblood pilgrim clowns afoot in a world gone predictably mad."[14]

8

Introduction

The Comparative Ethnic Studies Department at the University of California, Berkeley, mounted a new locked display case on the wall outside the main office to promote the faculty and their recent publications. The case is decorated with academic praises, and the faculty is pictured with copies of book jackets. For a few months there was a picture of me and the cover of *Shadow Distance: A Gerald Vizenor Reader*.[15]

Elaine Kim, chair of the department, ordered the removal of the book cover from the display case because, she told a reporter for the *Daily Californian*, "I feel an obligation to the women of this department who are always subjected to sexual harassment in the media. I too am sick of naked ladies—and men too, for that matter—in the media."

The cover of *Shadow Distance* is a color reproduction of an original painting by German artist Dirk Görtler. The expressionistic montage of totemic and trickster scenes from *Bearheart*, pictures, on the right, a portrait of the author and a Conoco truck stop sign in front of a bear. An androgynous nude trickster figure faces the bear; the omega letter is painted on the back of the trickster. The word *muralts*, a neologism, mounted on the truck stop sign over the head of the trickster, and omega, the end, are ironic, not erotic. A mongrel waits between the bear and the author, and at the bottom of the montage, the back of an automobile is pictured with the name "Cherokee Chief." These, and other obvious expressionistic ironies in the cover art, were censured by anonymous accusers.

Elaine Kim ordered the removal of a work of art, an act of oppressive manners; she seemed, at the time, not to have an ethical sense of responsibility as a university professor to discuss and honor the ordinary rights of a constitutional democracy. Once more, the ethnic censors and gender saviors became the dictators of manners and artistic taste. "I know what the nude figure is supposed to be," Kim told the reporter. "But for all intents and purposes, this looks like a woman."

No anatomical orifices, pubic hair, or sexual protuberances are pictured on the *back* of the omega trickster; the censorious notice was political not visual. The concern must return to the students who created the perversions on the back of an androgynous trickster figure. Dirk Görtler is an artist, not a documentarian; he is a visionary. The conversions pictured on the cover are ironic, not representation of the real; the censors must twist

9

creative expression to cause their own aesthetic simulations of victimry.

Kim announced in the *Daily Californian* that the content of the display case, the photographs of the faculty, and book covers, was a "party decoration," and "if people don't like the decorations, I will take it down. It's not even his expression. I decided to put the case up."[16]

The censors are erratic, the pieties twisted, and the educative perversions of narcissism are extreme, but some censorious actions are overturned with ironic humor in a constitutional democracy. The *censures* are institutive dominance, and that concomitance, ethnic or not, must be bared at universities.

Missionaries and social scientists have been the masters of moralistic and causal translations of trickster stories for more than a century. The Tianjin University censors were in absolute control of the library and photocopier. Elaine Kim maintained a fatuous but feudalistic control over the "decoration" of a faculty display case in a public space at the University of California.

AESTHETIC VINDICATION

Thomas Jefferson advised more favor to *indians* than to blacks and, at the same time, he denounced slavery. The active discourse that trained the rights and answerability of the new constitutional democracy were obvious in his service but not in his notions on race, reason, and countenance. "If we are made in some degree for others, yet in a greater are we made for ourselves," he wrote to James Monroe in 1782. He was determined to retire after "thirteen years engaged in public service." Three years later, however, he served as minister to France, then secretary of state, and the third President of the United States. "It were contrary to feeling & indeed ridiculous to suppose that a man had less right in himself than one of his neighbors or indeed all of them put together. This would be slavery & not that liberty which the bill of rights has made inviolable and for the preservation of which our government has been charged." His notice was wise, but at the time, and in the course of his private concerns, he undervalued the inviolable rights of blacks and *indians*; the *other* was a separation, a disunion of reason.

Five years later, not entirely pleased with the proposed constitution, he furthered a bill of rights. "First the omission of a bill of rights providing clearly & without the aid of sophisms for freedom of religion, freedom of the press, protection against standing armies, restriction against monopolies, the eternal & unremitting force of the habeas corpus laws, and trials by jury in all matters of fact triable by the laws of the land & not by the law of nations," he wrote to James Madison in 1787.[17]

Jefferson created a presence of natives, a representation that was not common in narratives; in earlier journals the *indian* was an absence in histories. That absence has become a theme of romantic tragedy. Many natives have turned that absence into a fugitive pose.

Jefferson observed in *Notes on the State of Virginia* that blacks "have less hair on the face and body. They secrete less by the kidnies, and more by the glands of the skin, which gives them a very strong and disagreeable odour." He used these racialist notions to construe that black "griefs are transient," that "their existence appears to participate more of sensation than reflection," and, comparing "them by their faculties of memory, reason, and imagination, it appears to me, that in memory they are equal to the whites; in reason much inferior." He would, however, advance a contentious proposition to emancipate slaves.

"Some have been liberally educated, and all have lived in countries where the arts and sciences are cultivated to a considerable degree, and have had before their eyes samples of the best works from abroad," asserted Jefferson. "The Indians, with no advantages of this kind, will often carve figures on their pipes not destitute of design and merit. They will crayon out an animal, a plant, or a country, so as to prove the existence of a germ in their minds which only wants cultivation. They astonish you with strokes of the most sublime oratory; such as prove their reason and sentiment strong, their imagination glowing and elevated. But never yet could I find that a black had uttered a thought above the level of plain narration; never see even an elementary trait of painting or sculpture."

Jefferson was not certain that the racial notions he described, and contradistinctions he concocted, would ever be assuaged by notice, reason, or legislation. "Deep rooted prejudices entertained by the whites; ten thousand recollections, by the blacks, of the injuries they have sustained; new provocations; the real distinctions which nature has made; and many other circumstances, will divide us into parties, and produce convulsions which will probably never end but in the extermination of the one or the other race."[18]

Jefferson denounced "slavery on almost every ground, from moral issues to practical economics," notes I. B. Cohen in *Science and the Founding Fathers*. Jefferson was a scientist, and his notions of race were based, for the most part, on the discernible differences between whites, *indians*, and blacks; however, he was not persuaded that countenance or race was an excuse of slavery. Clearly, his redoubtable renunciations of slavery were not moved by a romantic expectation of racial harmony.

Cohen points out that Jefferson's comparative praise of *indians* and "disparagement of the abilities" of blacks in *Notes on the State of Virginia* has puzzled many historians. "Jefferson's 'vindication of the American Indian' has been described by Merrill Peterson as a 'vindication of the American environment.' Jefferson could not similarly envisage 'a natural place in that environment' for African-Americans and so 'his solution for them was not amalgamation but expulsion.' "[19]

Jefferson created a presence of natives; that, however, was not an obvious vindication. Natives were represented in narratives, and in the comparative notions of race, but not in the foundational sense of the nation. The reasons of vindication were aesthetic; natives were named in connection with the vast distances of an unexploited nation, and as a potential threat to the government. Natives, not slaves, had negotiated treaties and formed alliances with other governments; these associations were considered to be dangerous to the new constitutional democracy. Natives, in other words, were removed as a vindication of the environment. The *absence* of the *indian* in the histories of this nation is an aesthetic victimry.

RELUCTANT TOURIST

Ernesto Che Guevara observed as a tourist in Caracas that discrimination and poverty unite blacks and Portuguese "in a daily battle for survival but their different attitudes of life separate them completely: the black is indolent and fanciful, he spends his money on frivolity and drink; the European comes from a tradition of working and saving which follows him to this corner of America and drives him to get ahead."

Che wrote *The Motorcycle Diaries* more than a century after Thomas Jefferson commented on blacks in *Notes on the State*

Introduction

of Virginia. These two authors seemed to avow much the same notions on countenance and race, but not on an *indian* presence. Che noted that the "blacks, those magnificent examples of the African race who have conserved their racial purity by a lack of affinity with washing, have seen their patch invaded by a different kind of slave: the Portuguese. And the two ancient races now share a common experience, fraught with bickering and squabbling." Che created his travel narratives in Argentina, Chile, Peru, Colombia, and at last in Caracas.

Cuzco is evocative, an "impalpable dust of other ages covers its streets, rising in clouds like a muddy lake when you disturb the bottom," a ceremonial city two or three distinct evocations.

Cuzco, "navel of the world," once a native empire, now that "plaintive voice is heard in the fortress destroyed by the stupidity of illiterate Spanish *conquistadores*, in the violated, ruined temples, in the looted palaces, in the brutalized indians. This Cuzco invites you to turn warrior and club in hand, defend freedom and the life of the Inca."

Cuzco, the "gentle harmony broken by the cupola of a baroque church," the "narrow streets," the "native people in their traditional costumes," and the colors. "This Cuzco invites you to become a reluctant tourist, to glance at things superficially and enjoy yourself under the beauty of a leaden wintry sky."

Cuzco is the evocation of another city, vibrant, and a "witness to the formidable courage of the soldiers who conquered this region in the name of Spain, expressed in their monuments, the museums and libraries, in the decoration of its churches and in the distinctive features of the white leaders who still take pride in the Conquest." The monuments of colonial dominance.

"This Cuzco invites you to don armour and, astride a sturdy powerful steed, cleave a path through the defenceless flesh of a flock of naked indians whose human wall crumbles and falls under the four hooves of the galloping beast," wrote Che Guevara.

Che's Personal Archive, the transcription of his travel diaries, was edited by Aleida March de la Torre, the second wife of the author. *The Motorcycle Diaries* are expressionistic, touristic commentaries, and histories on time, place, people, and cultures in Argentina, Chile, Peru, and Colombia.

Che missed at least two other evocations of that ancient native city. Cuzco, the stories of the natives, and natural reason; that sense of nature, and the presence of the seasons. These are not the *indian* but native evocations and connotations of survivance. Natives and their stories actuate a presence, not an absence. The *indians* in the many diaries of reluctant tourists are simulations, and the seasons are aesthetic.

The *indians* are the romantic absence of natives; and the name "indian" is printed lowercase in his travel diaries. He mentioned that the "indians no longer worked the barren earth," and a museum was created "by a scholar of pure indian blood." Near the river, he noted, to "find savage tribes you have to follow the tributaries deep into the interior."[20]

NATIVE CONNOTATIONS

Racial and cultural names, nouns, and capitalization are never decided in dictionaries. The various meanings of words change, of course, and lexicographers must consider the current usage in new editions of dictionaries. For instance, in the "United States in the 1920s, a parallel protest movement, aimed at the compulsory capitalization of the initial letter of the word *Negro* and the abandonment, except among black inhabitants of the United States, of the world *nigger*," observes Robert Burchfield in *Unlocking the English Language*. Dictionaries "were among the main targets, and here, too, the lexicographers replied that if writers, including the editors of newspapers, used a capital initial for *Negro*, they would themselves be happy to include this form in their dictionaries."[21]

Newspaper editors were slow to consider the capitalization of the initial letter of the word *Native* in Native American. My stories as a journalist for the *Minneapolis Tribune* continued the use of the word *Indian*, and at times *Native American*, but the style changed sooner than at many other newspapers. The *Indian* is a simulation and loan word of dominance; the *indian* is an ironic crease.

The ironic use of the noun *indian* lowercase and in italics is so controversial that lexicographers might consider it in subsequent editions of dictionaries. *The New Shorter Oxford English Dictionary* includes the word *Indian* with five references to the meaning: the first is a "native or inhabitant of the subcontinent of India"; the second is a "member of any of the aboriginal peoples of America." Other meanings include the "language spoken by any American Indian people" and an "indigenous inhabitant of the Philippines."

14

More than thirty special collocations are listed, such as *Indian ink,*
Indian tobacco, Indian path, and *Indian giver.*

The simulation of the *indian,* lowercase and in italics, is an
ironic name in *Fugitive Poses.* The Indian with an initial capital is
a commemoration of an absence — evermore that double absence
of simulations by name and stories. My first use of the italicized
indian as a simulation was in *The Everlasting Sky.* The natives
in that book were the *oshki anishinaabe,* or the new people.[22]
Since then, natives are the presence, and *indians* are simulations,
a derivative noun that means an absence, in my narratives.

My vocabulary in these five essays includes several new and con-
notative words; these new words, *transmotion, varionative, pene-*
native, postindian, and *interimage,* are derivative. Other words,
listed in historical dictionaries, such as *indian, sovenance,* and *sur-*
vivance, are used with new connotations. For instance, survivance,
in the sense of native survivance, is more than survival, more than
endurance or mere response; the stories of survivance are an active
presence.

The *indian* has no native ancestors; the original crease of that
simulation is Columbian. The native stories of survivance are
successive and natural estates; survivance is an active repudiation
of dominance, tragedy, and victimry.

The *indian* is a simulation, the absence of natives; the *indian*
transposes the real, and the simulation of the real has no referent,
memories, or native stories. The *postindian* must waver over the
aesthetic ruins of *indian* simulations.

The *varionative* is an uncertain curve of native antecedence;
obscure notions of native sovenance and presence. The *varionative*
traces of ancestors are scriptural, episodic, and ironic in narratives.
The *penenative* is the *autoposer,* the autobiographical poseur, or
the almost native by associations and institutive connections.

Native *sovenance* is that sense of presence in remembrance, that
trace of creation and natural reason in native stories; once an
obscure noun, the connotation of sovenance is a native presence
in these essays, not the romance of an aesthetic absence or victimry.

The connotations of transmotion are creation stories, totemic
visions, reincarnation, and sovenance; transmotion, that sense of
native motion and an active presence, is *sui generis* sovereignty.
Native transmotion is survivance, a reciprocal use of nature, not a
monotheistic, territorial sovereignty. Native stories of survivance
are the creases of transmotion and sovereignty.

The simulations of the *indian*, as the absence of natives, are the documents of discoveries, cultural studies, and surveillance. Native transmotion and sovereignty are complementary, not possessory.

The *anishinaabe* word *manidooke* means, in translation, to "have spiritual power" and to "conduct a ceremony." The word is entered as an "animate intransitive verb" in *A Concise Dictionary of Minnesota Ojibwe*. The head word *manidoo*, or *manitou* in earlier dictionaries, means "god," and "spirit," a native sense of creation in translation.[23] The wider sense of the word is spiritual motion, or transmotion, an active spiritual presence that is not determined by a direct object.

Bishop Baraga, more than a century earlier, entered the same word in his *Dictionary of the Otchipwe Language*. The actual oral sounds of words vary as do the orthographic transcriptions. Baraga boldly translated *manito* as "spirit," and "ghost," and *manitoke* as "I practice idolatry," and "I worship idols."[24]

Clearly, in this earlier translation is a crease of monotheism and dominance. The word *manidooke* in the most recent dictionary is defined as a sense of spiritual power, presence, and the transmotion of native sovereignty.

Native "sovereignty is inherent, an essential right that has been limited but not given by the government."[25] The many treaties with natives are the documents that secure traces of transmotion and, at the same time, modernist reason of sovereignty. Treaties were historical notice and evacuation, but not mere gratuities or benefaction; treaties were both concessionary and complementary. Today, treaties are a presence, the recurrence of transmotion and intrinsic native sovereignty.

The connotations of native transmotion would counter cache, means, and dominance; that sense of natural reason, and stories of presence, are neither servile nor unitary. "Life *beyond utility* is the domain of sovereignty," asserts Georges Bataille in *The Accursed Share*. "In theory, a man compelled to work consumes the products without which production would not be possible, while the sovereign consumes rather the surplus of production. The sovereign, if he is not imaginary, truly enjoys the products of this world—beyond his needs. His sovereignty resides in this."

Native sovereignty is transmotion, and the rights of motion are personal, totemic, and reciprocal; not base line surveys, futurity, or possessory. Bataille argues that it may be "*servile* to consider duration first, to employ the *present time* for the sake of the *future*, which is what we do when we work." No master could bear the natural reciprocity of native sovereignty. "The sovereign restores to the primacy of the present the surplus share of production, acquired to the extent that men submitted to the primacy of the future. The sovereign, epitomizing the *subject*, is the one by whom and for whom the moment, the miraculous *moment*, is the ocean into which the streams of labor disappear."[76]

WOUNDED HEARTS

Ohiyesa, the "winner," was a dedicated, beleaguered native medical doctor. The Santee author and name giver was born four years before the 1862 Minnesota Massacre. Many Lightnings, his father, was arrested and condemned for his resistance, but his death sentence was commuted by President Lincoln.

Mysterious Medicine, his uncle, trained the young man to be a warrior and to avenge the death of his father: the family did not know that Many Lightnings was alive and in a federal penitentiary. "To avenge the death of a relative or of a dear friend was considered a great deed," writes Charles Eastman in *Indian Boyhood*. "My uncle, accordingly, had spared no pains to instill into my young mind the obligations to avenge the death of my father and my older brothers."

Many Lightnings was released after three years and returned to his family as a native conversionist, a Christian with a new name, Jacob Eastman. He encouraged his son to attend school.

"He had brought me some civilized clothing. At first, I disliked very much to wear garments made by the people I had hated so bitterly. But the thought that, after all, they had not killed my father and brothers, reconciled me, and I put on the clothes," wrote Eastman. "My father was accustomed every morning to read from his Bible, and sing a stanza of a hymn. I was about very early with my gun for several mornings; but at last he stopped me as I was preparing to go out, and bade me wait."

Ohiyesa listened "with much astonishment" to a hymn and to the word *Jesus*. "This conversion made a deep impression upon my mind," and he became Charles Eastman. "Late in the fall we reached the citizen settlement at Flandreau, South Dakota, where my father and some others dwelt among the whites. Here my wild life came to an end, and my school days began."[27]

Eastman first attended a mission school. "At age fifteen he had spoken only Sioux. By the time he received his Bachelor of Science degree from Dartmouth in 1887, at age twenty-nine, he had become a powerful speaker and writer of English and had studied Greek, Latin, French, and German," noted Frances Karttunen in *Between Worlds*.[28] He continued his studies at Boston University Medical School.

Doctor Charles Eastman was named the physician at the Pine Ridge Agency in South Dakota. He arrived on the reservation only two months before the Seventh Cavalry massacred the families of Ghost Dancers at Wounded Knee on December 29, 1890.

Elaine Goodale, the supervisor of native education on the reservation, met the doctor at the time of the massacre. Wounded Knee was buried in snow and Eastman was caring for the few survivors. Christmas ended overnight, the decorations were removed, and the church became a trauma hospital. Eastman and Goodale lectured and wrote about the horror at Wounded Knee. Six months later they were married in New York.

Eastman practiced medicine for several more years, in both private and government service; then he directed native programs for the Young Men's Christian Association. Later, he was associated with the Boy Scouts of America. His last position, however, may have been his most significant service to natives. He was named a *name giver*, and his "job was to provide families with surnames that were acceptable to them and to the United States legal system." He was aware that natives needed surnames to "assert their claims to land allotments and cash settlements."[29]

Many Lightnings, once a warrior, was a conversionist to the cues of monotheism in the penitentiary. Charles Eastman, his son, was a conversionist in two other dimensions: a native of mission education, and a medical doctor who returned to natural reason with a wounded heart. He encircled the horrors of that massacre in stories of native courage and survivance. That sense of presence, rather than absence or aversion, is natural reason and a source of native identities. The doctor enunciated his visions, memories, and totemic creations as an author. Clearly, his autobiographical stories are native survivance not victimry.

Eastman, once a native outcast and taunted as a warrior, endured the severe turn of seasons; later, as a doctor, he treated the survivors of a military massacre. His totemic visions, conversions, and traumatic memories are the traces of *tragic wisdom* in his many stories. Tragic wisdom, in the native sense, is the ecstatic nature of creation and chance.

Friedrich Nietzsche "believes that a tragic wisdom would restore good conscience to action, selfhood, and responsibility by affirming the fatality of historical being in the comprehensive sense demanded by *amor fati*," or the love of fate, observes Mark Warren in *Nietzsche and Political Thought*. The native sense of chance and survivance, and the dionysian *amor fati* are much the same in the metaphors of ecstatic creation. "Nietzsche intended his concept of tragic wisdom to evoke an awareness of the worldly conditions of individual power," writes Warren. "Tragic wisdom involves an acceptance of the historicity of the human condition."[30]

Nietzsche must have rushed the "eternal recurrence," and now the cause encircles our names, and the constancy of trickster creation stories. "I have the right to understand myself as the first *tragic philosopher*," he wrote in *The Birth of Tragedy*. "I had discovered the only parable and parallel in history for my own inmost experience — and thus became the first to comprehend the wonderful phenomenon of the Dionysian."[31]

The foremost sources of the native self as a personal identity, and sense of presence, are visionary; the presentations are families, communities, contrariety, and the politics of nations. These, the most obvious associations, are the public references to a personal sense of presence in the world. The foremost connections, however, may not always reveal the most significant sources of self and identity in the native stories of chance and survivance.

Eastman wrote about the moral and ethical values of natives; he created an aesthetic native world, and he simulated the *indian* as sovenance, the absence as a presence. "Indian children were trained so that they hardly ever cried much at night," he observed in *Indian Boyhood*.

I was a little over four years old at the time of the "Sioux massacre" in Minnesota. In the general turmoil, we took flight into British Columbia, and the journey is still vividly remembered by all our family. A yoke of oxen and a lumber-wagon were taken from some white farmer and brought home for our conveyance. . . .

The boys found a great deal of innocent fun in jumping from the high wagon while the oxen were leisurely moving along. My elder brothers soon became experts. At last, I mustered up courage enough to join them in this sport.

That was his "first experience with a civilized vehicle," and he was glad when they abandoned the wagon.

"The Indians are a patient and a clannish people; their love for one another is stronger than that of any civilized people I know. If this were not so, I believe there would have been tribes of cannibals among them," asserted Eastman. "White people have been known to kill and eat their companions in preference to starving; but Indians — never!"[32]

These are the stories of native endurance and survivance; the stories that create a sense of presence, a native self, a teasable self in names, relations, and native contingencies, but not victimry. That sense of self is a creation, an aesthetic presence; the self is not an essence, or immanence, but the mien of stories.

Eastman created an *indian* self as a warrior, doctor, lecturer, father, name giver, and author. Surely, his teasable self is as much a source of native presence as visions; he was teased by his peers, and later persecuted by *indian* agents. The *indian* self is not the same as the native self of personal visions; and the previous or historical self is not the same self created in autobiographies. The self is a tease of identity. My self is an interpretation of creation and history.

"The search for a foundational subject, as history teaches, tends to lead either to a mysticism wherein the existence of the self is assumed but cannot be demonstrated or to scepticism concerning the whole enterprise," notes Paul Kerby in *Narrative and the Self.* The self is a narrative construed "not as a prelinguistic given that merely employs language, much as we might employ a tool, but rather as a product of language."[33]

Native survivance is a sense of presence, but the true self is visionary. The true self is an ironic consciousness, the cut of a native trickster. Stories of truistic selves tease the originary. "The self is probably not constituted in such a way that it can see or express itself," observes Francis Jacques in *Difference and Subjectivity.* "It is a remarkable fact that it is no more possible to accept a self that is known as an object in the world than it is a self that sits behind consciousness as a knowing subject."[34] Native selves are stories, traces of discourse, and the tease of presence.

Frances Karttunen reports that ridicule "was a principal means of social control. Sioux children became exquisitely sensitive to it and would plunge into all sorts of hazardous or painful behavior to avoid being mocked."

Eastman, a decade after the massacre, was named the medical doctor at the Crow Creek Reservation in South Dakota. He moved with his family to the agency. At first he was content to carry out the crucial public health needs of that community. Regrettably, a new *indian* agent "took over, and soon he was accusing Eastman of being a troublemaker and an agitator. Eastman tried to keep out of the way, but once again he found himself serving under an agent who was trying to get his physician transferred elsewhere. This time, to the list of complaints about Eastman speaking with the Sioux in their native language and being uppity were added complaints about negligence and sexual misconduct. Eastman did what he could to hang on and continue to treat patients, but again he was forced to resign."[35]

Native identities are more than nominal considerations; there are theoretical causes and historical situations that abet the agencies of dominance. True, natives have endured centuries of separation, proscription, removal by treaties, and *disappearance*, but the tragic wisdom of their survivance has been converted by many academics to an aesthetic victimry. Clearly, the foremost stories of traumatic memories and worried hearts on this continent are native; however, the modernist consideration of an "identity crisis" in the nation was attributed to Erik Erikson. World War II veterans, he observed in clinical studies, sensed a loss of "personal sameness and historical continuity." Erikson observed the "same central disturbance in severely conflicted young people whose sense of confusion is due, rather, to a war within themselves."[36]

The clinical studies in the 1960s would include those of native students on reservations. Congressional investigations revealed horrible conditions at federal *indian* boarding schools. For instance, more than a thousand Navajo children attended the Tuba City boarding school in the late 1960s. Senator Walter Mondale, a member of an *indian* education committee invited me, then a journalist for the *Minneapolis Tribune*, to travel with him to several remote schools on reservations in Arizona and New Mexico.

Mondale compared the boarding school at Tuba City to the Rough Rock Navajo Demonstration School. There were only two Navajo teachers at Tuba City. At Rough Rock more than half of the staff, teachers, and assistants were Navajos. Rough Rock was built by the Bureau of Indian Affairs and turned over to the Navajo in 1966. The school had been in operation for two years at the time we visited. Rough Rock students studied first the structure of their native language, and then English.

Psychiatrist Karl Menninger observed at the time that you "damage a child still more when you destroy his first stone of identity, when you tell him his language is no good, when you tell him that his color is not right or imply it by surrounding him with people of a different color, habits, and status."[37]

The past studies, and narratives on the native "identity crisis" in the tragic ruins of reservations, seem to have turned, in this generation, on a critical sense of historical *absence*; the academic conversion of the native *victime*, the real sufferer, to the modernist pose of aesthetic victimry.

"My own identity crucially depends on my dialogical relations with others," observes Charles Taylor in *Multiculturalism and "The Politics of Recognition."* Natives create their identities in "dialogical relations" with many others, with nature, and with those who must bear the *indian* simulations of dominance. Natives have sustained over many centuries a *dialogic circle* of natural reason, resistance, the tease of presence, and communicative mediation over names, histories, and sovereignty.

Taylor points out that "our identity is partly shaped by recognition or its absence, often by the *mis*recognition of others, and so a person or group of people can suffer real damage, real distortion, if the people or society around them mirror back to them a confining or demeaning or contemptible picture of themselves. Nonrecognition or misrecognition can inflict harm, can be a form of oppression, imprisoning someone in a false, distorted, and reduced mode of being."[38] This misrecognition of natives as *indians* is both oppressive and a prison of false identities.

CHAPTER ONE

Penenative Rumors

SECOND NATURE

N ative American Indians actuate the stories of this continent, and natives are the traces of natural reason, the
aesthetic fugitives of the originary. Native stories are the
canons of survivance: the tease of seasons, scent of cedar, oneiric
names, shamanic creases, and the sure transmotion of sovereignty.

Natives have resisted empires, negotiated treaties, and, as diplomatic strategies, embraced the simulations of absence to secure
the chance of a decisive presence in national literature, history,
and canonry. Native resistance to dominance is an undeniable
trace of presence, but even these memories of survivance in a
constitutional democracy are cast as narratives of absence and
victimry.

Natives actuate the "second nature" of the essay.

The essay is resistance, not tradition; the essay is contention,
the salvos of mediation, not the hest of separation, absence, or
the manners of dominance. The essay is a venture, the tease of
creation, the tricky stories of winter, but not the cause of modernist
histories. The native essay is a trace of survivance and sovereignty.

The essay *must* tease creation; the tease and version of natural
reason, consonance, and affinity. The tease must reverse modernist
theses, models of the social sciences, and the narratives of a native
absence as an *indian* presence. The native essay is not observance,
mere reversion, or the deceptive virtues of cultural immersion;
and never the course of dominance. The essay is a native tease, a
trace of survivance, not the overseer of scientism.

The essay is "related to rhetoric," probably an "adaptation to
communicative language," and, unmediated, the "essay retains,
precisely in the autonomy of its presentation, which distinguishes
it from scientific and scholarly information, traces of the communicative element such information dispenses with," observes

Theodor Adorno in *Notes to Literature*. "Instead of 'reducing' cultural phenomena, the essay immerses itself in them as though in a second nature, a second immediacy, in order to negate and transcend the illusion of immediacy through its perseverance."[1]

The "second immediacy" of the essay is a trace of resistance, survivance, and native sovereignty. This "second nature" cocks the ecstasies of the native past over the cause of history. The past is a thesis of creation and culture, the constructions of a "false society." The native past is enacted in theses, the creation of a traditional absence and cultural distance; transcendence becomes a notion as nameable as the myth of *mother earth*, a metronymic commodity.

Truly, native stories, the tease of creation, and nicknames are the shadows of a presence; intransitive shadows, the transmotions of a native presence in stories. For instance, the word *agawaatese*, in the oral stories of the *anishinaabe*, could mean a shadow, or casts a shadow, as a bird in flight; *agawaatese* is a presence in stories, an intransitive, inanimate, avian entity. That native sense of a presence has been mediated amiss by theistic discoveries, social science theses, the "final vocabulary" of dominance, and master narratives.

The vocabulary "is 'final' in the sense that if doubt is cast on the worth of these words, their user has no noncircular argumentative recourse," the words we use to "formulate praise of our friends and contempt for our enemies," asserts Richard Rorty in *Contingency, Irony, and Solidarity*. "Those words are as far as he can go with language; beyond them there is only helpless passivity or a resort to force."[2]

The essay is contingency, not the secession of native time or nature, because there is no final, absolute measure of creation or the unnameable. Tradition, then, is a dialogic immediacy. Consider the "discoveries" of culture and, in turn, the absence of natives, as the cut, not the crease of presence; that separation, redoubled in the invention of the *indian* is a simulation and commodity.

"The essay is what it was from the beginning, the critical form par excellence; as immanent critique of intellectual constructions, as a confrontation of what they are with their concept, it is critique of ideology," writes Adorno. The essay "wants to heal thought of its arbitrary character by incorporating arbitrariness reflectively into its own approach rather than disguising it as immediacy." The native essay is the transmotion of nature, culture, and sovereignty. The sense of a native presence is a "second immediacy."[3]

The absence of natives as an *indian* presence is a simulation that serves the spurious histories of dominance. Likewise, the essential sources of native cultures, the mythic in translation, are theses of the social sciences. There is no referent of native absence, no second historical observance of native vanishment; not even the creation of absence is a presence. The native past is not an absolute referent in the course of time; rather, absence is an event created in discourse. There is a native trace, but no sense of presence, no native diachrony in the absence of a dialogic interaction.

Discoveries, cultural observance, casuistic evidence, names, and narrative denouement are events; dominance is an event but not a discourse. Surveillance is a pretense of being, and not a trace of native presence, as these events are simulations and must counter even the narration of native vanishment. The "event of being" is a dialogic act, a second presence, but neither simulations of absence nor mimetic interaction of presence are originary.

"The human sciences are a surveillance; the exact sciences are an observation," writes Michel Serres in *The Limits of Theory.* "The first are as old as our myths; the others, new, were born with us, and are only as old as our history. Myth, theater, representation, and politics do not teach us how to observe; they commit us to a surveillance." Surveillance is relational; myth, theater, and politics have no object. Myths are poor, "without objects," he asserts. "I call poor the theater, deprived of things; theories are poor; politics is poor." Human sciences, and our "philosophies are poor and miserable." Communication, however, "renders presence useless" and "makes surveillance obsolete."[4] Serres, then, seems to assert that myths, simulations, and representations "without objects," and most likely the *indian,* a simulation with no referent, are obsolete in his catchy panopticon. Natives, as natives are the absence of an *indian* presence, are a much wiser notice as objects, in a dialogic second presence, than as exotic myths in the cultural theses of the social sciences.

That originary sense of a native essence, the *philosophia prima,* is a translation, the *litera scripta* of an eternal presence. The *manidoo* of the *anishinaabe,* that spirit and trace of an unnameable creation, intransitive native shadows, and the *names* of shamanic visions, are either autotheistic poses, natural reason, or dialogic creation; the *manidoo,* and that ironic sense of a native presence in narratives, are events *in* language. The trace in nature is an event in language, as *bimikawaan*, a track, or footprint, is a presence of an absence in nature and narratives. The trace is natural reason, a native presence; the culture of the *indian* is a simulation.

"The differences between a life lived in nature and one lived in culture are sufficient grounds for honoring the distinction between natural events and human events," observes Hayden White in *The Content of the Form*. "Narrative is at once a mode of discourse, a manner of speaking, and the product produced by the adoption of this mode of discourse." Moreover, as native narratives are traces of natural reason, then one "can produce an imaginary discourse about real events that may not be less 'true' for being imaginary. It all depends upon how one construes the function of the faculty of imagination in human nature."[5] Nature, shamanic visions, oneiric presence, and the simulations of culture are true in imagination, not discourse; one is survivance, the other is commodity. Native stories are creation, natural reason, and actuate the essay.

The "final vocabulary" and promotion of native absence over the contingencies of presence is an anachronism, a casuistic history. "There is neither a first nor a last word and there are no limits to the dialogic context," observes Mikhail Bakhtin in *Speech Genres and Other Late Essays*. "Even *past* meanings, that is, those born in the dialogue of past centuries, can never be stable."[6] Surveillance is dominance; the essay is a "dialogic context" of survivance, and that, a second nature, is the past and presence of natives.

"The essay abandons the royal road to the origins, which leads only to what is most derivative," writes Adorno. "Nothing can be interpreted out of something that is not interpreted into it at the same time." The essay "distrusts" the affirmation of the "single moment," the existence of the sacred. "Hence the essay's innermost formal law is heresy."[7]

Mikhail Bakhtin teased a literary sense of human unities and answerability. Natives are traceable, while the origins of consciousness are obscure. The *indian* is a simulation, not a trace; the *indian* has no referent, a counterfeit culture of a native absence, and the remission of surveillance. History is amenable, but "knows no past, present, and future; it knows no long or short time, no 'long ago' or 'recently'—as absolutely unique and nonconvertible moments," Bakhtin writes in *Art and Answerability*. "Art and life are not one, but they must become united in myself—in the unity of my answerability."[8] The *indian* and the absence of natives are united, as simulations, transmotions, aesthetics, and actual experience, in a "dialogic context," the conversions of answerability.

The studies of emergence and narrative histories are not "contained in the originary scene" as a "universal preformation," notes Eric Gans in *Originary Thinking*. "The modernist vision of the origin is prerepresentational: the existence of human beings as creatures of desire precedes language, and the scene of their art is modeled on the supposed intransitivity of this originary desire."[9]

John Pizer argues that most "historical research is driven by etiology, the striving towards origins." That "originary moment" is the tease of new historicism, and the tricky overtures of postmodern critiques. The *indian*, in this sense, is striven, a hyperreal simulation and, at the same time, the ironic enactment of a native presence by an absence in a master narrative.

Master narratives perpetuate an injustice, "a denial of the imagination, a denial of the right to respond, to invent, to deviate from the norm," asserts David Carroll in *Paraesthetics*. In "other words, the right to little narratives that are rooted in difference rather than in the identity established by the grand narrative."[10]

Natives are the native stories of their own diverse creation; the traces of native origins are intransitive, a tease of presence in the uncertain ventures of semiotic translations, and the transmotion of native sovereignty. "Authentic origins are inherently plural and divergent, and an extended mediation upon them both reinvigorates attention to history and subverts the supremacist claims of particular groups by showing that their ethnicity, religion, or discipline is 'always already' . . . entangled with others," writes Pizer in *Toward a Theory of Radical Origin*.[11]

The *indian* is a misnomer, a simulation with no referent and with the absence of natives; *indians* are the other, the names of sacrifice and victimry. Natives are a *native* creation in the stories of survivance. The *indigène* is the noble savage, the stoical warrior, evermore the metaphor of the native at the littoral, the passive native at the treeline. The history of the *indian* is an aesthetic sacrifice, an absence of natives that has become a perverse presence of the other, the modernist manner of a counter simulation, and that absence is a commodity.

Jean Baudrillard noticed an obscure curvature of the real, an elusive transition of allegories in the ruins of representation, and a turn to simulations. "To dissimulate is to pretend not to have what one has. To simulate is to feign to have what one doesn't have. One implies a presence, the other an absence," he writes. "Simulation is no longer that of a territory, a referential being, or a substance." The *indian* has never been real in the mirror, or a name of presence in the simulations of history. Simulation "is the generation by models of a real without origin or reality: a hyperreal."[12]

The *indians* are cultural narratives of an absence, the absolute misnomer of a native presence and the originary. Natives are the curvature of presence, an eternal trace of presence; the mimetic representation of that presence in other situations is either sophistic or a parody.

In the past century the representation of objects has turned to the literary discussion of the *referent*, as a mediation of objects in language. The persona of natives is a referent, not an object, in the sense of a literary presence. The persona is natural reason, a trace of native stories, and not a racialist separation; the native persona is mediation, and always "entangled with others." Natives are the run of seasons, the rush of rivers, and tricky creation stories, but natives are not analogies by surveillance, by cultural substitution, by social science remissions, or simulations of an ethnic originary.

"Taking analogies to be identities is a delusion, but rendering the analogous void by treating it as just another difference is an even more radical delusion," writes René Girard in *Job: The Victim of His People*. "Nothing is more difficult to resolve in the cultural sciences than the role of analogy. In the nineteenth century, a great deal was made of the slightest analogies. Broad theories were derived from a limited number of misunderstood analogies."[13] The *indian*, of course, is a "radical delusion," the other as a cultural analogy.

AESTHETIC SCAPEGOATS

Job is the sacrifice of a dramatic theocracy. The stories of that sacrifice endure as moral parables. The simulation of the *indian* is an aesthetic sacrifice in a theistic democracy. Not the sacrifice of the unnameable natives, but the factitious *indigène*, the *indian* of a contrived diachrony in literature and history.

The histories of discovery, dominance, racialism, civilization, noble and demonic savagism, are the sacrifice of the *indian* as the double other.[14] The simulation of the *indian* is an aesthetic sacrifice

28

in the tragic parables of racialism and nationalism. These obvious misnomers, and the absence of natives, are the complete theses of victimry. Naturally, native stories, trickster stories of resistance and survivance, are eversions of tragic victimry.

The trickster is "one of the two great theologies to evolve as a result of the sacrilization of the scapegoat," observes René Girard in *The Scapegoat*. The two theologies, divine caprice and divine anger, provide "solutions to the problem that faces religious belief when the victim," and in this sense the scapegoat is the *indian*, "becomes the means of reconciliation." Native tricksters tease their own histories and are comic healers in stories. Tricksters are seen as wise, wicked, deceptive, stupid, and naive. The motivation of tricksters is never obvious, as the transcendence of the characters is never a sacrifice, and seldom amounts to very much at the end of stories. "These both compromise the desired result and yet ensure its outcome by creating the unanimous opposition to the blunderer necessary for the good of the community."[15]

Jarold Ramsey points out in *Reading the Fire* that native tricksters are imaginary figures "*whose episodic career is based upon hostility to domesticity, maturity, good citizenship, modesty, and fidelity of any kind.*" Tricksters are transmutative, mythic, "mediative figures."[16]

The trickster is a native estate; the natural state of the earth is a mighty rumor, but not a rumor of balance, and not the *penenative* notions of peace. Clearly, natives and the earth are uneven; natives and nature are ever out of balance. Mythic peace is not a balance, but the cause of manifest manners and dominance. The notion of a counterbalance is a theistic covenant in the structural themes of savagism and civilization. The trickster is evermore eversive, the transmutative menace to the dominion of peace. The trickster is an aleatory creation, the transmotion of the seasons, the endurance of humor in winter, and the natural craver of an aesthetic earth out of balance. The trickster, even in translation as the *indian*, must hold reason on a tether and mock the desire to sacrifice a scapegoat.

"I would rather be at war in the cities than at peace in a tame wilderness," said the character Bagese in *Dead Voices*. The choice is a "chance of tricksters" or the "drone of cultural pride on the reservations." That peace "ended our war, ended our chance, and that peace comes back to us now in plastic beads and bones. The dance scars are shown with no stories in the ear. We must go on."[17]

The trickster *naanabozho* in *anishinaabe* stories mounts the obvious and exotic, metamorphosed as *makwa*, bear, *nikan*, bone, *waabooz*, rabbit, *niinag*, penis, and other oneiric conversions and mutations; the wild eversion of cultural incoherence. Trickster stories are the *coherence* of natural reason and native survivance.

Will Wright argues in *Wild Knowledge* that if "the idea of objective nature is incoherent, then the technology, and social actions, derived from that idea will also, very probably, be incoherent, and in particular they will probably be ecologically and socially debilitating." He points out that the "idea of knowledge must remain critically 'wild' in the sense that it cannot be 'captured' and 'tamed' by some particular set of social institutions, the institutions that are uniquely compatible with the 'true' knowledge of absolute 'reality.' "[18]

The narratives of cultural balance—the tamed, educated, and civilized— are notions of incoherence; the tricksters of wild manners—mutations, and eversions—are the traces of natural reason and the coherence of native survivance. Trickster stories are not the exercise of tragic victimry.

Greek tragedy presents the contradictions of equilibrium and violence. René Girard notes in *Violence and the Sacred* that the "relative nonviolence guaranteed by human justice must be defined as a sort of imbalance, a difference between 'good' and 'evil' parallel to the sacrificial difference between 'pure' and 'impure.' The idea of justice as a balanced scale, an exercise in exquisite impartiality, is utterly foreign to this theory, which sees the roots of justice in differences among men and the demise of justice in the elimination of these differences."[19] The mutations of the trickster in stories and the coherence of natural reason are the traces of native differences, justice, and survivance.

The continuous discoveries of *indians* and cultural treasures are the obvious desires of salvors and nations; uncovered bones, and stones, unearned ruins, objets d'art, are the missions of museums and scriptors of dominance. The misnomers and simulations of *indian* names are the most common possessions of institutions and nations. Native stories, the curvature of creation and presence, are erased by possessory desires and the mimetic representations of civilization over savagism; dominion by surveillance, incentives, violence, and cues of tragic victimry. That differences exist outside the cultural order is "terrifying because it reveals the truth of the system, its relativity, its fragility, and its mortality," notes Girard.[20]

The *indian* is the scapegoat, the aesthetic sacrifice of the other; severely, the simulation of the double other, as the absence of the native is the presence of the *indian* by surveillance, separation, and dominance. These mimetic motives, cultural tries, delusions, and aleatoric persecutions, are exacerbated by the contradictions of desire, envy, and admiration, the very causes of tragic victimry.

"Shakespeare possesses the sharpest possible eye for the human tendency to arbitrary scapegoating and the manner in which the dissolving of significance in mimetic violence destroys everything in its wake," asserts Girard in *A Theater of Envy*. The playwright "must have been tempted by nihilism and threatened by madness," as natives were in their resistance, a century later, to the merchants of dominion, envy, and "mimetic desire." Shakespeare's "awareness of the victimage mechanism and its religious consequences . . . reached an anthropological vision that has remained undeciphered to this day." That vision "is finally becoming intelligible, thanks to the same mimetic theory that enabled us to unravel the significance of the comedies."[21]

The myth of civilization over savagism is a sure and ironic cue that sacrifice "restores order by restoring difference: between the sacralized victim, arbitrarily chosen, and the rest of the community, which is unanimous in its expulsion of violence," observes Andrew McKenna in *Violence and Difference*. "The selection of the victim is aleatory; all that is necessary is an insignificant mark."[22]

Girard points out in *Violent Origins* that in the "psychosocial connotations" of violence, scapegoating "enables persecutors to elude problems that seem intractable. But scapegoating must not be regarded as a conscious activity, based on conscious choice." There must be an element of delusion.[23]

The *indian*, the simulation of the scapegoat, has no referent more than sacrifice and violence; the causal histories of *indians* are analogies not identities. The *indian* is the double other, the absence as a presence, the occidental simulation of desire that is at once the contradiction of emulation and aversion. The *indian* as scapegoat is a double sacrifice; the national epiphanies of tragic victimry.

"Violence is the true 'referent,' " Girard notes in *Job: The Victim of His People*. "Society is very aware that it has a good thing in its victim, a successful purge for ill feelings. It is equally aware that the process is as dangerous as it is beneficial." Compared to a "bolt of lightning, the scapegoat mechanism suddenly frees all men without being answerable to anyone except perhaps to the victim himself, who is likely to become an idol after his disappearance." The *indian* is the unanswerable scapegoat, and the *indian* has freed a theistic democracy.

Girard points out that rivalry, in the absence of moderation, "is such a natural result of the imitation of desires that mimesis comes to regard the triumphant rival as indispensable. The obstacle supersedes the model." The simulation or "model is chosen for its function as obstacle. If nothing thwarts it, mimetic masochism ceases to desire. There is no longer a model worthy of imitating."[24] The tease of trickster stories oversets *indian* simulations and the desires of aesthetic sacrifice; the mimetic representations of the other are deconstructed in ironic native stories.

The critical mention of mimesis is an imitation of action that, in the sense of a tragic mode of literature, arouses the emotions of an audience; for instance, the mimetic representation of *indians* as the other, the narrative pleasure of "pity and fear," is an imitation of tragic victimry.

"Tragedy is essentially an imitation not of persons but of action and life," noted Aristotle in *Poetics*. The imitation arouses "pity and fear" and is a "complete action." The "finest form of tragedy" must avoid certain forms of plot: succinctly, the good man to bad fortune, or a bad man to good fortune. Such stories may arouse emotions but not pity and fear. "There remains, then, the intermediate kind of personage, a man not preeminently virtuous and just, whose misfortune, however, is brought upon him not by vice and depravity but by some fault, of the number of those in the enjoyment of great reputation and prosperity."[25] Tobin Siebers argues in *The Ethics of Criticism* that "tragedy fails, in Aristotle's estimation, when characters intend to do evil and reverse themselves at the last minute."[26] The *indian*, as an imitation of action, might arouse "pity and fear," but tragedy is not a secure literary theory to represent native stories.

The *indian* is a simulation, of course, that imitates both many misfortunes and faults: the misfortunes of either noble or demonic savagism, and the faults of civilization, a contradiction of the exotic and mundane, and discrepancies of the absence and presence of action that arouses emotions. The *indian* denouement is tragic victimry.

The simulation of the *indian* is a "tragic pleasure." The motive to own the other, once a rave interdiction, now a race in season, is a common mimetic representation of modernity; the cravers, but not the *indian*, tout an ironic referent. The conversions of the mimetic other are possessive, the mince of savagism and civilization. The *indian* is a fugitive object, the uncut cord of colonial dominance.

The New Age criers over the *indian* are the aesthetic cues of their solace, remission of winter, a "tragic pleasure." The "treasure" of the other has no real waste, and the outcome of that lonesome race with the simulation of *indians* is the theistic rememoration of tragic victimry.

Fear and pity are aroused in the contradictions of envy, admiration, and the aversion of the other; the double other of invention and imitation in scripture and governance. The *indian* as aesthetic scapegoat is the imitation of the "complete action," and the cause of cultural contention, fear, and pity. The denouement is the aesthetic sacrifice of the *indian*, once more the presentation of tragic victimry.

"The object of poetic mimesis, then, is an action that may or may not be fictional but must in any case bear a certain relation to universals dealing with human behavior," observes Paul Woodruff. He argues that "Aristotelian tragedy makes us respond emotionally to representations as if they were real, and that this involves one kind of poetic deception. Now we see that a second, more subtle, kind of deception is involved in tragedy: in so far as a tragedy represents universals, it makes us respond to them as if they were particulars."[27]

Native motion is sovereignty, and native stories of survivance are transmotions, not the mere imitation of motion or action in the tragic mode of literature. The choices of identity, then, are redoubled in the critique of tragic victimry. The native, an inscrutable persona, is a referent in stories: the *indian*, a mimetic representation of the other as scapegoat. The native is the trace of ethical transmotion and sovereignty.

CHANCE CONVERGENCE

George Steiner, the literary essayist, says that the "best acts of reading are acts of incompletion, acts of fragmentary insight, of that which refuses paraphrase, metaphrase; which finally say, 'The most interesting in all this I haven't been able to touch on.' But which makes that inability not a humiliating defeat or a piece of mysticism but a kind of joyous invitation to reread."[28]

The invention of the *indian* is an ethnographic metaphrase, a cultural traducement; the minutes and evidence of that surveillance are not the best invitations to reread the *indian*, a ruined presence in the representations of the social sciences. Natives and *indians* are not read as the same stories; the *indian* is a cued simulation, a native absence that becomes a logocentric presence, and that simulation of presence is the successive closure of differences.

Jacques Derrida critiques *logocentrism*, the "metaphysics of presence" and signification; moreover, causal reason, closure, and the repression of differences are undone by the space of *différance*, by the wordsters of variance, and testy deconstructions. That *différance* combines the meaning of "difference" and "deferral," the chance of time and space in language, over the heavy hand of true representations. "Thus, *différance* is the name we might give to the 'active,' moving discord of different forces," he writes. The motion of *différance* is not a "present being, however excellent, unique, principal, or transcendent," because the *différance* "governs nothing, reigns over nothing, and nowhere exercises any authority." The *différance* is more native trickster than the manner of the last word. There is "no kingdom of *différance*, but *différance* instigates the subversion of every kingdom."[29]

Natives and the *indian* are purported to be the other by second nature in written narratives. The *indian* is the simulation of a logocentric other; the *différance* is a deconstruction of a cultural absence, and the absence is evermore deferred, but not as a presence. The "meaning" and differences of native experience are *deferred* to other unnameable situations, at other times; the *différance* of native identities is deferred to other native stories.

Derrida's "logocentrism replaces ethnocentrism as the name for the debasement of writing and the use of 'writing' as a category to rank peoples," writes Tobin Siebers in *The Ethics of Criticism*. "The theory of difference makes the structure of language not a prison-house but the ethical model and signature of a hypothetical equality based on difference not identity." Ranking "peoples according to separate categories, placing some closer to nature through the use of terms such as 'primitive' and 'savage,' ends by refusing them the constitutive qualities of human beings," and the ethics of a *différance* in literature.

"Deconstruction seeks a reversal of values, conferring a new kind of meaning on those elements of literature that critics have traditionally ignored," observes Siebers. "Whereas literary criticism has most often focused on similarities, unities, coherence, systematic ideas, and the body of the work, deconstruction draws attention to contradictions, obscurities, discontinuities, interruptions, margins, and plays of the signifier. . . . Deconstruction acts to combat all forms of theory because it equates systematic thought with the violence of power."[30]

The *indian* is a mundane romance, the advertisement of the other in narratives. Natives are elusive, the traces of presence are unnameable in literature; the origins are deferred, and the acts of reading native stories are the *différance*, a *postindian* "fragmentary insight." The tricky native, not the racialist simulation of the *indian*, is an invitation to a "pleasurable misreading."

The simulation of the *indian* is the absence of the native, and that absence is a presence of the *other*, the eternal scapegoat, but not a native past; the native is a trace of presence. The *indian* is the absence of the native, but the native is the presence of the *indian* in name. These chiastic inversions of *indian* simulations, the mock unities of culture and exclusion, are the ironies of representation, and deconstruction; the *différance*, and the anticipation of native stories over the margins of ethnographic documents.

The chiastic inversion is not the same as synecdoche, or the part to the whole, as the trace of natives is to the simulations of *indian* culture. The inversion is a difference, one name or sense to another, and the differences are natural reason, a native coherence. There is a "tendency to transform the chiasmatic relationship from one of difference into one of identity," observes Brook Thomas in *The New Historicism*. "This replacement of difference by identity leads to another tendency—that of disciplinary imperialism, masquerading as interdisciplinary work."[31] The *indian* is the simulation and difference that becomes the culture, the totalization of unnameable native identities.

Native identities are more chance than the inheritance of an organic culture; the pronouns that bear a persona, a trace, a name, and native stories, are a chance convergence in language.[32] The trace of presence is a natural chance in stories; once an oral creation of native pronouns, the scriptural representation is the convergence of identities at a distance, and in silence. The pronoun is the absence of the noun; that absence has a referent, and the trace of presence in a name. The *indian* has no referent but a simulation. Surely, native identities are more than the absence of a common name. Survivance stories and the tease of native identities are traces of the originary.

The first person is not the true pronominal of native identities; neither is the second, or third person. Pronominal representations of identities are mimetic, the imitations of others in the absence of the noun or name; the first person is the ninth letter of the alphabet, an abbreviation, and one letter is the presence of the author, narrator, or consciousness in a story. The second person pronoun, *you*, is a much trickier absence; *you* are the one, and the *one* is the author, the absence that is the presence of the narrator. The narrator is the *you*, the *you* is the author of the *you* as narrator, the reader. The native *you* is a trickster pronoun with no obvious antecedence. The *you* is the transmotion of the other, the transcendence of the *indian* as the other, the narrator, and the reader.

The *indian* author is the other in a name, and the narrator is the other in a pronoun. The narrative presence of natives is undone as *indian* by the reader and by the convergence of the unnameable; otherwise natives and *indians* would always be together, a fantastic unity with everyone in every pronoun. The author observes *you* as the *indian*, *you* the reader, the absence that would be the inversion of the narrator, a second person to bear the uncertainties of the name.

Native identities are in the words, to be sure, and in traces of wind and water; the distance of pronouns in a summer rain, the run of a thunderstorm, is as much an assurance of native survivance as the chiastic inversions of the names. That reversal of the pronouns, the second person as a tease of a native presence in the reader, could be an obscure trace of the obviative, the silence of the fourth person, that pronominal shadow of the unnameable native. In other words, the fourth person could be a native presence in third-person stories or narratives. That obviation is a contrasted third person, a distinct narrative entity, or shadow, in certain native languages.

Leonard Bloomfield observes in *Eastern Ojibwa* that, in any close narrative context, "one animate third person, singular or plural, is proximate, and any other animate third persons are obviative." Bloomfield notes, for instance, that the word *mekkwa*, bear, or *makwa* in a more current dictionary, is *mekkwan*, and *makwan,* in the obviative. The obviative, or fourth person, could be read in new critical interpretations as a shadow presence of some other person in oral stories or written narratives.[33]

The *indian* is the simulation of a third person, and the absence of the native. The native is the double other: a fourth person in the obviation of the *indian,* and the native is a trace, the shadow of an unnameable presence.

That obviative could be a *manidoo,* the fourth person spirit in *anishinaabe* stories; the shadows of the *manidoo* in narratives. The *manidoo* is a trace of presence in the *silence* of a native name; native shadows of creation and the fourth person are unnameable.

RADIANT CREATION

Native identities are traces, the *différance* of an unnameable presence, not mere statutes, inheritance, or documentation, however bright the blood and bone in museums. Native identities must be an actuation of stories, the commune of survivance and sovereignty.

The *indian* is a universal simulation, the other in a vast mirror of moods and temperance; at the same time, miniature conversions of an unnameable native, an obscure crease of a second nature. The two dimensions, one a simulation of the real, and the other a trace of the real, converge in the minutes of surveillance and the imagination of a "second immediacy."

Vladimir Nabokov was hushed by the "luminous hues" of the "translucent miniatures." Then, nigher the silence and precision of his notice, an insect's organ, radiant "under the microscope," and "magnified for cool study," he observes in his memoir. "There is, it would seem, in the dimensional scale of the world a kind of delicate meeting place between imagination and knowledge, a point, arrived at by diminishing large things and enlarging small ones, that is intrinsically artistic."[34]

Nabokov, in a "review of a book on butterflies," asked if "there does not exist a high ridge where the mountainside of 'scientific' knowledge joins the opposite slope of 'artistic' imagination," notes Vladimir Alexandrov in *Nabokov's Otherworld.* Nabokov, in an interview, said that "he tended 'more and more to regard the objective existence of *all* events as a form of *impure imagination.*'"

So, whatever "the mind grasps, it does so with the assistance of creative fancy." The novelist explained "that 'pure imagination' must come into play when the individual tries to apprehend the events constituting cosmic synchronization."[35]

The *indian* is a simulation of impure imagination. Natives are the trace of an unnameable presence. Natives and *indians* are the convergence of imagination, surveillance, knowledge, and cosmic irony. The New Age myths of *mother earth*, and the counterfeit unities of *indian* cultures, are causal revisions, the mundane myths of balance. The cosmic *indian* is a material, postindian simulation at the end of modernity.

Modernity, that mirror of science, material culture, and the courier of the other as *indian*, causes the disenchantment of essence, traditional authority, and overruns natural reason. The scrutiny of traditions, however, is never the same in the case of *indians* or natives. The *indian* is a case of cultural nostalgia, the presence of tradition in a chemical civilization; on the other hand, the *indian* is the very absence and inexistence of reason and literature. Natives are secured as the unnameable, an aesthetic niche, the obscure entries on a bourgeois cruise of cultures. The *indians* are writable, an extrinsic presence in the theses of the social sciences. Certainly, many natives teased a worldview of natural reason and survivance that counted the seasons, the moves of shamans, tragic wisdom, and the stories of nature—stories that are never in balance.

The modernists must have conceived of the native other in the cosmopolitan consciousness of a cultural distance; separations of the real as the countenance of pieties, presence, and manners, are mere simulations of an unanswerable native absence. Consequently, the concoction of the *indian* is evermore a commodity.

Clearly, these modernist convictions, and points of view, are curious conversions of natural reason and native transmotion; cultural dominance at the hest of new social science theories. The objective possession of the other, however exotic the fugitive pose, has no comparable value, as theories and simulations of *indians* must be new, otherwise the truly fake artifacts would be rated as no more than kitschy. Ironically, the hyperreal, kitschy simulations "authenticate," in the course of modernist reason, the bourgeois worth of ancient, worn, and real native artifacts. For instance, the cost of a fake wing-bone choker, or a modernist doorstop coyote, is a kitschy reverse of the assessment of a ghost dance dress or a chief's blanket at auction in New York City.[36]

Consider the *indian* writ of modernity, the aesthetic caste of the other, as you name me an *indian*, or *postindian*; the *penenative*, obviative crossblood in literature. The *indian* runs in the absence of the native and does so with a postmodern name; *indian* cuts to natural reason and, at the same time, entertains an external union and "communicative action" with modernity.

"The theory of communicative action takes into account the fact that the symbolic reproduction of the lifeworld and its material reproduction are internally interdependent. . . . Reason is by its very nature incarnated in contexts of communicative action and in structures of the lifeworld," observes Jürgen Habermas in *The Philosophical Discourse of Modernity.* "Mythic traditions cannot be revised without danger to the order of things and to the identity of the tribe set within it. Categories of validity such as 'true' and 'false,' 'good' and 'evil,' are still blended with empirical concepts like exchange, causality, health, substance, and wealth."[37]

Natives and *indians* are the savage in the pieties of civilization, nationalism, and modernity of a constitutional democracy. Natives are an absence in histories, and that national vanishment has many names and contingencies. The *indian*, on the other hand, is the counter discourse of modernity. The savage is named the cause of national paranoia in captivity narratives and, in other frontier stories of sacrifice and redemption, a cultural hyperparasite and structural scapegoat; one parasite is the host of the other in the course of savagism, civilization, and victimry. Nostalgia, remorse, the row of tradition over reason, are the natural deconstruction of the *indian* as a simulation of modernity.

"Nationalism is the ideology of banality," testy kitsch, more kitschifacient, or the kitschy action of modernity, and "*paranoia*, individual and collective paranoia," writes Danilo Kis in *Homo Poeticus.* Nationalism "has no universal values, aesthetic, or ethical."[38] Likewise, the racialist ties of *indian* identities are creases of paranoia and dominance, the banal ideologies of victimry. The *indian* must sacrifice the uncertainties of individual experiences and count a *kitschifacient* simulation as a real native presence. The new enemies of the *indian* kitschymen are natural reason, wordsters, and spiritistic consumers. Truly, the fickle crystal setters in search of the authentic and overreal were crossed by the kitschymen. The chance of native stories and trickster hermeneutics is sure to deconstruct the *indian* simulations of a consumer presence.

The tricky theories of author intentions turn with the seasons; the native stories of creation, trickster transmutations, and the everlasting variations of stories, are intention movements, a motion that names other motions, or transmotions in literature. The sound and silence of native stories, the oral and written versions, are the seasons and motions of the author; intentions are obscure outside of the *indian* ordinal of penance and victimry.

The *manidoo* is the shadow of motion and trace of spirit, that shadow of the fourth person in native stories; the *manidoo* is more than the intention of the author, the interpreter, or even the tease of native stories. Native stories commove a sense of presence, and that intention movement is second nature. Pronouns are the intention of authors, the tease of survivance and constancy.

The historical situations and hermeneutics of native stories must consider the intentions of the author, the transmutations of culture and character, and the resistance of causal motivations in trickster stories. The *manidoo* is a trace of presence, consciousness, and native identities in stories. Winter is more than the name, and the *manidoo* is more than a season. Native shadows are a presence in the name, but not everyone has a sense of that presence.

"Language makes possible something like intention, and not the reverse," observes David Couzens Hoy in *The Critical Circle*. "On the other hand, 'language' is not an unembodied phenomenon; it manifests itself only in particular situations. When someone talks about language, he is talking about use; and use, roughly, precludes bringing in the notion of consciousness." The *manidoo*, as the fourth person in native stories, is not a "notion" but a *trace* of presence and consciousness. The author is an absence, and the text has intentions; the *manidoo* is a trace, not a cause.

Hermeneutics is a mediation of presence, experience, and the sleeves of silence; extensions of the text are interpretations. "The intention is thus not something different from the poem, nor does it 'accompany' the poem," writes Hoy. "It *is* the poem. Yet it is what the poem shows, not just what it says. That is why people often look beyond the text for the *author's* intention; they have not yet seen what is being shown." Lastly, the hermeneutic theory of "interpretive *dialogue*" is how the "intention of a text is determined by the interpreter."[39]

Many native stories have been traduced in translation and reduced in social science interpretations to serve the intentions of culture, the objectivism of historical dominance. The author, reader, and text are named by the culture masters. The *manidoo* is a trace of native presence in a name, a nickname, and stories. "Language is possible because it strives for the impossible," and inherent in language, "at all its levels, is a connection of struggle and anxiety from which it cannot be freed," posits Maurice Blanchot in *The Work of Fire*. "The cruelty of language comes from the fact that it endlessly evokes its death without ever being able to die."[40]

OTHER DIMENSIONS

Novelist D. H. Lawrence declared natives dead, "dead and unappeased," dispossessed, and unforgiving. "The Red Man died hating the white man." He does not believe in "our civilization, and so is our mystic enemy, for we push him off the face of the earth," he notes in *Studies in Classic American Literature*. Curiously, the spirit of a place does not exert "its full influence upon a newcomer until the old inhabitant is dead or absorbed."

Lawrence doubted that "any real reconciliation, in the flesh, between the white and the red" was possible. "There is no mystic conjunction between the spirit of the two races." His mystic want, erotic ipseity, and minimal tease of natives, are racialist simulations of the other. The lonesome, nostalgic, bourgeois occidental, bored or broken by the rational authority of modernism, would discover, once more, a secular salvation in the exotic "traditions" of the other; in the tone and caption of tragic victimry.

The *indian* is loved and hated, and the "desire to extirpate" and "glorify" are "rampant still, today." However, a "minority of whites intellectualize the Red Man and laud him to the skies. But this minority of whites is mostly a high-brow minority with a big grouch against its own whiteness. So there you are."[41]

So, here we are.

The *indian* is a daemon, a modernist simulation of the other in the wicked cause of savagism and civilization. The *indian* daemon is a perverse misnomer, a concoction of aversions, curious notions, and "traditions" in the name of a native absence. The eversion of native stories in translation has been cited as *indian* in cultural studies and histories. That eversion is an inane union of other names, such as *indian* traditions, *indian* shamanism, *indian* values, *indian* humor, *indian* arts, *indian* identity, the *indian* way, *indian* alcoholism, *indian* scapegoat, and the *indian* tragedy. The *indian* as mythic daemon, and the new *indian* as natural ecologist, are secured in social sciences theses, motion pictures, literature, and in national histories. The *indian* daemon is maintained by the enervation of native reason, and the absence of native differences; the *indian* is the absence of natives in the course of modernity.

The *indian* and *alien* are inscriptions of the other; the *indian* is a simulation of an absence, and aliens are an arcane presence, the entities of other dimensions. The *indian* as natural ecologist, in the paradoxical notions of *mother earth*, is a daemon of reversions. The *indian* countermines reason with interior "traditions" and, at the same time, the *indian* is a simulation of modernity. The alien is the other, the fantastic *native* outside of reason, the extreme of reason, and the *exterior* of other dimensions; the alien is the overreal other of modernity.

"The red people had no need to consider migration from their nature-based system," writes Ed McGaa in *Rainbow Tribe*. "Their land was kept pure and clean." The postindian sun dancer, retired combat fighter pilot, and law school graduate seemed to succor the absence of natives, a tragic victimry. McGaa asserted that such "treasures" as "harmonious sociology, unselfish leadership, warm family kinship, and honest justice" proliferated in traditional tribal cultures. His sense of nostalgia is a renunciation of modernism; the manifest sanction of tradition over reason and liberal contingencies in a constitutional democracy.

The conceivable outcome of a "rainbow tribe," and overreal *indian* traditions, is absolute boredom and melancholy. Consider the consumer manners of *indian* casinos and the mores of *indians* in commercial movies as the measures of competition for tradition and other "rainbow" ventures.[42]

"Simulation is the ecstasy of the real," states Jean Baudrillard in *Fatal Strategies*. "Every strategy we invent is in the hope that it will unfold unexpectedly. We invent the real in the hope of seeing it unfold as a great ruse." People "are not looking to amuse themselves, they seek a fatal diversion. No matter how boring, the important thing is to increase boredom; such an increase is salvation, it is ecstasy." Perhaps, he asserted, the "only one, fatal strategy" is theory.[43]

McGaa is a veteran of fatal strategies, the aesthetic reversions and simulations of *indian* traditions; an increase of boredom. More than two decades ago he announced to some eighty farmers and townies in Waseca, Minnesota, that excessive materialism and the loss of respect for *mother earth* are the cause of problems in the world. "Our ways come from a woman, your ways come from a man," he told the audience. "Anytime you get away from the natural way you're going to get into trouble. You have to get back to tribal thinking." Getting back to the present must be a trickster story.

McGaa shared the lectern that night with Arthur Harkins, a future-studies teacher at the University of Minnesota. McGaa, the *indian* revivalist, evacuated the presence of modernism for the fatal strategies and simulations of *mother earth*; the audience was bored by their own need for diversions.

Harkins, in his lecture, evacuated modernism for the fantastic galactic frontiers of the future. "Until we develop the technology on the basis of solar power, or fusion power to take us away from this vale of tears, we are pretty much bound by a conservation ethic," said the futurist. "To really know ourselves is to become at least temporarily alien to ourselves," and in "order to advance as humans we may have to become temporarily other than human."

The futurist and the revivalist renounced the enlightenment, in a sense, and espoused the antithetical simulations of absence over presence; the fatal strategies, and conversions of modernism, were the same ruse. The revivalist enlisted more than a dozen good citizens to take part in a sacred sweat lodge ceremony. The futurist, however, had the last word that night. "I think that we are all faced with the problem of controlling technologies whether it is a chemical compound or a tomahawk."[44]

Russell Means, at about the same time, swore to jurors in federal court that "all living things come from our sacred *mother earth*." He was on trial for alleged violations of federal laws in connection with the armed occupation of Wounded Knee, South Dakota. "It is our philosophy that because all living things come from one mother, our mother," he stated, "we have to treat one another with the same respect and reverence that we would our own blood relatives." The federal judge dismissed the charges. Means, since then, has continued the fatal strategies of his activism as a movie actor.

Dennis Banks, on trial at the same time, swore to the jurors in his opening statement that the "piercing of the skin is a reminder to me that I truly owe myself to *mother earth*," and "when the flesh was torn from me I realized what a great injustice it would be to lose the Oglala Sioux Religion." Banks, since the federal court trial, has turned his attention to corporate investments on reservations, one more postindian fatal strategy. Banks is *anishinaabe* and converted to the Sun Dance Religion. "I should have been a capitalist years ago."[45]

Jean Baudrillard has asserted that the universe "moves toward extremes, and not towards equilibrium." The simulation of *mother earth* — the ecstasy of the real — is the banal balance of creation and nature; *mother earth*, the model, is named the real in the contest of ecstasies. The seduction of an unnameable native absence becomes an *indian* tradition. Then, the transcendence of the *mother earth* simulation is an ironic absence of the other ecstasy.

There is no obvious transmotion, no creative curve of stories, in the banal simulations of these revivalists, futurists, and activists. The consecration of *mother earth*, the evacuation of presence, alien transmutation, and the renunciation of modernism, are over-real, the fatal strategies of simulations. That sense of survivance in stories is native transmotion, not an escape to tradition or futurity.

"Today, in order to survive, illusion no longer works; one must draw nearer to the nullity of the real," observes Baudrillard. "Even revolution can take place only if there is the possibility of spectacle; what people of goodwill deplore is that the media has put an end to the real event."[46] These revivalists, futurists, and activists are men of the media, the fatal strategies of *indian* simulations over native survivance.

VISIONARY RUMORS

The incantations of *mother earth*, a truistic native association, otherwise a pious metronymic custom, and synecdochic reversions of *indian* traditions, are comparable to the sinewy estates of *indian* captivity narratives and relative to the fantastic realities of the alien other in futurity; *indians* and aliens are not, by any means, exclusive ties, simulations, or experiences in time or place. Namely, the stories of alien abduction are relative, as summaries, to the simulations of the *indian* other, and to the sentiments of savagism in captivity narratives. The simulations of aliens and the other are the scares and aversions of nature, atavistic visions, ecstatic severance, the daemons of the unconscious, and the ruse of cultural nationalism.

"The connection between humans and beings from other dimensions has been illustrated in myths and stories from various cultures for millennia," observes John Mack in *Abduction: Human Encounters with Aliens.* "Across many epochs, humans have reported making contact with a multitude of gods, spirits, angels, fairies, demons, ghouls, vampires, and sea monsters."[47] The *indian* has been named a demon, but not a fairy; cast as a god, but not a vampire; a trickster transmutation, but not a monster of science. The noble alien in some stories, the *indian* is the loathsome shaman in others, and the simulations of both sin and salvation. These motives are conversant with a monotheistic culture of tragic victimry.

Mack, a medical doctor and professor of psychiatry at Harvard Medical School, noted that the "mystic or the shaman, like the abductee, makes a pilgrimage, usually with ardor, to receive a new dimension of experience or knowledge." He treated nearly a "hundred cases of alien abduction" and observed that "the abduction phenomenon is not simply traumatic. Experiencers may be left with fears, nightmares, and some sequelae of severe stress," but they are not mere victims of abduction encounters. Some are shamans and healers, others are teachers. "My own impression, gained from what abductees have told me, is that consciousness expansion and personal transformation is a basic aspect of the abduction phenomenon."

New Age trances and romances announce much the same transpersonal experience and "consciousness expansion" as named in encounters with aliens, *indians,* and the other. The truistic cut and measure of these experiences would, of course, be the ecstasies of simulations. Likewise, the stories of postindian visionaries are ecstatic. Such experiences are not the same as the severe visions of a shaman: the chancy, portentous silence and separation in other dimensions. Shamanic visions and that trusty, unnameable sense of healing are seldom consummated outside of the politics of native communities.

"Virtually all the abductees with whom I have worked closely have demonstrated a commitment to changing their relationship to the earth, of living more gently on it or in greater harmony with the other creatures that live here," writes Mack. "Each seems to be devoted to transforming his or her relationships with other people, to expressing love more openly, and transcending aggressive impulses." He points out that many abductees "experienced a dual

45

identity as both a human and alien being." They see the world from both perspectives.[48] Consider the tension of redoubled identities, the native and *indian* in separate dimensions, and the experiences of captives on the frontier.

Fanny Kelly, for instance, was captured at age nineteen by "an overwhelming force of hostile Sioux" on an emigrant train west of Fort Laramie. She was a captive for five months. "Reader, imagine my feelings after the terrible scenes of the day previous; the desolate white woman in the power of revengeful savages, not daring to speak, lest their fury should fall on my defenseless head," she wrote in *My Captivity among the Sioux Indians*. "My great anxiety now was to preserve my sanity, which threatened to be overcome."

Kelly mentioned another sense of time and presence, a second perception of her experiences as a captive. "I was ill at ease among my new friends, and they told me that my eyes wore a strangely wild expression, like those of a person constantly in dread of some unknown alarm." She suffered hunger, thirst, and many privations. "Once more free and safe among civilized people, I looked back on the horrible past with feelings that defy description."[49]

The narratives of slavery, captivity, abduction, and servitude by slavers, colonists, natives, *indians*, and others have in common a moral resistance to dominance, the case of survivance over victimry. The narratives of *indian* captivity and alien abduction are created as ordeals, transmutations, and end with an escape or return to family and community. Richard VanDerBeets notes in *The Indian Captivity Narrative* that this "ritual passage" or "archetypal journey of initiation," a variation of the death and rebirth archetype, is a mode and pattern of *indian* captivity narratives.[50]

America is the source of most alien abduction stories and reports of Unidentified Flying Objects. Carl Jung named the *objects* "psychic products" and the stories a *"visionary rumour."* The flight of these rumor objects "resembles that of a flying insect" and "the occupants are about three feet high and look like human beings, or, conversely, are utterly unlike us," he writes in *Flying Saucers*.[51]

C. D. B. Bryan attended an Abduction Study Conference on "encounters of the fourth kind" at the Massachusetts Institute of Technology and reported that the "descriptions of the aliens by abductees are consistent." The aliens, named the *small grays*, were described as "smooth featured" and hairless. John Mack, at the end of the conference, "suggested that the data accumulated on the abduction phenomenon was so revolutionary that it was necessary for us to abandon our traditional scientific methods and adopt some other approach."[52] Consistently, natives have presented natural reason, the *manidoo* of the *anishinaabe*, shamanic elation, or *élan vital*, the unnameable, but not vitalism, the tease of trickster stories, and other traces of survivance, as mighty sources of consciousness.

Clearly, aliens are not *indians* by conception or description, but the experiences of abductees and captives are similar. John Mack identifies "five basic dimensions" to consider in the explanations of "abduction phenomena." The dimensions of abduction by *small grays* are relative to the experiences reported in *indian* captivity narratives.

Mack noted a "high degree of consistency of detailed abduction accounts," told with emotion by "reliable observers." The second dimension is the "absence of psychiatric illness or other psychological or emotional factors that could account for what is being reported;" the third, "physical changes and lesions affecting the bodies of the experiencers;" and fourth, the "association with UFOs witnessed independently by others while abductions are taking place." The fifth dimension is the "reports of abductions by children as young as two or three years of age."[53]

Budd Hopkins investigated hundreds of curious accounts and observed that "abductees are neither paranoid nor suffering from delusions of grandeur; they are honest people who have suffered traumatic experiences they do not understand." The abductees are victims "in every sense of the word," he writes in *Intruders*. "And yet, unasked, they are also pioneers. For good or for ill, they have seen the future."[54]

The aliens and *indians* are simulations of the other in stories and narratives. The abductees and captives are pioneers in their stories, and they encounter the other in adverse dimensions: the savage, an awesome renunciation of modernism; and aliens, the small grays of technocracy and futurity. The captivity narratives and abduction stories are diverse literary frontiers, and neither relative pioneer has a referent. The avian aliens seem to be in need of some contact with "primitives" on earth, the *indians* are the absence of natives, and neither has a presence.

Conceivably, the *anishinaabe* pictomyths, or paintings of humanoid figures on rocks, are of none other than the aliens; the pictomyths of the spirit, *manidoo*, and the trickster, *naanabozho*, painted on rocks near the water, and also inscribed on birchbark, could be a native archive of the small grays near the Great Lakes. The *anishinaabe* "claim that the pictures were the work" of the *manidoo*, noted William Jones. "It is said that tiny folk amuse themselves sliding down the slant" in the rocks near the water. The *anishinaabe* "say that the little people were seen on the rocks when their ancestors first came to the island." The "little people" vanished into the water.[55]

This is an ironic ethical situation, as the simulations of aliens and *indians* are a marvelous presence of the victims who created the other in stories and narratives. What remains are "two different intelligences that lack a common plane of understanding," suggests Hopkins. The simulation of the alien is a "morally ambiguous and self-contained external reality. A reality, I should add, that none of us understands."[56]

The *indian* captivity narratives are a "sensational literature" with a remarkable consistency in at least two distinctive periods. Jules Zanger pointed out that the first narratives were "both concrete evidence and symbolic testimony." The Puritans wrote of religious conviction and mercy. "The religious intensity of the early narratives was replaced in the eighteenth century by a merely formal piety, and the narrative became increasingly a propaganda vehicle concerned in the main with revealing the cruelty and barbarity of the savages," he notes in his introduction to *My Captivity among the Sioux Indians* by Kelly. "The female captive, because of her greater potential for pathetic effects and because of the excitement she created as an object of sexual interest, all but crowded the male captive off the scene."[57]

There is no evidence that the narratives were related to psychic disturbance, psychiatric illness, or psychological problems. Fanny Kelly included affidavits and testimonials by several *indians*, military officers, and many other notables attesting to the authenticity of her narrative. Spotted Tail and other *indian* chiefs and warriors, for instance, swore that "We, the undersigned, chiefs and head men of the Dakota and Sioux Indians, do hereby acknowledge and certify to the facts set forth in the foregoing affidavit of Mrs. Fanny Kelly, as to her captivity and to the destruction of her property by members of our nation."

Spotted Tail and the other *indian* chiefs acknowledged the experience of the captivity but not, of course, the veritable narrative. The signatures of these *indians* were five marks certified as valid by a notary public. The "authentic" *indians* were not readers of the narrative. *My Captivity among the Sioux Indians* and many other captivity narratives are ironic in the sense that the five marks of attestation are undermined by the context of the implied reader and the commercial concerns of the publisher. Fanny Kelly, the ironist, created a frontier experience in a captivity narrative that was more readable with an *indian* warrant of authenticity.

The certification of captivity narratives is comparable to the serious investigation, assurance, and treatment of the traumas of alien abduction. The experiences of abduction are consistent, and causes of the experience cannot be explained as emotional problems. Consider, in this sense, the ironic archive on aliens and *indians*, the discrepancies of warrants and documents: the experiences of captives, abductees, and others in cosmic servitude are vouched true, and the narratives of captivity, the tricky stories of survivance, are creative, forever dialogic, and literary.

Carl Jung observed that the "*visionary rumour*" of fantastic, cosmic intervention is a human projection. The "love of adventure" and "technological audacity" may be the motives of "futuristic fantasies," but the "underlying cause," the impulse and spin of such fantasies, is "a situation of distress." He noted that the "universal mass rumour was reserved for our enlightened, rationalistic age." The *indian* has been both the absence and the presence of reason in the visionary rumors of modernity. Jung asserted that the "present world situation is calculated as never before to arouse expectations of a redeeming, supernatural event. If these expectations have not dared to show themselves very clearly, this is simply because no one is deeply rooted enough in the tradition of earlier centuries to consider an intervention from heaven as a matter of course."[58]

TRANSETHNIC TRIAGE

Clement William Vizenor, my father, was born on the White Earth Reservation in Minnesota. He moved to the city in search of employment during the Great Depression. The stories of natives on the move are common; the natural traces of native transmotion and survivance. My father moved with his mother, brothers, and sisters, in more than one dimension to the city. He was a native emigrant, a man of uncommon stories in a constitutional democracy, and wise to the mundane exclusions of the 1930s — the cut and count of *indian* simulations and identities. He was sure of the moment, neither a newcomer to the contingencies of poverty, nor a poser in the name of victimry.

Clement was never hired as an *indian*, but he was counted as *one* on the census. My father was not asked to name his tribe or his proportion of "*indian* blood" in the U.S. Census of 1930. However, his parents were asked questions on the reservation about identity and native affinity in an earlier national census; my father and his generation were enumerated as *indians*, the first national census simulation; the votive politics of assimilation, and transethnic triage.[59]

"Transethnic" in the sense that the simulation of the *indian* is the absence of the native, and the *indian* is the other in the archive of *institutive* simulations. Triage, the decisive sacrifice of the *real*, the unnameable, and the antecedence of natives, to save the *indian*, is the "archive fever" of preservation, and the cause of narrative dominance. Natives are evermore the other, twice the other in the transethnic studies of *indian* victimry.

"*There is no archive without a place of consignation, without a technique of repetition, and without a certain exteriority*," asserts Jacques Derrida in *Archive Fever*. Moreover, "*every* archive . . . is at once *institutive* and *conservative*." Traditions, preservation, death, and deconstruction are the causes of the archive, the curious traces of the other, the outside, the radical separation of public and private contingencies.[60]

The *indian* is an archive; the simulations, discoveries, treaties, documents of ancestry, traditions in translation, museum re-mains, and the aesthetics of victimry. Cultural and transethnic studies are common access to the *indian* archive, but not to a native presence, that unnameable sense of difference. The archive is *institutive* and, at the same time, it is the conservation and deconstruction of the *indian* in literature and history.

Minnesota, at the time my father moved to the city, counted only about eleven thousand *indians*, about three percent of the state population; some ten percent of the total *indian* population in the nation lived in urban areas, three percent more than were counted a decade earlier in the census. The national enumeration of the *anishinaabe* was 21,549 in 1930, compared to more than a hundred thousand today.[61]

My father was *anishinaabe* by reservation ancestors and an *indian* by simulation; the census counted him as *indian*, the absence of a native presence in the city. He was the other in the archive, and the double other in the enumeration of *indians* on the census; the exclusion in national documents of his *anishinaabe* experience and sense of privacy.

Michel Foucault points out in *The Archaeology of Knowledge* that the common "will to knowledge" establishes "certain functions" of observance, measure, and classification of objects. He notes that "this will to knowledge, thus reliant upon institutional support and distribution, tends to exercise a sort of pressure, a power of constraint upon other forms of discourse." He considers that in "every society the production of discourse is at once controlled, selected, organised and redistributed according to a certain number of procedures."[62]

Clement, his brothers, and other natives in urban areas were *indians* by simulation, transethnic by separation, but native in their stories of survivance. One contractor refused to hire my father and uncles as housepainters because they were *indians*; the contractor reasoned that *indians* never lived in houses, and therefore would not know how to paint one. Consequently, my father, uncles, and other natives had to present themselves to subsequent contractors as some other emigrant; at last my father and uncles were hired to paint houses as Italians. Their stories are a counterpoise, one simulation to outcant the other, a tricky outcome of the "will to knowledge" about *indians*; their pose in a culture of painters secured a presence in the name of survivance.

Alice Mary Beaulieu, my grandmother, was born January 3, 1886, and nineteen years later she married Henry Vizenor. They were both born on the White Earth Reservation. Sixteen years later, abandoned by her husband, she moved with her children, first to rural towns in the state, and then to the city. The family lived for several years in a cold-water flat in downtown Minneapolis.

My grandmother was an *indian* on the reservation and an emigrant in the city. She endured the seasons of poverty and the winters over tricky stories but never lost her soul to victimry. She teased the lonesome and, in her late sixties, married a generous, sightless, younger man.

Alice never summoned the reservation shamans; the causes of their wounds, and the unrest of their visions, were onerous and not the newsy stories of survivance in the city. She must have been wary of reservation men and their traditions; yet, she teased chance and mentioned the *miinidiwag*, the native "giveaway" in *anishinaabe*. She never used the word *potlatch*, in the sense of native economies, but surely understood the ceremonial give and game of wealth and power.

Alice lived on social security, a minimal income, and told ironic stories about lace, music, medicine, motorcars, and more, not as envies, and not as rue, but as a trace of the potlatch in the creative, narrative giveaway of her uncommon experiences. She had always been a mighty healer, and then, on the move with her blind husband, she became an unnameable reassurance to lonesome women lost in suburbia. She told curative stories in an ironic giveaway.

Earl Restdorf and his native stunner set out, once a week at times, on a metropolitan bus, and rode to the end of the line; there, they went door to door and sold brushes and brooms to housewives. My grandmother told me that they were always invited into fine houses by lonely women. They were served a nice lunch and then shown pictures of children and families; the reservation native, a newcomer to the envies of the bourgeois, was evermore the warm and worthy listener to the contingencies of economic histories.

Alice could heal a worried heart with a natural tease, the most common unities in trickster stories—just the right touch of survivance. She was never bothered that they seldom sold a brush or broom in the suburbs; the venders must have heard the envies of parvenuism, the vent and concessions of modernity. Together, my grandmother, the native emigrant, and her sightless husband conceived of a new giveaway ceremony. There, at the end of the bus line, they had so much to give in the suburban estates of victimry.

There are two crucial dimensions of the native potlatch: the ceremonial distribution of wealth and the destruction of personal property. The distribution of resources is a common convention in native communities, otherwise named a giveaway; philanthropy, charitable donations, tithe manners, and even certain measures of taxation could be considered in a wider sense of the custom, but there are marked distinctions. The destruction of resources, and the curse of wealth, is a tricky convention to understand as a differentiation of power and prestige.

The mastery of native resources and the desecration of the environment as sources of wealth and power are abstruse cues of obligation, and misuses of the potlatch in any culture. Philanthropy is the second notice of institutive power, a mask that covers the separation, and the ruins of natural resources in many national economies.

"Once the resources are dissipated, there remains the prestige acquired by the one who wastes," observes Georges Bataille in *The Accursed Share*. "The waste is an ostentatious squandering to this end, with a view to a superiority over others that he attributes to himself by this means. But he misuses the negation he makes of the utility of the resources he wastes, bringing into contradiction not only himself but man's entire existence." Bataille points out that the potlatch is "like commerce, a means of circulating wealth, but it excludes bargaining. More often than not it is the solemn giving of considerable riches, offered by a chief to his rival for the purpose of humiliating, challenging and obligating him. The recipient has to erase the humiliation and take up the challenge; he must satisfy the *obligation* that was contracted by accepting. He can only reply, a short time later, by means of a new potlatch, more generous than the first: He must pay back with interest."[63]

Strictly speaking, notions of the potlatch, "should be reserved for expenditures of an agonistic type, which are instigated by challenges and which lead to responses," argues Bataille in *Visions of Excess*. "It is only through loss that glory and honor are linked to wealth."[64]

Alice, and many other natives, seemed to actuate a postmodern potlatch in the city. My grandmother teased the sacred, that moral mime of *indian* traditions, and earned new trickster stories in the suburbs; the outcome was a giveaway. She waited on the chance of humor over sacrifice and of native survivance over victimry.

The potlatch ceremonies, once crossed by missionaries and outlawed by the government, were connected to the resistance of the Kwakiutl, or *kwakwaka'wakw* in the language of the *kwakwala*, more than any other native culture. "Potlatches are held to name children, mourn the dead, transfer rights and privileges from one generation to the next, and conduct marriage exchanges."[65] The name *potlatch* is a word in Chinook Jargon, a fur trade language, and the custom is worldly, a giveaway.

The White Earth Reservation was instituted by concessions, coercion, and a treaty, a caricature of native sovereignty. The treaty was an invitation to a perversive giveaway, and a century later, the due conscience of that ironic covenant would be the raison d'être of casinos, that crafty union of avarice and sovereignty.

The treaty removal of *indians* to federal exclaves was never historical evidence of a native culture; *indian* culture is a simulation, not a resistance to the converse giveaway. Julia Spears had moved from Madeline Island to the Chippewa Agency near Crow Wing in Minnesota, and then, on June 4, 1868, she was removed to the White Earth Reservation. "It was a year after the treaty before all the Indians could be persuaded to leave their old home," she wrote in a letter.[66] Native stories are tragic wisdom and survivance, not the countenance of *indians* or the counterfeit heirs in the histories of dominance.

My grandmother conceived of the reservation in stories, not in the metes and bounds of land allotments or in the wily timber concessions; she created a homeland in the memories of native humor, a trickster survivance, not in a nation of traitorous *indians* and federal agents and never in the rites of tragic victimry. These ironies, teased at the heart of scorn, deceit, and at once false pity, were the very counter sources of her humor, natural reason, mediative ethics, and new giveaway stories in the city. She teased the sunrise at the windows, the crowns of winter, teased tricksters to the bone in stories, and she reassured the lonesome heirs in the suburbs that the old traces of dominion were erased in a native giveaway.

Native giveaways, the wink of trickster stories, and memories of a comic nation, and reservation, are creases outside the institutive surveillance and sway of the government. Always, the double agents of the social sciences were abused by their own measures and could not bear the tease and humor of trickster stories. My grandmother, a mighty storier, was deft and worthy of laughter and the tease of native reason. Native stories are a natural giveaway, and laughter is the response; the obligation is literature.

"Laughter frees consciousness from the confines of its own discourse, and this freedom is the first prerequisite for the creation of literature," writes David Patterson in *Literature and Spirit.* "Laughter thus manifested in the word is not simply a reaction but is a response that in turn seeks a response. Laughter, then, is a form of discourse that turns discourse back on itself."[67]

Mikhail Bakhtin observes that "Europe knew neither the mysticism nor the magic of laughter; laughter was never infected, even slightly, by the 'red tape' of moribund officialdom. Therefore, laughter could not be deformed or falsified as could every other form of seriousness, in particular the pathetic. Laughter remained outside official falsifications, which were coated with a layer of pathetic seriousness." The simulation of the *indian* is an occidental case of "pathetic seriousness," the course of tragic victimry. Therefore, he notes in *The Dialogic Imagination*, "serious genres" and "high forms of language and style" are "drenched in conventionality, hypocrisy and falsification. Laughter alone remained uninfected by lies."[68]

Many native authors have actuated a literary giveaway in their stories, and a narrative deconstruction of cultural dominance. William Apess, Luther Standing Bear, D'Arcy McNickle, N. Scott Momaday, Leslie Silko, James Welch, Louis Owens, Thomas King, Kimberly Blaeser, Gordon Henry, and others have created a transmotion of native consciousness, a literature of laughter, tragic wisdom, and survivance. Native stories are a giveaway.

Owens, in an autobiographical essay, honored the motion of his father. "Once we had left Mississippi for good, we moved about a great deal, never living in the same house longer than two years and often as briefly as a few months before the rent couldn't be paid or a new job beckoned my father. Sometimes we moved just a few miles from where we had been, always staying in the country where we could hunt right outside the backyard. My father labored on farms and ranches driving tractors, working cattle, building fences, fixing machinery, and generally doing whatever could be done. A man of extraordinary broad skills, he could do or fix anything, it seemed."

Owens created a narrative of survivance, a native giveaway. Natives have been on the move since the creation of motion in stories; motion is the originary. The novelist is answerable to the hue of transmotion, that mighty curve of the unnameable, in native survivance stories. Owens reasoned that "writing novels is the most exciting thing in the world, an exploration into the unknowable, each one a new world."[69] Now, the memories and stories of transmotion are a natural giveaway. Native stories are national obligations, the gift of power, and the wise antidotes to modernity.

The "authentic consumption" of the *potlatch* and, in a sense, the giveaway, "ought to be solitary," but the action would not be complete. "And this action that is brought to bear on others is precisely what constitutes the gift's power, which one acquires from the fact of losing. The exemplary virtue of the potlatch is given in this possibility for man to grasp what eludes him, to combine the limitless movements of the universe with the limit that belongs to him," writes Bataille.

Today, "society is a huge counterfeit," and the "*truth* of wealth has underhandedly slipped into *extreme poverty.* The true luxury and the real potlatch of our times falls to the poverty-stricken, that is, to the individual who lies down and scoffs. A genuine luxury requires the complete contempt for riches, the somber indifference of the individual who refuses work and makes his life on the one hand an infinitely ruined splendor, and on the other, a silent insult to the laborious lie of the rich. . . . One might say, finally, that the lie destines life's exuberance to revolt." The *indian* is a counterfeit; native stories are resistance, survivance, and the "lasting obligation" of a new giveaway. "To give is obviously to lose, but the loss apparently brings a profit to the one who sustains it."[70]

CONSTATIVE ARCHIVES

Pierre Bourdieu, in *The Logic of Practice*, points out that a "man possesses in order to give. But he also possesses by giving. A gift that is not returned can become a debt, a lasting obligation."[71] Native stories are a literary giveaway. The debt is a lasting, moral obligation of the nation.

Foucault argues that "we need . . . a new economy of power relations" in the "theoretical and practical sense" of economy. The point here, in the absence of natives, is to counter the enterprise of reason that sustains the *indian* as a social science simulation of modernity. "The relationship between rationalization and excesses of political power is evident. And we should not need to wait for bureaucracy or concentration camps to recognize the existence of such relations." He notes that "we should investigate the forms of resistance and attempts made to dissociate these relations."[72]

The American Revolution, for instance, that celebrated war of independence, was the second, not the first, mighty revolution on this continent. The first was the native resistance to missionaries and colonial dominance, and that revolution was executed almost a century before the second revolution that overturned the British Empire.

Natives of the southwest executed the first united revolution on August 10, 1680, and defeated the Spanish Kingdom of New Mexico. "This dramatic episode represented one of the bloodiest defeats ever experienced by Spain in her overseas empire," observes

Marc Simmons in the introduction to *The Pueblo Revolt.* "And, as historians are accustomed to say, it was the first successful battle for independence fought against a European colonial power in what was to become the United States."[73] Natives in these communities were united by their resistance and distinctive theocracies.

The American Revolution became the reason for dominion over natives; at once, natives lost their sovereignty in the historical contradictions of a constitutional democracy. The Constitution of the United States commences with a national, editorial pronoun; the *we* embraces others in the name of a "more perfect union." The *we* was not native, but the other in the archive of democracy; the *indian* was named twice in the discourse of constitutional governance.

The Preamble announces the reasons to remove and restrain natives on federal exclaves, or reservations, as measures to "insure domestic tranquillity" and "secure the blessings of liberty." Clearly, natives have served the nation in many wars, and natives have been protected by treaties and court decisions based on the Constitution.

The First Amendment provides for the "freedom of speech," but this constitutional right has been actuated on reservations only with unusual courage. For instance, the editor of *The Progress,* the first newspaper published on the White Earth Reservation, declared in the first issue, March 25, 1886, that the "novelty of a newspaper published upon this reservation may cause many to be wary in their support, and this from a fear that it may be revolutionary in character. . . . We shall aim to advocate constantly and without reserve, what in our view, and in the view of the leading minds upon this reservation, is the best for the interests of its residents."

The dedication of *The Progress* was enough to threaten the federal *indian* agent, T. J. Sheehan. He confiscated the press and ordered the removal of Theodore Beaulieu, the editor, and Augustus Beaulieu, the publisher, both of whom were members of the White Earth Reservation. Sheehan wrote to the editor and publisher that they had "circulated a newspaper without first obtaining authority or license so to do from the honorable Secretary of the Interior, honorable Commissioner of Indian Affairs, or myself as United States Indian Agent."

The second issue of *The Progress* was published more than six months later on October 8, 1887. The U.S. District Court had decided in favor of the editors, confirming the right to publish a newspaper without government permission or restraint. This was the first constitutional case that maintained the freedom of the press on a reservation. "By referring to the date on the first page of this issue, our readers will observe that we made our bow, or rather, more strictly, we began to bow, but a heavy hand was laid upon us, and we have not been able to resume the perpendicular until now," wrote Theodore Beaulieu in an editorial. "The court asserted and defended the right of any member of a tribe to print and publish a newspaper upon his reservation just as he might engage in any other lawful occupation, and without surveillance and restrictions."[74]

The Fourth Amendment to the Constitution provides for the "right of the people to be secure in their persons, houses, papers, and effects against unreasonable searches and seizures." Natives on federal exclaves and treaty reservations have seldom realized this basic protection of personal and communal privacy. The dominion of reason, in governance and the social sciences, has been established over the right of natives to be secure at home, a sense of native sovereignty. The means of cultural surveillance, causal theories, simulations, and material vanities, are institutive; these measures, the manner and mien of the national archive, are more than aesthetic violations of constitutional rights. The simulation of the *indian* as the other, the representation of absence, is a moral and ethical contravention of native sovereignty.

According to Gary Gutting, Foucault maintains in *The Order of Things* "all social scientific knowledge is based on a particular conception of human reality, the conception of *man*." "Man is defined as that entity for which representations of objects exist. To assert the reality of man in this special sense is to posit a being with a puzzling dual status; something that is both an object in the world and an experiencing subject through which the world is constituted. Modern thought takes this conception of man as definitive of human reality." Foucault argues that this "one contingent construal" of reality "will soon pass."[75]

This "modern concept of man" is given, and the outcome is a contravention of native worldviews, tricky origin stories, privacy, and a sense of presence, by surveillance, transcription, translation, and elaborate transmission; the institutive sanctions of social science reason have decorated the simulation of the *indian* over the traces of native presence and resistance on this continent.

The Constitution of the United States has not always protected natives from the violations of their right of privacy by federal agents, archeologists, and social scientists; various agencies of the federal government, in fact, continue to encourage and subsidize an "archive fever" of research that countervenes the native right "to be secure in their persons." These institutive archives, national repositories, and the excessive studies of the other over the past century are evidence enough to document the violation of privacy and the rationalization of dominance over natives. Native memories, shamanic visions, and the unnameable, have been construed as absence; the *indian* is the world soul, and the object of reason in the archive of victimry.

CHAPTER TWO

Wistful Envies

F ranz Kafka cut to the wise of the native and created a rave
consciousness in his stories, a "fierce light" of awareness,
an intense, "immense tenderness, oddly good humor, and
a certain severe and reassuring formality." He was the *one* who
teased the absence of natives over a pronoun in translation, "If
one were only an Indian."

The author is native, a byword of chance on a "racing horse,
leaning against the wind" in an unsure sentence, aesthetic spurs
and reins thrown away, "for there needed no reins, and hardly saw
the land before one was smoothly shorn heath when horse's neck
and head would be already gone."[1]

Kafka was the *one*, evermore the native pronoun of aesthetic
transmotion and metamorphoses in stories, the sensitive cue of
mutual nouns and antecedence; never the weal and woe of a mere
literary missionary, he created a sense of pronominal action, the
"instantly alert" native as a presence. He teased the absence of
natives as others have done in their stories and autobiographies,
the romance of natives as the uncertain simulation of deliverance
and salvation. Yet, in the absence of a native noun, the oneiric one
is an ironic salvation in literature.

"Kafka was not very good at living; he lived only when he was
writing," notes Maurice Blanchot in *The Work of Fire*. "Kafka asked
more of literature, and got more from it, than many others have.
But he had first of all the honesty of accepting it in all its forms,
with all its constraints, as both craft and art equally, as a task and
as a privileged activity."[2]

God is a "language of absence," muses Edmond Jabès in *The
Little Book of Unsuspected Subversion*. "Writing outside time, always *beyond*, yet readable in the words it transcends: a writing
out of bounds then, outlandish even, which would weigh on our

writing with the infinite weight of absence."³ Consequently, the real native, as the *one* "outside time," must tease that transcendence and turn to the natural reason of creative literature, the presence of survivance over absence and victimry.

Jacques Derrida considers the ancient wounds of severance, the passion and endurance of writing, in his essay on "Edmond Jabès and the Question of the Book." Derrida could have mentioned the "incommensurable destiny" of natives "born of the book," as he so knowingly regarded the writing of our mentor Jabès. "For there could be no history without the gravity and labor of literality." Jews and natives surely create a comparable presence in the literature of survivance.

"The only thing that begins by reflecting itself is history," writes Derrida in *Writing and Difference*. "And this fold, this furrow, is the Jew. The Jew who elects writing which elects the Jew, in an exchange responsible for truth's thorough suffusion with historicity and for history's *assignment* of itself to its empiricity."

Jews and natives, an election and wise convocation of writers, retold by much the same assignments of severance: that a "poetic discourse *takes root* in wound" and is enunciated in literature and history. Jews and natives, the folds of tragic wisdom, and these "separated ones" who must now trust traces, "must become men of vision because we have ceased hearing the voice from within the unmediated proximity of the garden."⁴

Natives must bear the visions of the "separated ones" in the traces of oral stories; that tease of presence, the chance of natural sound, and the motion of the last tricky stories of lakeside winters. Our memories of the last native seasons are autobiographies; we are in the book. We are the traces of ancient wounds, the visions in the creative literature and histories of survivance.

"The world exists because the book does. For existing means growing with your name," notes Jabès in *The Book of Questions*. "To be able to say: 'I am in the book. The book is my world, my country, my roof, and my riddle. The book is my breath and my rest.'"

Jabès and natives are in the book, and the "book is the work of the book. It is the sun, which gives birth to the sea. It is the sea, which reveals the earth. It is the earth, which shapes man. Otherwise, sun, sea, earth, and man would be focused light without object, water moving without going or coming, wealth of sand without presence, a waiting of flesh and spirit without touch, having nothing that corresponds to it, having neither doubles nor opposites."[5]

Jabès is the trace of our vision in the book, a sure signatory of presence, and we are natives in the book; his endurance is more than a mere "defendant in this dialogue" of the "allegory and literality" of blood, passion, and the wounds of exclusion in history. He emerges "from the book only within the book," notes Derrida. For "Jabès, the book is not in the world, but the world is in the book."[6]

Listen, our presence is a native trace in the book, and this essay is a retrace of the others—a tease of theories, a critique of certainties and testimonies as second nature in the literature of survivance. "My words are 'alive' because they seem not to leave me," writes Derrida in *Speech and Phenomena*. Words seem not "to fall outside me, outside my breath, at a visible distance; not to cease to belong to me, to be at my disposition 'without further props.'"[7]

Derrida observed, as natives have in the tease of motion and the creation of presence in oral stories, that to understand the "power of the voice" and "being as presence," the "objectivity of the object" must be considered. The voice, and native oral stories, are ideal objects, the "*technical* mastery of objective being," since "its presence to intuition . . . has no essential dependence on any worldly or empirical synthesis, the restitution of its sense in the form of presence becomes a universal and unlimited possibility."[7]

The sound of stories in the ear is a sure sense of presence; the trace of that native presence is an absence, a causal notion or representation in the silence and distance of pictures and print. Native oral stories are creations of fugitive motion, a sense of presence that must be heard, and these oral creations are evermore; otherwise, our presence and restitution of sound and seasons would be traced to the sinecures of literature.

Walter Ong points out that oral "cultures indeed produce powerful and beautiful verbal performances of high artistic and human worth, which are no longer even possible once writing has taken possession of the psyche." Human consciousness, he notes, has an even greater potential in the creations of written literature. Writing, however, "separates the knower from the known and thus sets up conditions for 'objectivity.'" Orality "forms unities," but print isolates. "Print encourages a sense of closure" or completion and contributes to the "romantic notions of 'originality' and 'creativity'" compared to that sense of presence and empathetic transcendence in oral cultures.[8]

"What is neither true nor false is reality," writes Derrida in *The Post Card*. "But as soon as speech is inaugurated, one is in the register of the unveiling of the truth as of its contract of properness: presence, speech, testimony." Speech "is not full of something beyond itself which would be its object: but this is why all the more and all the better, it is full of itself, of its presence, its essence." The "living and animated" text, he observes, in the context of the tropes of presence, and the *folds*, or complications of the text, "full and authentic, will be of value only by virtue of the speech it will have as its mission to transport. Therefore, there also will be full texts and empty texts."[9] Natives are the tropes of presence in the book, the traces of oral stories—the virtue, vision, and mission that transports the literature of survivance.

Native presence is the voice, natural sound, and a trace in the book, but not silence, as silence is aesthetic, endorsed outside nature and the trace of seasons to the words. Artistic silence in oral stories is an instance of creation, neither coercion nor obedience; silence is an aesthetic transcendence, an unnameable pause, not a cause in memories and stories. Silence is not the cause of native absence, not a wise resistance, or the cure of faux reason, as causes "demand the incomplete. *Causes demand relative disorder*," argues John William Miller in *The Paradox of Cause*. "Cause pretends to offer us unity and order," but cause is both universal and restricted, anarchy and unity. "Cause is a dynamic concept because it describes an ideal, the ideal of the intelligibility of nature. For nature is in large part a mystery, and causal coherence is but one of the keys to its progressive solution."[10]

The translation of native oral stories is an absence, never the natural haunt of presence. The transmutation of sound, the voice, and the trace of memories into written sentences is, at best, an artful pose; an aesthetic absence at the instance of the creation of native stories. Surely there are traces of native presence in translations, but the cause of authored renditions is both a cultural discovery and a literary enterprise, and poses as a union of memories; the creases on the verso are cultural restriction and dominance. The sound of stories in the ear is our presence, and the other traces of that nature are survivance.

The traces of native presence, the voices and shadows of oral stories, that ubiety of creation, are not the same as the structural intercessions of signs and representations. The sound of the voice, and the trace of that presence, has no cause of preservation or simulation, no rush of memories in the desire and silence of a written sentence. There are intimate traces of native presence in the book, but the insinuations of traces are not the cause of scriptural identities. "The living present springs forth out of its nonidentity with itself and from the possibility of a retentional trace," observes Derrida. The trace is motion, "not an attribute" of presence, but "always already a trace." The "self of the living present is primordially a trace" of that creation and presence. "Originary being must be thought on the basis of the trace, and not the reverse."[11]

In *Positions*, Derrida reasons that the *différance* of presence, "the systematic play of differences, of the traces of differences," and what "defers presence . . . is the very basis on which presence is announced or desired in what represents it, its sign, its trace." The differences are generative movements, "the effects of transformations, and from this vantage the theme of *différance* is incompatible with the static, synchronic, taxonomic, ahistoric units in the concept of *structure*."[12] Natives are in the book, the *différance* of motion in the literature of survivance.

The native traces of presence are insinuations of the originary. The sound and motion of stories are survivance, the absence of discovery, dominance, and victimry. For instance, the Ghost Dance, a native trace of revitalization movements, is a spiritual vision of voice and presence; other natives would return in oral stories, and that sacred restitution of presence is the natural absence of others, the waves of newcomers to the continent.

Jack Wilson, Wovoka, the oracular creator of the Ghost Dance, moved natives to dance and warned, "do not tell the white people about this. Jesus is now upon the earth. He appears like a cloud. The dead are all alive again. I do not know when they will be here; maybe this fall or in the spring. When the time comes there will be no more sickness and everyone will be young again."

Wovoka and the endurance of his vision are in the book. His message of survivance was transcribed in English by Casper Edson, an Arapaho, who had been a student at the Carlisle Indian School.[13] Wovoka, a Paiute, was once separated by racialism and scientism; he is now the trace of an obscure vision in translation, a presence in a dialogic circle, and the gravity of literality.

Native presence is that trace of oral stories in the literature of creative resistance and survivance. Written sentences must bear the traces of our presence, and bear our *identité*, the same native presence of the continent. Likewise, sentences are the traces of our written absence, the caste of names, loan words, cut of manners and dominance, and the adnominal dependence on description as the real absence, the case that was never a presence.

Men "flee presence," notes John William Miller. "They are escapists," he asserts in *In Defense of the Psychological.* "Presence means responsible action, a burden, but also an excitement." Not much of presence endures in the aesthetic seasons of our names, but the trace of presence is not escapable, as the trace is altogether the *evasion* of absence. "Psychology defines no presence and so no extension of it into a world."[14] Natives, in this sense, would have escaped the animation of seasons and the presence of oral stories; however, absence, the unsure cut and reverse of presence in the aesthetic silence of the written sentence, is much more burdensome than the tease of native creation and the motion of sovereignty.

DIALOGIC CIRCLES

This essay is a creative consideration of the esoteric presence of natives, and the indications of varionatives in a "dialogic sphere" of survivance literature.[15] The tricky traces of varionative antecedence, the uncertain estates of names and memories, the ambiguities of nativism, the weighty reigns of pious ontologies, and the tease of an aesthetic absence as a native presence are some of the dialogic circles of creative autobiographies. The many simulations of cultures and the comments on native countenance by adventurers, ethnographers, and travel posers, otherwise the connoisseurs of the *indigène*, are "fragile" immersions of themes and characters "in a second nature, a second immediacy."

Mikhail Bakhtin observes that there is a "false tendency toward reducing everything to a single consciousness, toward dissolving in it the other's consciousness." There are "advantages of outsideness," since emotional empathy alone is neither the "placement of the self in the other's position," nor a translation of understanding the "other's language."

Natives have been reduced to that "single consciousness" of *indians* in the rhetoric of dominance. Natives in a "dialogic sphere" are distinctive, and the interpretations, evaluations, and diverse un-derstanding of the "other" are "creative by nature." Clearly, in this sense, creative understanding is active, and the meanings of vari-onative consciousness are multiple and continuous. "Creative un-derstanding continues creativity, and multiplies the artistic wealth of humanity" and the "creativity of those who understand."[16]

American *indians* are secured as international simulations, the faux memories and reasons of an untraceable real, and with no antecedence outside the histories of dominance. The native, in the hemispheric sense of that name, is a communal trace, a union of native *others* in oral stories and narratives. Lastly, varionatives are the native *différance*, the postmodern variations, differences, the contingencies of native memories, and cultural practices at the end of objectivism and modernity; varionatives are the positivities of native experiences.

The creative poses of varionative authors, and the tease of aes-thetic traditions in autobiographies, are dialogic circles of native chance, literature, and humanity. Many cultural ambiguities are the treasons and contradictions of national *indian* simulations, since most varionative authors are stateless in their literary cre-ations. Clearly, the political reversions to exclusive consciousness are the sudden closures of creative understanding and survivance.

The synecdochic turns in native names are ironic and romantic in translation, but the elaborate reductions of varionative con-sciousness to the simulations of pithy traditions are the perver-sions of dominance. Most varionative autobiographies are creative narratives, not the service of traditions or the mere rush of con-servative manners and histories; varionative autobiographies are the dialogic circles of survivance.

HIGHWATER TRACKS

Jamake Highwater, one of the most notable varionative authors, vowed that his mother "somehow retained much of the special *inclusivity* which I identify with the very heart of the primal world." She was tolerant and "always capable of sustaining utter faith in the most contradictory realities," he wrote in *The Primal Mind*. She "managed to keep alive her innermost identity as an Indian." Highwater reminisced that his mother, who could not read or write, "spun her recollections" in Blackfoot and French. He learned from his mother that "everything is real." His father, however, was not "traditional," and "knew very little about his Eastern Cherokee heritage despite his intense pride in being Indian."[17] The *indians*, of course, are simulations, the absence of natives, and the reminiscer turned out to be the absence of the *real* in his own varionative poses and stories.

"I am an Indian only because I say I am Indian. I am not enrolled on the reservations of my mother or father," asserts Highwater. "I came by my heritage through the legacy of my mother and my own long efforts to reclaim an obscure identity." Apparently that notice and reclamation was enriched when he was decorated with a native name "to honor my achievements on behalf of my people."[18] The Blackfoot ceremony he mentioned is comparable to the honors described by the native *autoposer*—Sylvester Long Lance.

"There is some place in me where the animal tracks are still fresh," writes Highwater in *This Song Remembers*. The *indians* are artists, because "art is essentially a form of transformation." His metaphors may tease an atavistic nature, but his romantic tread is unnatural. "I am not a person, I am a people, a Blackfeet."[19]

Jack Anderson, the syndicated columnist, was roused more by the poser than by the vain tropes of his autobiography. Blackfoot or not, he "fabricated much of the background that made him famous."

Highwater "lied about many details of his life," reported the columnist. "Asked why someone of such genuine and extraordinary talent felt he had to concoct a spurious background, Highwater said he felt that doors would not have opened for him if he had relied on his talent alone."[20]

In *Shadow Show: An Autobiographical Insinuation*, published two years after the exposé by Jack Anderson and five years after the publication of *The Primal Mind*, Highwater wrote that the "greatest mystery of my life is my own identity." Indeed, the impostor is an artist, and his insinuations are clever simulations, but surely not a great mystery.

Highwater insinuated the absence of natives to case a romantic presence. Moreover, he once announced that he had earned a doctorate in cultural anthropology at age nineteen and that he could speak eleven languages, but none of these assertions have ever been documented.[21]

Mostly, his imposture and simulations were ironic; at times comic, even faux tragic, as some natives were truly heartened by his promise. However tricky, in the "second immediacy" of this essay, his varionative manners are more artistic, inclusive, and remissable than eugenic blood counts and other fascist certitudes of identity.

"Deception is very much with us, but that should be no cause for despair," notes David Nyberg in *The Varnished Truth*. "On the contrary, there are many reasons why we ought to be thankful for the inventive craft, and for all those agreeable and useful things it enables us to do."[22]

NATIVE SURVIVANCE

Native names and identities are inscrutable constructions; the ironic suit of discoveries, histories, memories, and many clusters of stories. Native identities and the sense of self are the tricky traces of solace and heard stories; the tease of creations, an innermost brush with natural reason, precarious visions, and unbounded narcissism. The *indians* are the simulations, the derivative nouns and adjectives of dominance, and not the same set as natives, the *indigène*, or an indigenous native, in the sense of a native presence on the continent. These are some of the immediacies in this essay. Native memories are intimate, the traces of wind over water, the rush of leaves, and the tease of seasons; bear in mind the accession of natural reason, and evermore that mythic sense of survivance in stories.

"The image of the indigene is perhaps most clearly defined in association with nature," observes Terry Goldie in *Fear and Temptation*. "The defeat of nature is thus a defeat of the indigene." Discovery is the absence and historicity the inevitable dominance and demise of natives. Goldie argues, in the context of natives in commonwealth literature, that "white technology *must* destroy the indigene because it must control nature."[23]

American *indians* are never the same as natives. The *indians* are that uncertain thing of discoveries, and the absence of natives, some*thing* otherwise in the simulations of the other culture. Natives are elusive creations; the *indigène*, that real sense of presence, memories, and coincidence is borne in native stories. The trick is to create a new theater of native names and antecedence that uncovers nativism and false memories; at the same time, native stories must tease out of the truisms of cultural exclusions and the trumperies of simulations. Dominance is sure to raise false memories, and the consequences are the autoposes of tragic victimry.

"A great sickness is coming; the signs are clear," warns activist and actor Russell Means in his autobiography, *Where White Men Fear to Tread.* "Just look at our powwows, those mockeries of our culture that shame us by fostering 'weekend Indians.' "[24] Richard White, in his review of the autobiography, points out that "Means locates real Indians in the past and, he hopes, in the future." The actor declares that with "honesty and therapy, my people can be made whole again." His autobiography is a "story about therapy," a "salvation story, whose form, if not its content, is Christian."[25]

American *indians* are ever associated with powwows and salvation, as the word *powwaw* alludes to those tricky shamanic ceremonies of the past; surely, the real "mockeries" of natives are more onerous in the simulations of Pocahontas, Geronimo, and Crazy Horse. Likewise, natives are ever and again the national allegories of discoveries, decimation, dispossession, dominance, and tragic victimry.

Michel Foucault considered two structural conditions and discursive practices of knowledge: the distinctions of "scientific domains and archaeological territories." The postmodern conditions of varionative consciousness and experience are both *connaissance* and *savoir* knowledge. The first refers to a "particular discipline," such as anthropology or economics, and *savoir* is "knowledge in general," or the "totality of *connaissance*," he writes in *The Archaeology of Knowledge.* "Knowledge is to be found not only in demonstrations, it can also be found in fiction, reflexion, narrative accounts, institutional regulations, and political decisions."

Foucault noted that by *connaissance* he meant "the relation of the subject to the object and the formal rules that govern it. *Savoir* refers to the conditions that are necessary in a particular period for this or that type of object to be given to *connaissance* and for this or that enunciation to be formulated."[26]

The histories of knowledge on varionatives are *connaissance* — objectively particular and reductive — and *savoir* — sensible, general, and at the same time, spoony simulations of natives. For instance, archaeological research, anthropological constructions of culture, climatological studies, evidence of diseases, and historical considerations of shamanism are *connaissance*; the stories of bears, beavers, and tricksters in various translations, narratives of treaties, government documents, consumer sun dances, postindian novelists, cinematic warriors, and other associations with natives are *savoir* conditions of general knowledge.

Ian Hacking patterned his theses, the science of memory and multiple personality, after the references of *connaissance*, or what he described as "surface knowledge as an analytical idea" to avoid a "value judgment about kinds of knowledge," and *savoir*, or "depth knowledge." Hacking studied the "politics of memory, the personal and the communal," and observes, in *Rewriting the Soul*, that group "memory helps define the group." The "politics of personal memories is, in contrast, relatively new." He points out that the "politics of personal memory. . . . is a power struggle built around knowledge, or claims to knowledge."

Hacking notes that if "some memories have been suppressed, deliberately, by whomever and by whatever means, then we may begin to think of false consciousness."[27] The suppression of native memories and, at the same time, the substitutive turn to *indian* simulations is a case of false consciousness, as the simulations of natives are faux real with no antecedence. Such encounters over memories and consciousness, faux native memories, the creation of recovered memories, and the power of knowledge are some of the obscure sources of varionative consciousness, the tricky postmodern conditions of survivance.

These tragic narratives of absence, the cures and curses of modernity, cinematic salvation, and the mercenary ruse of casinos, menace the very creation of autobiographies. Evidently, variona-tive memories are no more reckonable as documented correctness than any narrative; however, the pious suit of native memories, ei-ther true or faux, causes certain critical patterns of increased brain activity that could be enhanced by positron emission tomography.

Cognitive neuroscientists and many others are concerned that recovered memories have been used as prosecution evidence in criminal court convictions; clearly, memories are conversions, and in response to these concerns, recent studies have focused on the "fragile power" of memories. Positron emission tomography, for instance, is one of the most advanced "neuroimaging techniques" that scans distinct patterns of brain activity. Memories, faux or otherwise, may cause certain patterns of activity. The general rationale, observes Daniel Schacter in *Searching for Memory*, of "scanning experiments is that when a brain region is heavily involved in a cognitive task, it should become more active, and hence require more blood uptake, than a region that is little involved or uninvolved in the task."[28] This is "the first direct evidence from a normal human brain showing the way the brain functions differently in retrieving a true memory."[29]

Philip Hilts reported in the *New York Times* that the "truth of memory is infinitely hard to establish, as psychotherapists, lawyers and scientists know all too well. But for the first time, scientists may have captured snapshots of a false memory in the making." He notes that "in the images produced by these new brain scans, false memories can be clearly distinguished from those that are true."[30] Apparently, false memories, the memories of events that are more difficult to retrieve, activate different parts of the brain than true or "accurate" memories.

Schacter notes that the controversy over recovered memory "is fundamentally a debate about accuracy, distortion, and suggestibility in memory." He names three systems, or references of recollection, that give meaning to experience. The first is *semantic memory*, the references of facts and conceptual knowledge; the second is *procedural memory*, "which allows us to learn skills and acquire habits." The last is *episodic memory*, the references to explicit recollections of "personal incidents that uniquely define our lives."[31]

The semantic memories of natives are traces of treaties and other documents in narratives. The translations of cultures and the simulations of absence, otherwise the "generation by models of a real without origin or reality," are the common synthetic turns to the "hyperreal," as native "territory no longer precedes the map, nor survives it."[32] Procedural memories are performances, the native tease of seasons and natural reason, the care of hunters and warriors; episodic memories are a circle of names, ancestors, and the creation of native consciousness in stories.

Truly, the presence of varionative ancestors is conceptual, and it reveals the trace of political connections. Procedural memories are the masks of dancers, the habits of playing too many bingo cards, and forever riding bareback; ironically, episodic trickster stories are overcome at universities by the faux memories of victimry.

Last, the ecstatic visions of shamans and trickster stories of survivance are heart memories, the unnameable traces of creation in episodic narratives. These heart memories are animate, numinous, and tacit synchronicity.

"Memory is a central part of the brain's attempt to make sense of experience, and to tell coherent stories about it," writes Schacter.

"Our memories are the fragile but powerful products of what we recall from the past, believe about the present, and imagine about the future."[33]

Surely, stories and memories activate certain areas of the brain; these areas of neural activation, monitored as distinctive patterns, are measurable and could initiate a more precise narrative or scientific presentation of personal realities. Likewise, the true metes and bounds of that blood rush to the brain could be monitored as native memories, the actual measures of distinct and "authentic" stories. The scans and pictures of the brain produced by positron emission tomography could be used to conceive of truer varionative memories and to moderate faux memories and spurious allegories of exclusion and victimry.

Varionative identities are personal, achievable, episodic, and ironic narratives, as any sense of native presence must contend with the ambiguities of the absence of natives. The ironic narratives, in this case, tease the hyperreal, the simulations of natives with no origins, and are more than mere rhetorical devices.[34] Yet, concocted tribal traditions, and even resistance to the cause of romantic nativism, are construed by many observers as the true and absolute representation of natives in the monotonous theme of savagism and civilization. These are the contests over native memories, identities, and a sense of presence. The poses, pretensions, and catchwords of simulations are the obvious citations of dominance; the causes are so severe at times that casino cash, for instance, crosscuts varionative memories with new and serviceable traditions.

The crucial and enduring issue of personal identities, or who we are, is bound to what is real; in other words, native identities are personal creations of the real, not the decorative lace of metaphysics or the false memories of citatory dominance.

Joseph Notterman observes in *Forms of Psychological Inquiry* that "the question of *ultimate* reality *is* metaphysical in nature. But the rules and means whereby persons perceive their own identity, or their being, are psychological in character, and should not be dismissed as metaphysics."[35]

The traces of varionative chance have been structured and documented in the historical dominance of modernity. The creative tease of natural reason, or native contingency, is a postmodern discourse, and that narrative credence anticipated the "condition of postmodernity." The simulations of native cultures announced the "general failure" of modernity; the breakdown of historical truth as objectivism, facts, causes, and other cover certainties. "You cannot find a historical or geographical or scientific or literary discourse just out there, just growing wild," observes Keith Jenkins. Discourse is cultural, cultivated, fabricated, and "ultimately arbitrary."[36]

The creation of varionative identity is metaphysical and, at the same time, identity is sanctioned by government documents, a legacy of cultural dominance and the last ventures of modernity. Since the ultimate varionative narratives are postmodern, and a dialogic circle, then the crack of sure histories and causative truth must be mocked on the other side. Modernity and historical objectivism are the cause that would count and measure native "blood quantum" and then document the cold evidence of "authentic" identities; the vital juice of ancestors is a trope, of course, but consider the absurdity of a burette as a native blood measure. Varionative histories and identities are dialogic circles, not essential or sanguinary discoveries.

Hayden White argues in *Tropics of Discourse* that "in general there has been a reluctance to consider historical narratives as what they most manifestly are: verbal fictions, the contents of which are as much invented as found and the forms of which have more in common with their counterparts in literature than they have with those in the sciences."[37]

The current and most common measures of native identities are based on genealogical narratives, the recognition, rhetoric, and enmity of peers, service to native causes and communities, federal or reservation documents, and autoinscriptions, or the heritable names, assertions, and ethnic canons that endorse the mere simulations of identities.

The *indians* are simulations, as simulations are the absence of natives, and the cause of false memories. Varionative memories are the creation of personal identities and mythic narratives. Consider that recovered memories, vows in motion picture commissaries, the nurturance of simulations, and venture sun dances would not likely produce the same patterns of brain activities as actual varionative memories and stories. Surely, the stories and personal realities that create and activate certain patterns in the brain, distinct from false memories, are the most clever measures of varionative identities.

Treaties cut native heirs in and out of common and communal ties, rights, motion, and elusive boundaries; however, archival connections and historical treasons are not the same as the creations of varionative memories. Genealogies, reservation and church documents, nicknames, service cues, and casino envies are used and abused in the politics of race, the nonsense of *indian blood quantum* authenticity, and the poses of recovered memories. The real shadows of varionative memories, and the actual creations of native artists, are the tricky blood literature of a native presence. The traces of native shadows, stories, and memories are the "hermeneutics of survivance."[38]

Otto Rank reasoned that experience and artistic production overlap. "The artist takes refuge, with all *his own* experience only from the life of *actuality*, which for him spells mortality and decay," he writes. "And although the whole artist psychology may seem to be centered on the 'experience,' this itself can be explained only through the creative impulse—which attempts to turn ephemeral life into personal immortality."[39]

Since varionatives are the artists of their identities, their memories and stories are not discoveries or the actualities of experience, but the very creation of personal realities. Modernity and actuality would manifest the mere objective simulations of *racialism*, the crease of anthropologism, received cultures, and the complicities of tragic victimry.

The notions of race, and racialist cues at universities, are the politics of exclusion, the paradoxical separation and admission of the other in the common course of citatory dominance. Mention of that obscure truism, however, does not unburden the meanness of racialist doctrines, or the lasting concern over varionative identities.

"Racialist doctrine . . . is linked from the outset to the rise of science, or more precisely to scientism—that is, the use of science to establish ideology," and the doctrine "can be presented as a coherent set of propositions," observes Tzvetan Todorov in *On Human Diversity*. He presents five propositions that may not include marginal or "revisionist" versions of the doctrine. First, the affirmation and significance of the notion of race, such as "common physical characteristics;" second, the continuity of race and culture that would "explain why the races tend to got to war with one another"; third, an *ethnic* determinism, or racialism, as "a doctrine of collective psychology," that is "inherently hostile to the individualist ideology; fourth, the racialist "hierarchy of values"; lastly, the politics and "moral judgment" that puts the ideal racialist theory into the practice of racism.[40]

Natives were once contracted in name as "discoveries" and were the objects of racialist missionaries; however, racialist doctrines and practices were not coherent in a "hierarchy of values." Natives in the ironic course of racialist tropes, moved closer to civilization in the politics of land allotments and inheritable crossblood traits; at the same time, natives were celebrated as the eternal cues of a noble and romantic savagism, uncorrupted by urban civilization, the new creases of reason, objectivism, and modernity. Africans and slaves were not presented in the same romance: the racialist measures of slaves were absolute hierarchies, and black crossbloods were seldom seen as the coins of civilization. Africans remained black, and natives became white in the racialist ideologies of crossblood inheritance.

Natives and others are hounded by scientism, the reductive notions of anthropologism, and ideologies of representation. The mission, of course, has been cultural dominance. Scientism creates natives as objects, but the portrait of "humanity lacks analogy with any representation," notes John William Miller. "An object, and only an object, can be *re*presented. Only an object can be *presented*, that is, put into some relation with other objects."[41]

No discoverers, no scientists, no treaties, no anthropologists, no government agents, and no missionaries of scientism have ever had the moral cause or ethical authority to determine the outcome of native rights, consciousness, or sovereignty. Variatione memories cut our sense of presence to the bone, hue the tricky seasons, rush the turn of shadows, trace our names with the crows on the wire, and tease creation evermore in stories. The tease of our memories and stories is survivance not scientism, a presence not an absence.

LIGHT SOLILOQUIES

Charles Dickens traveled to several cities and traversed the prairie by stagecoach, railroad, and steamboat with an episodic literary manner and "a grateful interest in the country" for five months in 1842.

"It would be well, there can be no doubt, for the American people as a whole, if they loved the Real less, and the Ideal somewhat more," he wrote in *American Notes*. "It would be well, if there were greater encouragement to lightness of heart and gaiety, and a wider cultivation of what is beautiful, without being eminently and directly useful."[42]

That sense of national representation, the romance of the ideal, as an aesthetic "lightness of heart" in a travel journal, is an ambiguous treasure, picaresque at the unsure turns of the real, and the novelist vouches archetypes to understand the marvelous absence of natives.

The British Museum, he told the first native he encountered, has a chamber "wherein are preserved household memorials of a race that ceased to be, thousands of years ago." The native "was very attentive, and it was not hard to see that he had a reference in his mind to the gradual fading away of his own people."[43]

Dickens was certain to announce, unwearied of natural ruins, the romantic extinction of natives, a common treason of adventurers in the nineteenth century, and he did so with a curious aesthetic dominance. The actual presence of natives, the real encounters of the "racial" other, would summon in his journal a romantic representation of victimry.

Consider his "company at breakfast," a casual conversation with "a mild old gentleman, who had been for many years employed by the United States Government in conducting negotiations with the Indians, and who had just concluded a treaty with these people by which they bound themselves, in consideration of a certain annual sum, to remove next year to some land provided for them, west of the Mississippi," wrote Dickens.

"We met some of these poor Indians afterwards, riding on shaggy ponies. They were so like the meaner sort of gipsies, that if I could have seen any of them in England, I should have concluded, as a matter of course, that they belonged to that wandering and restless people."[44] That representation of the other, as a matter of course, is an incongruous narrative of racial dominance. The absence of natives is not in name, but in simulations, the turn to that "meaner sort" of presence by victimry.

V. S. Pritchett, in his essay on *The Mystery of Edwin Drood* by Dickens, notes that his "natural genius is for human soliloquy not human intercourse."[45] The omniscient novelist scarcely ever recounts the actual words of natives in his journal; the presence of natives is a romantic soliloquy of their absence.

Aleksandr Borisovich Lakier noted in his journal, some fifteen years later, a similar conversation with a government agent. "To my question of whether it might not be better to let the Indians remain in association with whites," he wrote in *A Russian Looks at America*, the agent "defended the customary" policy of segregation and "argued for ways to prevent any further mixing so as to save the last remnants of Indians, and to spare the government from the criticism that it allowed through negligence, or even worse, deliberately planned, the extermination of the Redskins."

Lakier observes that the government agent was "mestizo," and that was "partly evident in his face, with its white color, angular shape, and black, bristly, straight hair." The adventurer encountered an agent of reason but not enlightenment, one more "intermediary" with a narrative trace of his own absence. Decidedly, segregation of natives on reservations was not a case of preservation. The saviors of the "last remnants" were insincere, mere executors of dominance.

The agent explained that the "American government has the noblest of goals with respect to the Indians," wrote Lakier. "In no way does it want their extermination; on the other hand, neither does it want the white population to suffer from Indian raids and the Indian notion of unlimited domain."[46]

Dickens was aware of manifest manners but never certain of his readers. His travel soliloquy creates a sense of adventure, to be sure, but at a literary distance. He relates anonymous sources, such as the advice on a stern location because "steamboats generally blew up forward," but not a word of the pleasurable "long conversation" with a native on the steamboat was ever cited as a discourse. He quotes conversations with doctors, a railroad conductor, a turnkey in a prison, and a few "gentlemen," but not the actual words he heard with natives.

The novelist was on board the *Messenger*, a steamboat from Pittsburgh to Cincinnati, in the same year as the first expedition of John Frémont, and four years after the Trail of Tears. Dickens mentioned in his journal the great trees and the eternal solitude of the river, but he was unaware, one can assume, of the resistance of natives to federal removal, the immediacy of sovereignty, and the contingency of native presence in a constitutional democracy.

The sound of the steamboat was "enough, one would think, to waken up the host of Indians who lie buried in a great mound yonder," he wrote. "The very river, as though it shared one's feelings of compassion for the extinct tribes who lived so pleasantly here, in their blessed ignorance of white existence, hundreds of years ago, steals out of its way to ripple near" the native burial mounds. "Evening slowly steals upon the landscape and changes it before me, when we stop to set some emigrants ashore."[47]

Giacomo Beltrami mentioned the mounds of the "aborigines" nineteen years earlier in his travel journal. "The gods of ancient idolaters were probably only beneficent heroes, who were first the objects of their gratitude, and gradually of their adoration," he wrote in *A Pilgrimage in Europe and America*. He was eager "to see them more closely," but natives were the absence, not the presence of his discoveries. "The simple heap of earth which covered their remains would thus become an altar; and such perhaps was the origin of these Indian monuments."[48]

Aleksandr Lakier, aboard a steamboat in the same area but much later, wondered if the mounds were the tombs of heroes. "Americans rack their brains as to why the Indians built these burial mounds," he wrote in his journal. "It is difficult to believe they wanted to perpetuate a memorial to themselves. That concept was too sophisticated for a nomadic people who lived from day to day and did not do anything remarkable."[49]

Alexis de Tocqueville observed the same mounds and rated the natives as "hospitable when at peace" and "merciless in war." They "could live without wants," and, like others, "these savages believed in the existence of a better world." The mounds, or "heaps of earth" were the traditions of "another people more civilized," he reasoned in *Democracy in America*, because the "Indians of our time are unable to give any information relative to the history of this unknown people." He rated the absence of natives as "more advanced" than their presence; the romance of obscurity and tragic victimry over native habitancy. "Their languages are lost; their glory is vanished like a sound without an echo; though perhaps there is not one which has not left behind in some tomb in memory of its passage. Thus the most durable monument of human labor is that which recalls the wretchedness and nothingness of man."[50]

Robert Bieder notes that by the early nineteenth century there were two contrary views of the obscure mound builders. Bishop James Madison "held that the mounds were the work of a people no further advanced toward civilization than present-day Indians." Reverend Thaddeus Harris, on the other hand, "assigned their construction to ancient Toltecs."

The debate over the absence of the native mound builders was intense and elaborate. "The identity of the mound builders held implications beyond scholarly dispute, affecting even government Indian policy," observes Bieder. President Andrew Jackson, for instance, reasoned that if the "savage hordes" ended the civilization of the mound builders, then the cause of removal was otherwise justified. "The white race in the name of civilization would do to the Indians what the Indians had once done to the mound builders. The final victor would be civilization."[51]

William Warren, a learned historian and a native with a sense of presence, mentions in his *History of the Ojibway Nation* that "nearly all the tribes of the red man who lived in an open prairie country, before the introduction of fire-arms among them, were accustomed to live in earthen wigwams as a protection and defense against attacks of their enemies." Concerning the discovery of human bones "in these mounds, most writers have been led to suppose them as the graves or burial places of distinguished chiefs." Warren pointed out in his history, published fifteen years after *American Notes* by Charles Dickens, that the bones were the remains of the "former occupants" of the mounds.[52]

Dickens must have seen the mounds as the tragic allegories of decimation and dispossession; the removal and exclusion of natives. Clearly, he was eager to encounter a *real* native, since few natives endured the discoveries, diseases, and dominance. "Some tribes almost entirely disappeared as a result of disease and conquest," writes Robert Berkhofer Jr. in *The Frontier in History*. "Such severe demographic decline had profound implications for tribal leadership succession and the nature of governance, economic subsistence and patterns of survival."[53]

Old World diseases decimated natives, and smallpox "became the single most lethal disease Europeans carried to the New World," writes Henry Dobyns in *Native American Historical Demography*.[54] Russell Thornton, the native sociologist, notes in *American Indian Holocaust and Survival* that smallpox was the most "destructive during the nineteenth century." President Thomas Jefferson, in 1801, "caused the first American Indians to be vaccinated, rather than just inoculated. . . . Two years later, the explorers Meriwether Lewis and William Clark were instructed by the president to vaccinate Indians whom they encountered during their travels."[55]

The epidemics "weakened the Indian economic systems and dispirited the people, whose world order seemed to have collapsed in the face of unknown forces," observes Francis Paul Prucha in *The Indians in American Society*. "Many Indians and their white friends maintained that the proper status of the Indian tribes was as small independent nations under the protection of the United States."[56]

Dickens continued his adventures on the *Pike*, a steamboat from Cincinnati to Louisville, "which, carrying the mails, was a packet of much better class than that in which we had come from Pittsburg."

Peter Pitchlynn, a native aboard the steamboat at the same time, sent his name card to the novelist. The Choctaw leader had been in Washington to secure treaty annuities and native land patents and was on his way home to a farm near the Wheelock Mission north of the Red River in Indian Territory.

"There chanced to be one board this boat, in addition to the usual dreary crowd of passengers, one Pitchlynn, a chief of the Choctaw tribe of Indians, who *sent in his card* to me, and with whom I had the pleasure of a long conversation."

Pitchlynn "spoke English perfectly well, though he had not begun to learn the language, he told me, until he was a young man grown," wrote Dickens. "He was dressed in our ordinary every-day costume, which hung about his fine figure loosely, and with indifferent grace. On my telling him that I regretted not to see him in his own attire, he threw up his right arm, for a moment, as though he were brandishing some heavy weapon, and answered, as he let it fall again, that his race were losing many things besides their dress, and would soon be seen upon the earth no more: but he wore it at home, he added proudly."[57]

These chance situations, the manners, poses, and sovenance of native stories, are continuous adventures: the novelist casts his archetypes in a soliloquy, and the native retreats in the romance of his own aesthetic absence, cautious not to tease the ironies of his real presence on the steamboat. The coincidence of that nineteenth-century encounter, the tease of absence, and the episodic literary manner of a novelist, scarcely seem to ease the most obvious historical contradictions; only just in the reference to a portrait of Peter Pitchlynn, a lithography of the native in "traditional" attire by the artist George Catlin.

These encounters are the common pretensions of discovery, historical revisions, the poses of cultural dominance, and now, the estimable virtues of soliloquies and travel narratives in the "second immediacy" of this essay.

The novelist and titular presence of a real native is an obvious anachronism. My hand on that steamboat would overturn the romantic poses of native victimry. My resistance to the treasons of causal histories, a civilization of discoveries and dominance, more than a century later, is traced to the racial simulations of native identities, and the contradictions of native slave traders.

Peter Pitchlynn was born on a farm near the Noxubee River in Mississippi. His father was a prestigious white trader, a frontier diplomat, cotton farmer, and slave owner. Peter was an ambitious crossblood who studied at the Choctaw Academy in Kentucky and, for one year, at the University of Nashville. He was an active politician who became the secretary of the native delegation that negotiated the contentious removal treaty with the federal government at Dancing Rabbit Creek.

The United States "promised never to enclose the Choctaw tribe within the boundaries of any state or territory which it created," writes Vine Deloria Jr. in *Behind the Trail of Broken Treaties*. The Civil War, however, caused new enemies, and then new territories. The "Five Civilized Tribes offered to join the Union side, recognizing that their treaties bound them to the United States as military allies. But the Union forces rejected the overtures of the tribes, stating that the use of Indians against the Southern whites would be barbaric." The Confederates were at hand, much closer than the federal forces. The Choctaw "had little choice but to sign treaties with them."[58]

"Pitchlynn did not grow up in an Indian environment," writes W. David Baird in *Peter Pitchlynn: Chief of the Choctaws*. "Instead, his family's financial status and the visits of traders, travelers, and ministers made his father's home an outpost of 'civilization.' This, plus the growing frequency of contact with white settlers on the very frontier of the tribal domain, meant that Peter was less a Choctaw than he thought he was, then and particularly later. Still, the advantages of his 'position' as the son of a wealthy white trader were not always realized, a fact that became painfully apparent to him with increasing outside contacts."[59]

Pitchlynn initiated a new native constitution as a resistance to federal removal from Mississippi to Indian Territory. He was a persistent diplomat with extensive political and social connections in Washington. The Choctaw, however, waived the esteem of their national representatives by a declaration of independence from the United States during the Civil War. Native delegates then signed a treaty with the Confederate States of America. Pitchlynn, loyal to the Choctaw, was elected chief near the end of that war.

The Choctaws considered many "promises from the rebel government," wrote a missionary teacher to the Commissioner of Indian Affairs. "Their treaty gives their representative a seat in the rebel congress, acknowledges the right of the Choctaws to give testimony in all courts," and "they have the privilege of coming in as a state into the Confederacy."

The United States government failed "to give the Indians, in season, the necessary assurance that they would be protected, no matter what might happen," writes Annie Heloise Abel in *The American Indian as Slaveholder and Secessionist*. Mistakenly, the natives were of no importance to the government, and such failures of policy "can not be too severely criticized."[60]

Dickens observed that Pitchlynn was "a remarkably handsome man . . . with long black hair, an aquiline nose, broad cheekbones, a sunburnt complexion, and a very bright, keen, dark, and piercing eye. There were but twenty thousand of the Choctaws left, he said, and their number was decreasing every day. A few of his brother chiefs had been obliged to become civilized, and to make themselves acquainted with what the whites knew, for it was their only chance of existence."[61]

That a few natives were "obliged to become civilized" is a backhanded observation, the cultural recourse to an absence in the narratives of dominance, not the reason of a native presence. The clever native reverse of the binary, savagism and civilization, is the combination of savagism as a presence. Natives were the past, and to civilize natives "was to triumph over the past," argues Roy Harvey Pearce in *Savagism and Civilization*. "Savagism could be known only in terms of the civilization to which, by the law of nature, it had to give way." So, to kill natives "was to kill the past."[62]

Dickens wrote about slavery in the last chapter of *American Notes*. "Slavery is not a whit the more endurable because some hearts are to be found which can partially resist its hardening influences; nor can the indignant tide of honest wrath stand still, because in its onward course it overwhelms a few who are comparatively innocent, among a host of guilty."[63] Surely, the novelist was not aware at the time that the native he so admired on the steamboat was, in fact, a slave owner and trader.

Pitchlynn, at the death of his father in 1835, "received a substantial inheritance in slaves," notes Baird. The record of his purchases of shoes and other materials "suggested large slave holdings. In fact, a census taken after 1866 revealed that 135 freedmen had once belonged to Pitchlynn, 32 of whom had also taken his family name."[64]

Dickens, unaware of his incongruous romance of the native other, wrote that the Choctaw "took his leave; as stately and complete a gentleman of Nature's making, as ever I beheld; and moved among the people in the boat, another kind of being."[65] Later, the crossblood sent the novelist the "lithographed portrait of himself." The original was painted by George Catlin.

Dickens "did not want Pitchlynn to cross cultures; he wanted him to be a 'real' Indian," writes M. H. Dunlop in *Sixty Miles from Contentment*. "Once Dickens and Pitchlynn got past the hard part of the conversation, they joked about buffaloes and then shook hands. Dickens invited Pitchlynn to visit England and assured him of good treatment there, but Pitchlynn shook off the invitation with the remark that 'the English used to be very fond of the Red Men when they wanted their help, but had not cared for them much since.' Then he left, and Dickens, watching Pitchlynn move away across the deck, characterized him as 'another kind of being,' thus preserving him as different from the common humanity milling about the deck."[66] The novelist, by ignorance, romance, and literary manner, preserved the only native he encountered as an obscure soliloquy of the other in *American Notes*.

DISCRETE DELIVERANCE

Our native ancestors were never secure, as names and stories lost their tease in translation; now, the heirs wear the obvious, new stories and simulations as traditions, a romantic spectacle in the absence of native names. Seasons cut the stones, bears rush our memories; the stories of creation trace our survivance. Silence and separation are not our nature and are never the absence of our nature; the best memories of the seasons, the heat, storms, crows, and river otter are carried in stories, not in spectacles, aesthetic separations, or the narratives of dominance.

Discoveries are the very cause of absence not the presence of natives; the outness of simulations are sure to bounce. Likewise, revisions and recoveries are neither the nature nor the presence of native names. New varionative stories are the tease of creation, the turns of tradition, and the traces of presence that overcome manifest manners and the causes of absence and dominance.

Traditionalists are the timeservers, those posers in the case of past manners. Traditional connections are causal simulations, the cuts, envies, exclusions, and faux pas of racialism, more ironic than irenic in native consciousness. However, there is one common, sure ancestral sanction: that our presence, our teases of instancies, and hints of coincidence, are more than the mere conversion of a native absence.

Traditions must await a timely reversion; the bruises of silence that pose as primal memories. Yet, as the seasons, the memories we arouse are never the same traces of silence or native identities. We *are* the seasons, not the absence; we *are* the traces of native reason, the tricky presence of nature, not the tin ears of lost civilizations. The tease of native stories, the sovereignty of motion and survivance, are greater memories than the tragic postures of victimry.

"All the arts of memory attempt to trick oblivion by making the past somehow the present," writes Philip Kuberski in *The Persistence of Memory.* "A memory without a self may well appear to be the opposite of recollection, simply an anonymous process. But this appears only from the viewpoint of the self whose very existence depends upon a separation from the world and so considers natural the idea that memory is a discrete fragment rescued from the past."[67]

Native names and stories are evermore construed as cultural distinctions, or separations, and, in other interpretations, as mere rescued memories. Many varionatives tease the absence as a sense of presence and court certain romantic revisions of the past, such as the stoical poses of *indians* in photographs by Edward Curtis.

Native ancestors are counted as unimpeachable connections, but progenitors are not the last word on the antecedence of presence; besides, identities are sometimes measured by peer recognition, reservation residence, government documents, intimations of cultural traditions, and many other political considerations.

Native memories of the heart are unnameable; our stories and seasons are traces of this creation. Social science theses, discoveries, and other documents are the simulations of outness on the bounce, not a true sense of varionative presence.

SANGUINE MODIATION

More than a hundred million natives lost their lives by disease, slavery, violence, and loneliness as a consequence of colonialism in the Americas. One of the casuistic promises of civilization was the exclusion of natives; at the same time, the absence of natives was the cue of a national romance of victimry. Civilization over savagism was a monotheistic cadence, a continuous musical pageant that celebrated the specious evolution of dominance. The exclusion of natives was a wicked and unnatural cause, and even those natives who pursued an education were burdened with the romance of their own absence in history. The certainties of romantic vanishment, and, at the same time, the counteractions of native simulations were common at the end of the nineteenth century. The blithe evidence of native absence was objectively documented at fairs, pageants, and in museums.

The *indians* were ever on the decline in the dramatic episodes of civic celebrations and pageants of the early twentieth century. That public decline became a romantic absence in later narratives, as natives vanished in the new creases of modernism, the objective contravention of traditions, and back matter of *antimodernism*—the favor of the idealized past over the present.

"Public historical imagery is an element of our culture, contributing to how we define our sense of identity and direction," observes David Glassberg in *American Historical Pageantry*. "Chronological time in pageants began with the arrival of the first white settlers and the 'inevitable' decline of the Indians. One popular pageant scene presents a 'Medicine Man' foretelling his race's decline shortly before the episode in which the whites arrive."

Nature was gentle, feminine, innocent, and natives waned on an essential landscape. The absence of natives was more than a pageant theme, as others performed the very roles of *indians*. For instance, the "St. Louis Pageant Drama Association decided not to use real Amerindians in the *Pageant and Masque*." The casting director declined "the offer from William Hole-in-the-Day to bring his band of Chippewa from Minnesota to participate in the pageant, even though for the same fee the traveling troupe would have staged a baseball exhibition as well. Pageant planners instead ladled out sixteen gallons of copper-makeup and distributed dozens of gunnysacks to transform local white residents into 'Indians' for the performance."[68] The late presence of natives is a simulation of their absence.

The New Age romance of holistic inclusion has reversed the absence of natives; however, the reversion is a contradiction because some natives have now initiated their own exclusion and avoidance of others by virtue of revised traditions. Obviously, one exclusion does not absolve another, and simulations of inclusion have never been a real presence in any state. The action of one exclusion is the puny reversion of the other, and the end of one is the end of the other, overturned in the great romantic myths of inclusion. Still, varionative connections, and the tease of a native presence, bounce readily in the stories of survivance. Clearly, the exclusion of natives must end, and the exclusion of others by natives must end without recrimination or victimry.

Casino riches, for instance, must be more inclusive of the world to avoid the envies of others. Alas, the situational treasures, the cash of others, the losers at traditional slot machines, have emboldened a new class of natives, and their interests, for the most part, are venture capital, not native virtues.

My father was not a cultural ritualist; he never surrendered to shamans, base traditions, or absence as the source of a native sense of presence. He and many others of his generation moved from reservations to cities some sixty years ago during a severe economic depression in the country. Their concern, and with a much richer sense of humor at the time, was survivance.

The Great Depression was not a time to pronounce a reserved victimry. Moreover, the exclusion of natives and others, based on the new and monstrous measures of race, the hue, hair, cheeks, bones, and countenance was not carried out with the same cause of civilization as it had been at many civic pageants, or in the aesthetic simulations of learned narratives.

Native resistance to removal and dominance in the nineteenth century is not comparable to the abstract exclusion of others in the current narratives of dominance. Exclusion *by* natives is not resistance; the simulations of a native presence, as a separation of the past, are not acts of courage or resistance. William Apess, Black Hawk, Pontiac, Tecumseh, Chief Joseph, Geronimo, Crazy Horse, Sitting Bull, Wovoka, and many other courageous native leaders would have traced their sense of union to an actual native presence, survivance, and the transmotion of sovereignty.

The absence of natives in most histories of the nation, and the severance of natives on exclaves and reservations, has become a serious critique, but not as critical as repressed memories, or the hidden native vengeance in response to that exclusion. The heirs of those natives who were once removed are now in a reverse situation to exclude others; ironically, certain others are natives, scored as not worthy in the new stories and measures of native sanguinity.

The removal, separation, and exclusion have never been right, no matter the reasons, reversion of scores, or, measure for measure, the wild taste of vengeance. Natives would be much wiser now to include others, to absolve the absence, embrace a common presence, and celebrate coincidence over exclusions. The reservation politics of sanguine modiation and blood count names is a curse of exclusion and dominance.

DRAMATIS PERSONAE

Consider these eight native theaters, or the obvious relations and connections of inheritance, creation, countenance, genealogies, documents, situations, trickster stories, and victimry as the most common sources of native distinctions, identities, and tries of the self. These eight theaters, or the traces of autoposes and variationive memories, are inclusions, not separations, racial divisions, exclusions, or the politics of piecemeal estates of identity. These obvious connections, embodied in native stories, histories, and conversations are the variationive theaters and estates of survivance.

Native by concession: The first connections and memorable representations of native identities are given, the common, inclusive, continuous variationive concessions. The obscure native, once the other, the romance of an aesthetic absence, is embodied here as a narrative presence; variationive identities are a common inheritance. Decidedly, everyone in the world could be native, in the sense of this theater, a common association and wise connection that would end racial separations and the manners of dominance. The entire world could celebrate, at last, a common native connection and estate, but this is *not* a theater of treaty rights. Jaime de Angulo, author of *Indians in Overalls,* Lynn Andrews, the "warrioress" who created Agnes Whistling Elk in *Jaguar Woman,* Carlos Castaneda in *Journey to Ixtlan,* and Jamake Highwater, who posed a native *inclusivity* in *The Primal Mind,* could be natives by common concessions; no longer impostors or outsiders. Such an inheritance of a native presence would eliminate the obvious need of authors and publishers to name, document, and simulate native genealogies, or native artists to suit the consumer protection provisions of the Indian Arts and Crafts Act.

Native by creation: The second connection to a native theater of identities is creation; native by artistic creation and imaginative thought. The creation of native characters has presented and secured natives in literature. Some readers may not share the pleasure of every character, but the creation of memorable native characters in literature is a connection. Many artists and authors would be native by the creation of characters in their novels and other publications. Karl May, the German author who created the warrior Winnetou, for instance, and *The Last of the Mohicans* by James Fenimore Cooper, *Hiawatha* by the poet and romancer Henry Wadsworth Longfellow, *Black Elk Speaks* by John Neihardt, *Scarlet Plume* by Frederick Manfred, *Bury My Heart at Wounded Knee* by Dee Brown, and *Turtle Island* by Gary Snyder, are native creations and connections, a sense of native presence. These, and many other authors, poets, and artists, such as the painter George Catlin and the photographer Edward Curtis, are native in a theater of aesthetics, as they created native characters and images that are forever in the artistic and literary history of the nation.

Native by countenance: Native appearance, facial features, the walk, talk, manners, and other characteristics are traces of identities. Native countenance is a simulation, a pose that is seen by others as the real score of native identities. For instance, the color of skin, hair, and eyes, is seen as native countenance; however, few natives are born with a "pure" countenance. There is no essential truth in the tone and hue of a cheekbone. Variationive identities are not the same as birth marks. The coincidence of color and native countenance is one of the most controversial connections, and the advance of one tone, hue, cut of nose, breast, or buttock over another has never been a reasonable trace of variationive identities. Native cast and countenance are not exclusive; rather, native sanctions and suits must be inclusive and waive the measures of blood, and end the wicked structures of cultural exclusions, racialist commerce, and new age phrenology. Iron Eyes Cody and many other movie actors used the coincidence of their native countenance, and some were more believable in the movies than real natives at universities.

Native by genealogies: Native identities seem to be clearly represented by names and parentage in genealogies. This native connection, however, is based on genealogical stories not visitant selections or ontology. Consanguinity and other traces of native ancestors are sources of identities, to be sure, but never the last word on a sense of native presence. "I needed to go back before I could go forward, and mark the intersections created by my heritage, my family, my education, and my father," writes Sidner Larson in *Catch Colt*. "Once these intersections were marked, they could be imagined as a part of natural change rather than as elements of destruction." Larson was born a "catch colt," an illegitimate child of the Gros Ventres. He writes that the "position of illegitimacy" is an "exquisite place from which to consider legitimacy. I have no father, I am part Indian, I am not wealthy, and I choose to live a life of the mind, all 'illegitimacies' in one setting or another."[69]

Natives who have been deserted in time or place, adopted, or misrepresented in genealogies, would be native by hint, practice, association, and endurance. Many natives who are *outside* by adoption, and many others, with no native ancestors and raised *inside* native communities, have obvious connections to native identities. Grey Owl, for instance, author of *The Men of the Last Frontier*, was a naturalist and lived native. John Tanner, and many others who were captured by natives in the nineteenth century, would be native by extreme association in this theater. Tanner married a native woman and lived in the woodland.

Native by documentation: Native identities are established by documents, such as birth certificates, reservation enrollment, named in attendance at federal and mission boarding school, sacred native sites, photographs, and portraits. The nicks, notes, names, numbers, and pictures, are considered by many observers as the most authentic citations of varionative identities. No document, however, has a sense of presence without a story. Ishi, for instance, was nominated by anthropologists as the last of his tribe. Today, his story is a native presence, but as an artist, he could be in violation of the Indian Arts and Crafts Act. Peter Pitchlynn, on the other hand, was eager to mention his autopose as a traditional native presence in a portrait by George Catlin.

Native by situations: Some native identities are earned by situational connections, or associations, such as marriage, service, economic virtues, and other circumstances that are honored by native communities. Situations are as much a connection to a native presence and identities as countenance and genealogies. Carl Hammerschlag, in *The Dancing Healers*, writes directly about his transformation as a medical doctor in native communities, a theater of native connections and realities. Santiago, a native at the Santo Domingo Pueblo, told the doctor, "You must be able to dance if you are to heal people." Hammerschlag learned how to dance in a native presence.

Native by trickster stories: The trickster is a trope, the wild figuration of shamanism, sovereignty, and survivance in many native stories. Trickster stories are a tease of creation, a ruse of manners, causes and connections in native literature. The traces of native identities are closer to the tricky pauses in common sense than to dickered histories and narratives of dominance. This varionative connection would include and embrace some national politicians, those who have been touched in a warrior headdress, tricked by peace pipes, teased by obscure adoption, and given the dubious gifts of descriptive names.

Native by victimry: The last native theater is the most wearisome, and one of the most common connections, or sources of varionative identities and historical condolence. This last estate is the perversive autopose of victimry. The natives in this theater are cast as representations, the racialist tropes of vanishment; the historical measures of dominance, concessions, desistance, and the vectors of durative victimry. These are the absolute victims of modernity. Angrily, some varionatives have created an aesthetic victimry. Others must bear evermore the causes of sufferance, the cues of miseries, and the absence of those who were murdered and died of diseases since first contact, and the foreign occupation of native communities.

Jimmie Durham boasted in an autobiographical essay that he "absolutely" hated this country. "Not just the government, but the culture" of Americans. "Why wouldn't I hate this country? Because you are a nice person? Because it makes you feel bad for me to hate this country? You want me to be properly indignant about 'injustices' and still be on the side of you and your friends who are also 'trying to bring about some changes in the country.' "[70]

Varionative aesthetic sufferance is an elaborate enterprise. Signatory miseries, perverse concessions, and venter narratives are sources of authority in education and entertainment. Natives are stoical representations in pictures, and the romantic, demonic, and tragic heroes in literature. The real natives are fugitives, the absence as the presence of natives in the theater of victimry.

Ward Churchill could trace his varionative autoposes to this theater of aesthetic victimry. Not so much his pieties, censure, and rancorous reviews, but his verbose incursions, and counter visions, that seem to serve the modernist cause of victimry.

Churchill announced a critical vision of the Indian Arts and Crafts Act of 1990. This federal statute, an obscure measure of consumer protection, provides an extreme "criminal penalty for misrepresentation of Indian produced goods and products." The artisans must be documented as members of a tribe, native nation, or arts organization to lawfully sell or display their work as *indian*. "I have a vision—a recurrent hallucination, if you will—of an installation summing up the state of contemporary 'American Indian art.' It is of a life-sized plastic Indian man, seated in a director's chair and outfitted in the high Santa Fe style: abundant turquoise, fur and leather, genuine piñon-scented aftershave or cologne, fashionably long but neatly razor-cut black hair, a blanket-vest over an open-necked silk shirt, his medicine bag filled with cocaine, a $5,000 antique concho belt and Gucci loafers," writes Churchill.

Once the brand-name bluster of his vision is manifest, many gauche allegories that mention "eugenics codes" and the "Ministry of Racial Purity of the Third Reich," he proscribes the very racialist statistics of victimry he would otherwise use to treat his enemies, and those *indians* and academics who counter his termagancy.

Churchill seems to have created his own scriptorial ministry of racial purity. He announces the enervation of true *indian* traditions, and uses a racial sum game in his critical evaluation of others. Ed McGaa, for instance, "is peddling a lie" because "it takes a lifetime of training to become a genuine Lakota spiritual leader." The word *genuine* is the racial sum game. McGaa, in his *Rainbow Tribe*, creates more nostalgia than uses tradition, an overreal simulation of native presence. *Mother Earth Spirituality*, however, cuts to a new mission of visions and sacred traditions. "One can only hope that the author of this culturally genocidal travesty didn't repeat the error of his predecessors by selling himself too cheaply," writes Churchill. The words "genocidal travesty" overbear a simulation of the absence of natives, the "fatal strategy" of boredom in a final racialist vocabulary.

The aesthetics of *indian* advocacy is noticed in the scriptorial ministry. "What is ugliest about the Indian Arts and Crafts Act is that it is being passed off as something demanded by native people themselves. Indeed, its most vocal and vociferous advocates have been—by some definition or another—'Indians,' " he contends.

"It's not that there are no Indians who understand the nature and dynamics of the colonizing and genocidal processes to which we are subjected. Nor is it true that no Indians retain the courage and integrity necessary to stand up and resist against tremendous odds, regardless of personal cost or consequences."[71]

Churchill counters his own essentialist autoposes; he avows factions as native histories, creates conspiracies in the name of art and native art literature; then, by sleight of evidence, the peevish author poses as an *indian* with no obvious treaty connections or reservation documentation. Churchill is a poster radical in print, and he would be varionative in this theater, an incursion of his own aesthetic traces of victimry.

Jamake Highwater mentioned much the same concerns twelve years earlier. "Native American exclusivity and snobbery have caused enormous pain and confusion. Many Indians don't feel that they came by their Indian heritage honestly." His notice then would become more than an obscure prevision.

"Why is there an inclination to context the authenticity of Native American painters, writers, actors and spokespeople who have attained a newly acquired intellectual and artistic maturity? Why has the career, for instance, of Fritz Scholder been marked by violent antagonism among Indians, who don't seem to know what Scholder's painting is all about, and whites, who are always anxious to uphold the elitist stereotype of an ill-informed Indian?"[72]

These stories, aesthetic narratives, and documents are the emotive vouchers of victimry. The authors are either varionative observers, nominees, successors of endurance, or witnesses to either the absence or presence of natives: presence as a trace of survivance, and absence as a reserve facticity.

The common associations in this theater are modernist, as the autoposes of victimry are never the traces or antecedence of a native presence. Death and the observance of souls in native stories are ventures not aesthetic commensuration; these stories are traces of the souls, a native presence, even shamanic visions, but not the modernist causes of tragic victimry. The tragic themes of sufferance are simulations of presence, and the accession of an audience to modernist tragedy is evidence of consumerism more than naturalism. The tease of natural reason, that sense of presence, tarriance, and sovereignty, are postmodern, anachronistic circumstances.

The *anishinaabe*, the natives of the northern woodland, once decorated the dead for a dance with the spirits; the dead were on the "road of souls" in the distance, not on a cursory march of revision and victimry. The customs of native mourners were seldom the same; some mourners were extreme, and other elders were obscure. Natives mourned the presence not the absence of the dead; the trace of spirits, and the journey of the soul to another presence. Mourning was not the mere autopose of victimry. The word *aanimizi* means "to suffer" in *anishinaabe*, a subjective experience, and other words refer to emotions, mind, and pain; the word *dapine* means to "suffer in a certain place," but there is no word in *anishinaabe* that indicates the abstract possession of victimry.[73]

"The Ojibway believes his home after death to lie westward," writes William Warren in *History of the Ojibway Nation*. "With the body are buried all the articles needed in life for a journey." This "road of souls," *chebakunah* or *gabekana*, "is represented as passing mostly through a prairie country." Warren noted that the elders at the grave used another word, *kewakunah*, or *giiwekana*, the "homeward road."[74]

William Jones, a native scholar, observed at the turn of the last century that the *anishinaabe* believe in "two souls." One soul leaves a person at death and enters the "spirit world. The other remains with the body and makes the grave its abode."[75] The soul is our distance in a shadow, the persona of an animal or bird on the road of eternal memories. The stories of the soul are sources of survivance not victimry.

CONTESTABLE VICTIMRY

The simulation of the *indian* is not the same as the possession of the victim; the absence of the *indian* is the new representation of victimry. What, then, is an *indian* victim? The modernist subject, the racialist object, or is the new representation of the name, based on a simulation, the very cause of aesthetic sufferance and dominance? Modernity is rational, a constitutional dominance.

Modernity is the very ideological possession of the other, the representations of *indian* cultures by the documents and languages of civilization. Our names are real, the hand and heart of presence, but love, hate, victim, and other common nouns, are obscure, and "such nouns have no reality," observes Erich Fromm in *To Have or to Be*? "Most of us know more about the mode of having than we do about the mode of being, because having is by far the more frequently experienced mode in our culture." The mode of having is the possession of an absence, not a sense of presence, and "refers to things and things are fixed and describable. Being refers to experience, and human experience is in principle not describable. What is fully describable is our persona—the mask we each wear, the ego we present—for this persona is in itself a thing. In contrast, the living human being is not a dead image and cannot be described like a thing." In other words, and in the new course of *indian* victimry, "Being refers to the real, in contrast to the falsified, illusionary picture."[76]

Native hands and hearts are traces of sound and stone, the tease of nature not science. That postmodern sense of presence in oral stories is the creation, the turn and tease of imagination, not the animation or representations of the manifest in written words. The letters wait to hear the hand, the shadow distance of the soul and stone.

Modernity is science, representations, civilization, timewise histories, and the manifestive creases of document cultures over nature. That sense of native presence is unnameable; the *indian* is a modernist persona, not the mania of lost connections. Modernity is in the histories of the surname, the simulations of culture, the motive of absence, and the closure of identities. The stories of names, native nicknames, are the nature of hands and hearts, the traces of our presence. Modernity is the intention, the case and cause of science, the beat and possession of nature into silence, not stone. There, more than animism, is evidence that modernism, by causal representation and cultural simulations, ruined that tease of a native presence in stories, stones, and the ironies of structural signification.[77] Consider that the manner to have a cut, a communion, a culture, is not the same sense of presence as to be creative, to be humane, to be a native healer, or to bear the tragic wisdom of survivance.

Modernity is the conversion of nature by science, the curve of connate survivance. This is the modernist course of representations and dominance. William Connolly observes that modernity insists on "taking charge of the world" and nature "becomes a set of laws susceptible to human knowledge, a deposit of resources for potential use or a set of vistas for aesthetic appreciation."[78] The conversion of nature is the possession of natives and our experience by name and manner; the native absence is a representation of aesthetic victimry.

The *victime* is the sufferer, the one who bears the experience of evil, torture, and termagancy. The victime, the one who suffers, is not the perpetrator of aesthetic miseries and not the one who owns the name of victimry. The arrogation of cultural victims is a sacrifice to the representations of modernity. The possession of sufferance is not an existence but a transmutation; the cause of exclusion and violence is redoubled to the victim, an aesthetic victimology. The victime, then, is not the cause or consent to violence, or the name of cultural revisions and representations. The victime is the one who suffers, not the author of aesthetic victimry. The victime is the one who restores a sense of presence and tragic wisdom in the stories of survivance.

Cultural representations of the native victime are inevitable distortions of experience. "Individuals do not suffer in the same way, any more than they live, talk about what is at stake, or respond to serious problems in the same ways. Pain is perceived and expressed differently, even in the same community," observe Arthur and Joan Kleinman. "This globalization of suffering is one of the more troubling signs of the cultural transformations of the current era: troubling because experience is being used as a commodity, and through this cultural representation of suffering, experience is being remade, thinned out, and distorted."[79]

Those natives who ensure a sense of presence in the absence of ordinary ancestral stories, the synecdochic possession of a native persona, must bear an obscure sense of answerability in the traces of sufferance. Some natives may suffer a common experience of "survivor guilt," that sense of blame for the very absence of native traditions.

The survivors of violence and actual traumatic experiences, and those who arrogate an aesthetic victimry, are redeemed only when the trauma "becomes the source of a survivor mission" writes Judith Lewis Herman in *Trauma and Recovery*. "Social action offers the survivor a source of power." Commodity sufferance and the aesthetic persona of the native victime could be a mission and source of the survivance narratives if the "traumatic imagery and bodily sensation" are not "barren and incomplete." Herman asserted that atrocities "refuse to be buried." Remembrance and true or actual stories "about terrible events are prerequisites both for the restoration of the social order and for the healing of individual victims."[80]

Modernity beset the *indigène* with cultural alternations, and the simulations of the native became the vanishing *indian* at the turn of the last century, a theme of absence, cultural dominance, and aesthetic victimry. Native visions and consanguinity were revised by name, treaty removal, exclusions, education, cultural osmoses, federal policies of assimilation and disappearance, and other cruel ironies. The nation was a monotheistic ordinance, an institutional civilization of manifest cultural uniformity.

The modernist possession of rational notions and scientific certainty, a national conceit, has never been without serious—and very dangerous—contradictions; the victime would suffer not by fate but by the revelations of reason and science. The conceits, on the one hand, were rational, the practices of separation and exclusion as the perverse measures of human distinctions; on the other hand, the ideologies of dominance, the possession of cultures, civilities, and uniformity. Jews, natives, evermore the simulations of the other, have endured the miscarried cause of modernity.

"Modernity meant, among other things, a new role for ideas," Zygmunt Bauman writes in *Modernity and the Holocaust*. The state relied "for its functional efficiency on ideological mobilization, because of its pronounced tendency to uniformity." Clearly, that tedious, haunted mission of civilization, was an "attempt to bring previously peripheral classes and localities into an intimate spiritual contact with the idea-generating centre of the body politic." Jews, natives, and others were cut to mean representations, but not for the same reasons, in the course of ideological uniformity; however, that cultural "efficiency" inevitably caused new separations. "Modernity brought the levelling of differences—at least of their outward appearances, of the very stuff of which symbolic distances between segregated groups are made. With such differences missing, it was not enough to muse philosophically over the wisdom of reality as it was—something Christian doctrine had done before when it wished to make sense out of the factual Jewish separation. Differences had to be created now, or retained against the awesome eroding power of social and legal equality and cross-cultural exchange."[81]

Modernity was the cause of the precise, the common, and the continuous; once native distinctions were obscured by the simulation of the *indian*, the case of cultural dominance, and, as most natives were embraced by a constitutional democracy, new traditions and cultural distinctions were created to separate the national *indian* from the actual, more elusive native. These modernist simulations of the *indian*, once seen as the fugitive on a course of disappearance, became the new measures of cultural diversity. Here, the new *indian*, trice a simulation, became the connate trace to nature, that tease of *mother earth*, and, at the same time, the other, an aesthetic absence in the course of dominance and victimry.

CROATAN COUNTENANCE

Sylvester Long was born black in Winston, North Carolina, on December 1, 1890. He was ambitious, adventurous, generous, a clever athlete, and an actor. The spectacles of his poses were admired by natives, and many others; however, his native stories, the natural recurrence of his memories, were elusive. His sense of a varionative presence was an absence; the severe master of masks and native simulations. Grievously, his poses ended in suicide.

Long Lance, as he was later known, was also born native, and white, but he was raised "colored," and that racial exclusion as a child became the cause of the miseries he would overcome as a clever impostor. Cherokee was his choice of daemons; his father was crossblood native, white, and some of his ancestors were slaves. His mother was crossblood native and white, and his maternal grandmother was "classified as 'Croatan,' the name given at the turn of the century to people of mixed Indian, English, and possibly African ancestry, a group now known as the Lumbee."[82]

He asserted native ancestors and, by varionative deceptions, was accepted to study at the Carlisle Indian Residential School in Pennsylvania. He was nineteen at the time but lied about his age because the "preferred age" of admission was "fourteen to eighteen." Later, he won a scholarship to St. John's Military Academy, an exclusive school in New York State, and, had he not failed one of the academic entrance examinations, he might have been the first native appointed to the United States Military Academy at West Point.

Long Lance wrote to President Woodrow Wilson on March 8, 1915, boldly asking for his "assistance in securing an appointment" to West Point. "I am of Indian ancestry, being a member of the Eastern Cherokee tribe." The chance was granted, but he did not survive the examinations. The *Washington Post* noted in an editorial that the "appointment by the president of a full-blooded Cherokee to a West Point cadetship comes as a recognition of educational qualifications in the appointee that promise to do further honor not only to his own race, but to the country as well."[83] Indeed, he was native, an obscure trace, but he could not document his ancestors, so he created a native absence as a presence, the varionative depositary of racial politics, chance, choice, and audience. How ironic that the same president who advanced racial segregation would name a native poser to West Point.

"His lies were becoming more compulsive and more outrageous," writes Donald Smith in *Long Lance: The True Story of an Impostor.* "In March, 1926, he was interviewed by the Minneapolis *Sunday Tribune.*" The Cherokee had already become a tricky chief in the native confederacy of the Blackfoot. "To the Plains Indians, Chief Long Lance is 'Big Boss,' " reported the *Tribune.* Many tribes, "in addition to the Blackfoot Indians of Alberta, are said to look upon him as a leader." His pose, manner, and countenance were plausible to natives and others.

Grey Owl, for instance, in an ironic turn of varionative poses, wrote that Long Lance, "though educated" was a "splendid savage" compared to other natives who were favored by civilization.[84] The Englishman Archibald Stansfelt Belaney, an adventurous hunter on the frontier, and an author, assumed the name Grey Owl. Archie never met Long Lance, but Agnes Belaney, his *anishinaabe* daughter, remembered the handsome actor in the movie *The Silent Enemy.* Long Lance "exploded in anger" at Agnes. "She had simply remarked to him that she had never seen an Indian with such dark skin," wrote Smith. "She asked him where he came from, to which tribe he belonged, and then said, 'You must be a different kind of Indian.' "[85] Long Lance was a movie actor; his pose was a varionative presence but not the true hue of the month. Surely, his creations were more native than his countenance.

William Douglas Burden hired Molly Spotted Elk to play Neewa, and Long Lance as Baluk, in *The Silent Enemy.* The 1929 silent film was set in the Temagami Forest in northern Ontario. Molly, an ambitious dancer and vaudeville performer, was born on the Penobscot Reservation in Maine. "Long Lance presented a captivating picture of chiseled manliness. His accomplishments matched his physical stature."[86]

Long Lance created the simulation of a presence, the pose of the native real with no source, reference, or antecedents; a common simulation, as many others have done in the past century. Truly, some of his obscure ancestors were native and, after all, he was a graduate of the Carlisle Indian School. He was an athlete, author, actor, and bon vivant who toured and performed in Buffalo Bill's Wild West Show, traveled with Jim Thorpe to the Stockholm Olympics, served in the Canadian Expeditionary Force in France, and fought in World War I. These were admirable deeds, triumphs, and adventures, at a time of curious spectacles, pretenses, and trickery in the nation; however, his descriptive names and native chieftaincy were honorary, an obscure variational presence. Long Lance cut a fugitive pose as a "chief" and "used it as an instrument to serve the needs of others."

Long Lance was twice wounded; at the end of the war he became a staff writer for the *Calgary Herald* in Canada. He lied to the editors that he was a captain in the war, that he won the *Croix de Guerre*, and that he was a graduate of West Point.

Long Lance, his autobiography, was first published in 1928. The reviews were positive. The Philadelphia *Public Ledger*, for instance, named it "a gorgeous saga of the Indian race." The *New Statesman* observed, "This book rings true; no outsider could explain so clearly how the Indians felt." Another reviewer noted that "Inevitably one is reminded of Hiawatha and Fenimore Cooper's adventure tales. . . . all told with verve and remembered with clarity."[87]

Anthropologist Paul Radin wrote a generous review in the *New York Herald Tribune*. An "authentic" autobiography and "unusually faithful account of his childhood and early manhood," he observes. "I cannot think of any work that could act as a better corrective of the ridiculous notions still prevailing about the Indians than this autobiography of Long Lance."

The African American who posed as Cherokee wrote an "authentic" autobiography as a Blackfoot. The "corrective" is ironic, more backhanded salvation than erudition or a native tease, and the notion of the "authentic" hints at a pure presence, an "unusually faithful" simulation of the absence of natives.

Radin, however, points out that the author "had done very little to illuminate the Indian mind." This, the anthropologist explains, served the "book's authenticity, for 'no Indian talks much about himself.' "[88] Once more, the silence of natives is either one of those "ridiculous notions" or evidence of the true absence of natives. Radin, who published *The Autobiography of a Winnebago Indian*, had studied with Franz Boas at Columbia University. How might the expert anthropologist have reviewed *The Education of Little Tree*, the controversial "autobiography" by Forrest Carter?

Today such praise seems ironic, romantic, and the contradiction of an actual native presence. Long Lance was an actor, a dapper celebrity, and many reviewers of his autobiography were romancers of the absence of the native. Time and reason, however, are not natural correctives of varionative romance. Consider the praise in recent reviews of other native autobiographies.

Where White Men Fear to Tread: The Autobiography of Russell Means, with Marvin Wolf, for instance, recounts the adventures and identities of a native activist, "his incarcerations in prison, the thirteen assassination attempts on his life, his intellectual transformation to an outlaw personality, his spiritual awakening, and his most recent reincarnation as a Hollywood movie star in *The Last of the Mohicans* and *Pocahontas*."

Oliver Stone wrote on the back cover of the autobiography that "Russell Means awakens the spirits of Sitting Bull and Crazy Horse in *Where White Men Fear to Tread*." Dee Brown noted that a "reading of Means's story is essential for any clear understanding of American Indians during the last half of the twentieth century." Senator James Abourezk, in his praise of the book, observed that "Russell Means has written a moving, entertaining and ultimately inspiring book that shows why and how he became the symbol of his people's aspirations."[89]

Donald Smith points out that "Long Lance was blessed, or cursed, with the novelist's imagination. He knew how to inflate a story to make it read well, and to enhance its sales potential." *Long Lance*, the autobiography, "was a success and sold well across North America and Europe. The first run nearly sold out" by the end of the first year. A special edition was released in England, and translations were published in German and Dutch. "Long Lance was about to become one of the most famous Indians of his day."[90]

Long Lance, an obscure varionative, created the native other in his own memories and stories, and each clever simulation was his concise assurance of a fugitive pose; the lonesome varionative in a cursory presence, enhanced by the praise of anthropologists, and the admiration of curious audiences. Yet, his pretense and audacious cut of presence would never be the sincere trace of native ancestors; he was the real absence of the native other. His native heirs were simulations; even his nicknames were lonesome, the bare narratives of celebrity. Long Lance was bold, but derivative; an aerobatic daredevil in a biplane, he was easily transposed by his own postindian simulations and fakeries.

"In the air he was not a 'full-blooded Indian' or a 'colored,' but a man alone against the elements," observes Smith. "There was nobody to report to, nobody to prove himself to, nobody to lie to. Among the clouds his only enemy was death, and he did not fear it. He escaped all the rumors and ugliness, literally rising above it all in the skies over New York. He would soon be brought down to reality." Long Lance was a member of the Explorers Club in New York, and often stayed there when he was in the city. However, he was not at ease, because rumors were circulating "that he was an impostor." He would never show "his inner torment."

Long Lance died of a gunshot wound to the head. Los Angeles police authorities investigated and ruled the death a suicide. He was buried on March 30, 1932, by members of the British Benevolent Society in the British Empire War Veterans' section of the Inglewood Cemetery in Los Angeles.[91]

NOTABLE WARRANTS

Ralph Ware posed as an academic, a manifest impostor, and his poses were so convincing at the time that he was nominated and might have been elected to serve as a member of the Minneapolis School Board in Minnesota.

That nomination, in fact, is what started the investigation, some twenty years ago, into the alleged misrepresentation of his credentials. Ware was not, however, a unilateral impostor in the community. His varionative poses and cajolery were abetted by those who would romance the very absence of a native in the exotic presence of the other as an academic. He assumed the imprimatur of the academy and did so with notable warrants.

Ware announced that he was a clinical psychologist and, based on his uncommon pose and manner, he "practiced" on natives for more than a year at Lutheran Deaconess Hospital in Minneapolis. "Ware would allow himself to be introduced as a doctor and he wouldn't correct the title," said one medical doctor. "We never told him not to do that but we kidded him about it." Ware was dismissed for "personal reasons early in 1973."[92]

Project Newgate, a corrections rehabilitation program for natives, hired the impostor as a consultant. Ware told the director of the program at the time that he had a doctor's degree. He was a member of the Mayor's Indian Advisory Committee, and he was an occasional lecturer in the American Indian Studies Department at the University of Minnesota.

The Citizens United for Responsible Education, a bipartisan association of education advocates, endorsed the nomination of Ware, and that of four others, to the Minneapolis School Board in 1974. At the time, the board conducted routine investigations of the nominees in preparation for a selection. Ware, it turned out, was not his pose, not even the least trace of any academic pose.

Ware clearly indicated on the background sheet presented to the Minneapolis School Board that he had earned a "bachelor's degree in nursing" and a "master's in clinical psychology" at San Jose State University in California. A magazine article noted that he had a doctorate in clinical psychology from the "University of Southern California at Berkeley." The investigation of his academic records indicated that the universities he listed had no knowledge of his attendance, and one institution did not exist.

"Ware's school board biographical sketch said that he was born in Oklahoma and enlisted in the Army at 13," reported the *Minneapolis Tribune*. The sketch indicated "that between 1949 and 1955 he served four years in the Far East as a combat medic, including 18 months at the front," presumably in the Korean War. The sketch noted that "he was decorated with two Purple Hearts, a Bronze Star, a Silver Star and a Distinguished Service Citation."[93] Several investigators, at the time, were not able to authenticate the case of his military service or decorations.

"They found it easier to talk and work with me as a human being by making me a doctor," said Ware. His poses, nonetheless, were active, as he participated in the prestige of being a doctor, and passive in the sense that he did not correct erroneous academic credentials. His poses were variational contingencies, the cruises of a doubled absence: the romantic absence of the native, and the absence of a verifiable personal history.

Ware practiced the cause of modernity. His moment of fame was an objective imposture, a variational simulation of victory over victimry. Natives have always created their own presence and sense of existence, and were teased in certain communities to announce their personal identities in oaths, nicknames, visions, and stories. The practices of native healers were once sustained by those who were healed; the politics of constituency and contingency. Modern professions, however, must establish and secure certain objective standards.

Native poses are creations, and in this sense, presence is conveyed by a constituency. The absence of natives is a romantic cause; the absence of traditional and academic credentials is not the same. Those who pose as doctors must overcome their absence and heal a wise audience. Otherwise, "modern standards have taken some of the fun out of pretending."[94]

NATIVE TROPARY

Washington Irving announced in "Traits of Indian Character" that a "frequent ground of accusation against the Indians is their disregard of treaties, and the treachery and wantonness with which, in time of apparent peace, they will suddenly fly to hostilities." The *indian* "nature is stern, simple and enduring; fitted to grapple with difficulties, and to support privations." These curious discoveries of natives in the early nineteenth century were romantic, the hospitable simulations and literary pieties that he would fault in other authors.

The aborigines "have been dispossessed of their hereditary possessions by mercenary and frequently wanton warfare; and their characters have been traduced by bigoted and interested writers. The colonist has often treated them like beasts of the forest; and the author has endeavoured to justify him in his outrages. The former found it easier to exterminate than to civilize; the latter to vilify than to discriminate."[95]

John Joseph Mathews, the prominent historian and novelist, was "fitted to grapple" as a native author; he was "stern" as an aviator, a "simple and enduring" student at the University of Oklahoma, at Oxford University, and in Geneva, Switzerland, the absence and the presence of those ironic traits noted by Washington Irving.

Mathews published his first novel, *Sundown*, in 1934, more than a century after "The Traits of Indian Character" in *The Sketch Book* by Irving. Challenge Windzer, the main character in the novel, is educated, like the author, and he returns to Indian Territory in Oklahoma. His mother is traditional, but an oil boom burdens the memories of the Osage. "The black derricks had crept from the blackjacks of the east, slowly over the hills," he writes at the end of the novel. "Then one day something happened," the people of the town "seemed to melt into the air." The roar of oil production had faded, and the "derricks stood black against the prairie," as the "husks of a life force" on the hillsides. "Mixedblood families came back to the old Agency from their homes in the mountains, in California, and elsewhere. They dropped their golf clubs and lost their homes and came back to wander aimlessly along the familiar streets. They asked with the other citizens of the town, 'S'pose it'll come back?' All agreed that it would, but they wondered just the same."

Virginia Mathews, in the introduction to *Sundown*, noted that her father was in the "vanguard of American Indian writers who brought their education, their sophistication, and their consider-able pondering on a dual cultural heritage to the service of their tribes and Indian people collectively."[96]

Mathews created characters who tease the ambiguities of native memories, and neither the author nor his characters were tragic victims. "*Sundown* is the story of a mixedblood living both in and out of his tribal culture, and it is a nearly fatalistic tale that at a su-perficial glance seems to mesh neatly with the popular naturalism of the twenties and thirties," writes Louis Owens in *Other Destinies*. "Mathews leaves open the possibility of 'another destiny, another plot,' for the American Indian, refusing any romantic closure that would deny the immense difficulties confronting the displaced Native American, but simultaneously rejecting the cliché of the Vanishing American as epic, tragic hero."[97] *Sundown* was the start of a new vision in native literature, a modernist presentation of a dialogic presence over a romantic absence.

Many characters in native literature have agreed that the old towns and traditions would come back, and "they wondered just the same." That curious cue, the eternal return of cultures, and sources of native memories, is more romantic than actual, more manner and awe than venture; yet, wonder and reversion are contingencies of a native sense of presence in literature. Not only characters in fiction, but the narrators of many native autobi-ographies tease the very absence of culture and tradition as the authentic narratives of an ethical presence. "The doctrine of the eternal return portrays each moment as a gateway where the past and future meet in a decision of the present," writes Tobin Siebers in *The Ethics of Criticism*.[98]

Arnold Krupat considers modern western autobiographies as "essentially metonymic in orientation." Comparatively, native autobiographies continue "to be persistently synecdochic, and the preference for synecdochic models of the self has relations to the oral techniques of information transmission typical of Native American cultures."[99]

Metonymy, in this sense, is a trope, a figurative device that indicates a common reference by replacing one name with another; for instance, *the pen is mightier than the sword*. Synecdoche, on the other hand, is a word or name that substitutes the part for the whole, such as a *head count, hired guns, weasel words,* and the simulations of *indian* cultures and traditions. Thomas McLaughlin points out in "Figurative Language" that metonymy "accomplishes its transfer of meaning on the basis of associations that develop out of specific contexts rather than from participation in a structure of meaning. A metonymy such as referring to the king by the phrase 'the crown' speaks of the king by means of an object frequently associated with him. It does not call for the magical sharing of meaning that a metaphor implies; instead, it relies on connections that build up over time and the associations of usage."[100]

Gemma Corradi Fiumara observed that the "paradox of a metaphor is that it seems to affirm an identity while also somehow denying it."[101] The tropes of native stories, and interpretation of autobiographies, are dialogic circles; that native sense of presence in stories could be seen as "metabolic" and evolutionary.

Kenneth Burke, in *Grammar of Motives*, "argues that metonymic usage is *reductive*, while synecdochic is *representative*," observes Hayden White in *Tropics of Discourse*. "Metonymy, being reductive in its operations, would provide a model of that form of explanation which I have called mechanistic," a cause and effect phenomenon. "Synecdoche, by contrast, would sanction a movement in the opposite direction, towards integration of all apparently particular phenomena into a whole."[102] Natives, in either of these motives and associations, are objects in the tropics of dominance. Natives might tease the seasons, natural reason, tricky visions, and the "intransitive motion" of shadows in a new tropary.[103]

White was not specific about autobiography, but in the course of historical representations, varionative autobiographies would be synecdochic and move in the direction of integration, or the latent cast of native traditions, rather than metonymic simulations, or reductive associations, as causal reason and other connections. Whatever the figurative directions, varionative autobiographies are dialogic circles, and the traces of presence are more originary, and generative, than structuralist representations. These literary devices and interpretations are neither the directions of narratives nor the thematic union of author intentions. The autobiographies of natives are creative visions and the "second immediacy" of the dialogic circles of survivance.

Krupat mentions that *The Confessions* by Jean-Jacques Rousseau and *The Names* by N. Scott Momaday seem to be "metonymic in their orientation." Distinctly, there are instances of "synecdochic representation of self" in *A Son of the Forest* by William Apess and *Life among the Piutes: Their Wrongs and Claims* by Sarah Winnemucca Hopkins, "whose very title proclaims her individual life as comprehensible foremost in relation to the collective experience of her tribe." *Storyteller* by Leslie Marmon Silko "conceives of individual identity only in functional relation to the tribe." Native autobiographies, "as far as one may generalize," seem to be "marked by the figure of synecdoche" in the "presentation of the self."[104]

Krupat observed in *The Voice in the Margin* that the native *dialogic* of the self in autobiographies "most typically is not constituted by the achievement of a distinctive, special voice that separates it from others, but, rather, by the achievement of a particular placement in relation to the many voices without which it could not exist."[105]

Synecdoche is an "essential theme" of absence over presence in certain varionative autobiographies; the coincidence of traditions, contingencies of mythic representation, and nativist associations by artistic substitution. Chance is an obscure aspect of "archaic ontology."

Mircea Eliade studies "being and reality" in *The Myth of the Eternal Return* and reasons that the "eternal return reveals an ontology uncontaminated by time and becoming." The "eternal return" is a mannered absence in native autobiographies, but the figurative "collective experience" is never a certain reverse of distinctive native histories.

"The chief difference between the man of the archaic and traditional societies and of the modern societies," writes Eliade, "lies in the fact that the former feels himself indissolubly connected with the Cosmos and the cosmic rhythms, whereas the latter insists that he is connected only with History."

Collective native memories, in this sense, would be synecdochic archetypes, as the native in a "traditional" culture lives "at the heart of the *real* since . . . there is nothing truly real except the archetypes." The contingencies of a native presence, the rise of natural reason, and resistance are dialogic circles of interpretation; synecdoche, as an overture of "oneness" in the interpretations of varionative autobiographies, is an aesthetic renunciation of human sound and a native presence, an aversion to the creative maneuvers and ambiguities of visions and memories.

Myths, of course, present a union of "sacred histories" in collective reminiscence, but not the tease of native presence, tricky ontologies, or the ironies of modernity.[106]

THEATER OF OKLAHOMA

Washington Irving was on a "voyage of personal discovery," notes John Francis McDermott in the introduction to *A Tour on the Prairies.* Personal, descriptive, and picturesque, his travel journal provided no "significant information about terrain," no scientific notes or notice of enterprise. Irving "had no purpose but to observe human behavior." The natives he encountered were not named as individuals, but those he noticed in his travel monologue were slight traces of presence; an original crease of native character in the early nineteenth century that is seldom found in the scientism of military and ethnographic observations. The natives were described as animated and humorous, not solemn, stoical, or heroic. Few other observers have ever mentioned the humor of natives in the theater of discoveries and dominance.

Fort Gibson and the Osage Agency in the Indian Territory of Oklahoma were the crossroads of natives, slaves, traders, hunters, frontier diplomats, pioneers, and adventurers. Irving, on a theatrical excursion of the prairies, was so anxious to see bison and wild horses "that he had almost concluded to hire some Indians to escort him to their camp by forced marches."[107]

Auguste Pierre Chouteau was a frontier trader and diplomat in Indian Territory. Irving, who had traveled with the rich trader from Independence to Fort Gibson, described the Osage Agency as "a few log houses on the banks of the river, and presented a motley frontier scene." Nearby he noticed natives with bare heads, "excepting a bristling ridge on the top, like the crest of a helmet, with a long scalp lock hanging behind," and they were wrapped in blankets.

"The Osage are the finest looking Indians I have ever seen in the West," observed Irving. "Roman countenances" he noted, "with broad deep chests," and they "have not yielded sufficiently, as yet, to the influence of civilization to lay by their simple Indian garb, or to lose the habits of the hunter and the warrior; and their poverty prevents their indulging in much luxury of apparel."[108] Irving would preserve the absence of natives here, the mere objects of cultural representation in the manner of a theatrical adventurer, but later in his journal he creates a native sense of presence, the contingency and discernment of character. The natives he mentioned were not the same as the "imaginary attributes" of natives "described in poetry." Irving might have had in mind the "Indian Burying Ground" and other sentimental poems by Philip Freneau.

Henry Leavitt Ellsworth, commissioner to the *indians* in the new western territories, mentions in his narrative that Irving "had expressed a decided objection in joining the Osages who were filthy in the extreme."[109] Irving, to the contrary, was more observant of a distinctive native presence than other adventurers at the time. The Commissioner, a former city mayor and corporate president, must have attributed to others his own objection to natives, as natives are the absence not the presence in his frontier narrative.

Irving observed that natives "among themselves" could not "be greater gossips. Half their time is taken up in talking over their adventures in war and hunting, and in telling whimsical stories. They are great mimics and buffoons, also, and entertain themselves excessively at the expense of the whites with whom they have associated, and who have supposed them impressed with profound respect for their grandeur and dignity."

The Osage, "sitting around a fire until a late hour of the night, engaged in the most animated and lively conversations; and at times making the woods resound with peals of laughter. As to tears, they have them in abundance, both real and affected; at times they make a merit of them."[110]

Irving was an adventurer on the prairie; a curious observer of the other, a travel writer, elusive biographer, and historian. The nostalgia and patriotism of his earlier narratives were outdistanced by the tease of natives, their tricky humor, and stories. The Osage, in his journal, were the trace of eternal ancestors. The trace, as not one native was ever named in a conversation; yet, the action and reason he portrayed were closer to the literature of survivance than to the simulations of scientism. He was quickened by natives, and humored in the scenes and sessions of the prairie. Irving is forever in the book with natives.

"Irving worked best when he traveled, and he knew that his writing depended upon an accurate evocation of place," noted Lee Clark Mitchell in *Witnesses to a Vanishing America.* "Curiosity about Indian cultures often led beyond respect, and those willing to shake off preconceptions sometimes felt a wistful envy."[111]

The native *one* in the book is a trace of presence; otherwise, the one is a simulation of absence, or the mere notation of victimry. The traces of native presence are originary. The seasonable pretenses of native names, uncertain situations, and documents over service to score a nonce, are simulations of presence. The one as an aesthetic severance, the native absence feigned as a presence, must ensure the vectors of victimry.

W. S. Penn, the novelist, and his sister, Patricia Penn Hilden, turn to the absence and obscure sessions of *indians* in the book; the authors mention in their own books the consonance of ancestral documents, nominal entitlements, and aesthetic connections to the Osage in Oklahoma.

Oklahoma is the natural theater of the nativist one, and that pose is in the book. Everyone is invited to construe the documents in the theater of absence; the simulations of a native presence in the narratives of absence. The one of absence is alone in the theater, and the poses of ancestors never close in the book.

"Everyone is welcome" to the "Theater of Oklahoma," wrote Franz Kafka in *America.* Why not, he might have created a theater of varionatives in Oklahoma? The one to live an absence, to learn the cut of seasons in mere names, time in passive narratives, a native presence in the connotations of an absence, is the one to leave the book and the theater. That leave is evermore an absence in a theater that never ceases; the aesthetic location of native ancestors in the theater of Oklahoma. To hint too much a real native presence in the book is to leave the world of the book. The insinuation of natives in names and documents, the ancestors of absence, is the absurdism of the theater. The one of no trace is the absence not the silence in the varionative theater of Oklahoma.

"Growing up, we knew we were Indian," writes W. S. Penn in *All My Sins Are Relatives.* "But we did not know how Indian. It was a piece of laundry disguised and hidden from us." That laundry, of course, was a varionative simulation and, at the same time, the very absence of ancestors who were Nez Perce and Osage. Then, "by luck," he "discovered a picture" in the archives at the Brooklyn Museum, "a picture of me taken in 1877 in Osage, Oklahoma." The *me* was named Albert Penn. The native waited with two other men in a backlighted studio photograph. He wears trousers high on his waist, and the shirt could be borrowed, as the sleeves are too short. Albert, the *me*, the *one* of absence, looks past the camera; his gaze is archival, not a presence, but a tacit trace of native ancestors.

William Penn, the author, the *me* that entered the photographic gaze, was born some three generations later than Albert Penn. The actual names, dates, and transactions are uncertain; consequently, the simulations of emulsion countenance and entreaties of his native ancestors must be more shamanic than documentable. Albert Penn is archival, a tenuous relation, but once the author "found" that native pose, a fugitive photograph in a museum, he could announce a surname connection to the Osage in Oklahoma.

Penn, the surname, "was given to my father and uncles by the Orthodox Quakers who were deeded the mission in Indian Territory by the federal government in its passionate interest to protect and raise the Indians it had shipped there by the hundreds and thousands."

William Penn, the author, bears the same name as his father, his grandfather, and, centuries earlier, the English Quaker and founder of Pennsylvania. Penn, the surname, is a trace of presence in national histories, but natives are the absence in the course of his name, an obscure antecedence in narratives.

William Penn, the founder of his own colony, practiced cultural and religious tolerance; the seventeenth century was not a time of concessions or sufferance, but he negotiated treaties with natives in their presence and established a relatively honorable course of land purchase. Penn was respected by many natives; later, his name was carried to reservations by missionaries.

Benjamin West painted *William Penn's Treaty with the Indians* in 1771. That painting became a popular image of national pageants for more than a century. David Glassberg noted that pageants borrowed "heavily from familiar images such as the painting" by West to portray "white displacement of Indians as a friendly, legitimate business transaction."[112] The trace and presence of natives in art was ruined in pageant representations.

The perseverance of honored names, the trace and assurance of native ancestors, is an aesthetic survivance. Native visions and memories are incommensurable, and never certain, but the stories of names and the tease of creation are a tricky consonance. Creation, the wit of heritable names and stories, wisps of native ancestors, and the cues of victimry are sources of varionative identities; these, and other traceables, are trained to three generations in *All My Sins Are Relatives.*

"Mother once devised a kind of family tree for me, a tree laddered with question marks and dead ends," writes Penn. "It was her nature and her upbringing to want us not to be Indian." She "meant well when she made up the family tree," but now the image of "Albert Penn standing in colorful silk shirt and neckerchief and high-waisted pants, his perpendicular ears disguised (though not hidden) by his long hair, the extent of Mother's wishful thinking in compiling that tree becomes astounding." He mentions that his mother held to a bitter marriage, caused his father to be "marginal, ancillary to the function of the family," and she "even managed the discipline" of the children. Patricia, his elder sister, was beaten "mercilessly across the bared thighs with the back of a metal hairbrush."[113] Family memories and stories are seldom, if ever, the same; his sister recounts their mother in a more generous manner. These autobiographical narratives, published in the same year, note many of the same names; otherwise, the connections in these two books might not have been obvious.

"Mother, anxious to teach us our cultural identity with every means available to her, bought us beading materials so that we could learn to bead belts and headbands," writes Patricia Penn Hilden in *When Nickels Were Indians: An Urban Mixed-Blood Story.* Anne Marie, her sister, reminded her of this experience. "I started much less enthusiastically, playing with the beads rather than stitching them neatly on the warp. . . .

"My sister also remembers that 'on one of our regular Sunday visits to Grams and Gramps, once all the other grownups were busy doing other things, Gramps took us into the spare bedroom where he dragged a small chest out of the closet, carefully opened it, and pulled out a feather headdress. I remember it was very old. I think he said it was my father's.' "

Penn Hilden points out that the "Penns, who lived in our childhood imaginations as pale . . . white people garbed in somber black hats . . . were only slightly English, if at all. Rather they, too, were Indians—Osages." William Penn, their Nez Perce grandfather, she resolved, was recorded at the Osage Agency. "Moreover, this meant that we were all much more Indian then we had known—a mixture of Osage *and* Nez Perce. Furthermore, some records indicate that the Osage part married a Mexican part as well as an English part at some point."[114]

The remarkable measures of varionative identities by rumor and allusive documents, and the rich mixture of native names, are the absence, not a presence of natives in *All My Sins Are Relatives* and *When Nickels Were Indians*. The metaphors, and the curious ambiguities of "some records" are incommensurable as sources of native identities. These are not native sessions or situations; rather, the cursive subordination of an *indian* presence to the abetment of names in government documents.

Penn Hilden could be the one to live an absence in the book or the one to hint at "much more" native mixture and leave the world of the book; the cut to measures, and the other "point" of a native absence, is a crease of remorse, an aesthetic desistance. "Trickster wasn't finished with me, it seems," she writes at the end of her story. "No sooner did we all begin to accept the transformation of the Pennsylvania Quaker Penns into Osages than another very old relative mailed *her* 'documents in the case.' " Charles Dickens is summoned to the name, another ironic dimension of victimry, as

victims caught in Victorian England's Chancery courts were never so muddled as this! A marriage certificate shows quite clearly that Grandfather's father, John Swain Penn, was really what we had thought all along: distant (and undistinguished) descendant of William, born in Philadelphia (stories say of mixed-blood parents, but no one knows what the mix was), a migrant to Indian territory where he met his Indian wife. It was she whose Indian blood was mixed. Family narratives continued to assign the Blue half of her to the Nez Perce tribe, Wallowa Band. Her other half, the Liptrapp half, although "full-blooded Indian," according to official records, may or may not have been Osage. No one, in fact, knows.[115]

113

The general records relating to education, boarding schools, allotments, leases, and other matters of the Osage Indian Agency are located in the official repository of the Federal Records Center at Fort Worth, Texas.[116] Doubtless, there are tricksters in the archives, the creases of an absence that would be a presence in other stories of dominance, desistance, and native survivance.

Little Tree is a sentimental simulation, an aeonian absence of natives in the common cast of "a true story." The autobiographical pose of the author, and hint of native ancestors, has enticed millions of readers to a romance and to the aesthetic remorse of victimry.

Forrest Carter created a narrative in the unreliable first person voice of a child. That literary innocence, a common want of authors and readers, is enhanced by the essence of nature and the veracious care of native elders. Nothing real or uncommon is named in this narrative, but the very presence of the author in the previsions of an autobiographical "authenticity" has raised once more the literary contingencies of voice, cultural association, and the tacit intentions of the author in the native content of the book. The author, not the native, is in this book. Neither readers nor literary historians can oust the author from the book. The author is the book. The critic is a hunter, the author an elusive creature; surely, to hint at a sincere narrative and construe the intentions of the author are not traces of a native presence in the book. The author is not the absolute trace of natives in a narrative; rather, the absence of natives is a romance and continues to entice readers. Jonathan Culler notes that the "reader becomes the name of the place where the various codes can be located: a virtual site."[117] So, how is the author to secure a site, or a native presence in a narrative? How is a tacit native presence traced to the author in the book?

There is no trace of a native presence in *The Education of Little Tree* by Forrest Carter. The pretense of a "true story" is the absence not the presence of natives, and the allusions to an autobiography are never certain, real, or precise, in any narrative; the reader has no mastery over the presence of the author in the book. The author is creation, a narrative transcendence, and the reader construes the stories in the absence of the author. The author is never there as a native, at the ear of the reader. Yet, the author is in the book.

"Print finally standardized the communication of knowledge, regardless of a particular speaker or manuscript," observes Donald Lowe in *History of Bourgeois Perception*. Consequently, this typographic "standardization shifted the knowable entirely to the 'content.' This meant a formalization of the known as content, detached from the knower. Previously, it was very difficult to separate the two, and certain bodies of knowledge depended on personal transmission by a master."[118] The author could be a native content, but not an oral presence in the book. Contrary to absence, narratives in the first person voice create a sense of presence, and even more presence in the content of a "true story" by a native author.

"Presence will be at the heart of autobiography," writes Robert Smith in *Derrida and Autobiography*. "Above all, presence stands for self-presence, being present to the self and thus making it bloom, bringing it alive and into the conscious presence of its being. Indeed auto-affection as 'presence' and 'life' are practically synonymous."[119]

Little Tree, an orphan, lived with his grandparents, who were both native. His grandmother was "full blood" and grandfather was "half" Cherokee. "I knew I was Little Tree, and I was happy that they loved me and wanted me. And so I slept, and did not cry," writes Carter. Later, the child was punished at school. "The Reverend reached behind his desk and taken up a long stick" to beat the stoical native. Little Tree learned from his grandfather how to bear pain. The *indian* "lets his body mind go to sleep, and with his spirit mind, he moves out of his body and *sees* the pain — instead of *feeling* the pain."[120]

Little Tree is concise and laconic; however, the "true story" is unreliable in the first person because the reader must sustain a sense of presence that the narrative is told in the omniscient voice of a native child. Later, that same voice is doubled in the narrative. Little Tree assumes the voice of his grandfather, and tells his memories as stories in the Civil War. Grandfather "moved back into a deep fern growth and kept his eyes on them," the Union soldiers. "They didn't scare him, for though he was only nine years old, Granpa was Indian-wise, and could move right through the whole patrol without them seeing him, and he knew it. . . . That night he got to figuring. He figured the Union soldier with the yellow stripes was up to meanness, and he determined he would warn the people in the old house that they was being watched. Next morning, he set himself to do just that."[121]

Carter is the one in the book, as the crease of a double narrator in concise sentences, but he is not the trace or presence of natives.

There are *indians* in the book, those curious simulations with no antecedence. The natives are the absence, and these are the wounds of severance in the literature of survivance.

Forrest Carter created a sincere narrative conscience that was not his own; the "true story" is the concoction of an accused racialist and fascist. "*The Education of Little Tree* is a hoax," asserted Dan T. Carter, a historian at Emory University. The author of this "gentle memoir" constructed a mask, "the last fantasy of a man who reinvented himself again and again."

Asa Earl Carter was his real name. "The Alabama native carved out a violent career in Southern politics as a Ku Klux Klan terrorist, right-wing radio announcer, home-grown American fascist and anti-Semite, rabble-rousing demagogue and secret author" of that infamous inaugural address and promise by Governor George Wallace of Alabama, "Segregation now! Segregation tomorrow! Segregation forever!"[122] That wicked promise lasted about six months, and then black students were enrolled at the University of Alabama. Later, he renounced segregation. Carter continued as a novelist and published *Gone to Texas*, or *The Outlaw Josey Wales*.

Dan Carter told a reporter for the *New York Times*, "This guru of new-age environmentalists was actually a gun-toting racist. . . . I have absolutely positive documentary proof." Forrest "took his new name from Nathan Bedford Forrest" the "slave trade and Civil War general who founded the original Ku Klux Klan in Tennessee in 1866." Forrest Carter died in Abilene, Texas, in 1979.[123]

The Education of Little Tree has sold close to a million copies, more copies sold than *The Way to Rainy Mountain* by N. Scott Momaday, which once was the best seller at the University of New Mexico Press. Rennard Strickland, in his foreword, "Sharing Little Tree," compared this "life story" to the *Adventures of Huckleberry Finn* by Mark Twain. Little Tree "speaks to the human spirit and reaches the very depth of the human soul," Stickland notes with no obvious sense of irony. "Students of Native American life discovered the book to be as accurate as it was mystical and romantic."[124] Romantic, indeed, but far from accurate in any sense of an autobiographical narrative.

Henry Louis Gates Jr. writes in the literary context of racial, ethnic, and gender suppositions that *The Education of Little Tree* "is only the latest embarrassment to beset the literary ideologues of authenticity, and its political stakes are relatively trivial." Gates asserts that what we read, and our "literary judgments, in short, remain hostage to the ideology of authenticity."[125] Clearly, the critic avowed no stake in the literature of native survivance. He rushed to trivia rather than to an authentic critique of the autoposers, those posers who were so admired by readers, even honored by librarians and teachers for their *indian* simulations. The critical issue is racialist fraud, not trivial literary reviews and reductions. Little Tree is much more than the moot trace of the author in the book.

Charles Dickens and Franz Kafka wrote of nature and natives and their extensive journeys in America. Dickens traveled by steamboat, railroad, and stagecoach for five months and published *American Notes*. Kafka toured the nation by imagination, and on his last creative excursion he wrote the novel *Amerika*. "My intention," he wrote in his diary, "was to write a Dickens novel, enriched by the sharper lights which I took from our modern times, and by the pallid ones I would have found in my own interior."[126]

Dickens recounted the exterior of the country, and seasoned the nation as a vast landscape; he held the mounds at a distance in a soliloquy, and mentioned the real absence, the absence in a museum, as the true presence of natives. Kafka teased an interior creation, an unnameable vision, a rush of wild light into the night; unshakably, he scorned the shadows at the borders of silence and memories. Then, near the end, he raved over names, heroic solitudes, and over the extravagant announcement of a future in "The Nature Theatre of Oklahoma."

Kafka teased creation, silence, and situations of the absurd as coherence. Grandeur and absurdities were his rave, the cause to hear ironies in names and common sentences, and in the *nature* of literature. "The absurdity is that the soul transcends its body so immeasurably," writes Albert Camus. "Whoever wishes to delineate this absurdity will have to give it life in this play of parallel contrasts. It is thus that Kafka expresses tragedy by the banal, and the absurd by logic."[127]

Amerika is a new world of hospitable absurdism, a landscape of creation and natural motion over the creases of want and reason. "The Nature Theatre of Oklahoma" is an invitation to artists who would be the new technicians, historians who would be the literary shamans of the archives, and native autoposers who would dare to be authentic in the absurdities of auditions, pictures, and documents. Kafka's "invention of a romantic America corresponds amazingly to the real one. His vision of this country proves to be surprisingly perfect," writes John Urzidil. "If he had ever actually visited America he could not have offered a more competent picture."[128]

Amerika is the creation of an absence, the hoax of discoveries, the hint of treasures, the tragic turn of haste, concision, manner, and that banal distance in the eye. America the creation is the nation of new representations, and consistent simulations of wild nature and the absence of natives.

Kafka is the one, that "fierce light" in the book, and he teased the absence of natives over their ancient pronouns; he mocked the absence of natives as the cause of reason, and tied presence to the absurdities of natural coherence. The last train of countenance, native autoposes, and documents is evermore on the move; a name, a noun, a native pronoun, and the contumacies of our ancestors are the most ironic auditions in the "Theatre of Oklahoma."

CHAPTER THREE

Literary Animals

The earth is a trickster creation; *naanabozho*, that *waabooz* storier, the foremost mind rabbit, and elusive conscience of native transmotions, teases the stone, hies beaver, bears, cranes, the chance of other creatures, and oversees the seasons in *anishinaabe* stories. That trickster *naanabozho* races with the sunrise over winter, to the summer in the spring, a ruse over manners and hierocracy.

The *anishinaabe* endure in these stories of survivance as the crane, loon, bear, martin, and catfish families, the first ancestors on the earth; the *odoodemi*, totem or "to have a totem," is that native presence and trace of the originary.

"Stories with animals are older than history and better than philosophy," writes Paul Shepard in *The Others.* "History tries to describe the world as if it began with writing and only humans mattered; philosophy attempts to abstract truth as if it were defined only by discursive thought and experience of the natural world were unimportant."[1]

The *anishinaabe* are named in "several grand families or clans, each of which is known and perpetuated by a symbol of some bird, animal, fish, or reptile," observes William Warren. The *ajijaak*, or crane totem, is the sandhill crane, a gray wader, a dancer with a red forehead, and a distinctive wingbeat. "This bird loves to soar among the clouds, and its cry can be heard when flying above, beyond the orbit of human vision." The native crane leaders in "former times, when different tribes met in council, acted as interpreter of the wishes of their tribe," the *anishinaabe* historian noted more than a century ago. "They claim, with some apparent justice, the chieftainship over the other clans" of the *anishinaabe.*[2]

Elias Canetti venerates animals and the crane, the trace of a great oratorical totem in his aphoristic memoir, *The Agony of Flies.* He observes the "dance of the cranes! Seeing it, how can humans still dare to take even a single step?"[3]

Keeshkemun, an orator of the crane totem, was a native leader at the turn of the nineteenth century on Lake Superior. He was the grandson of Kechenezuhyauh, the first leader of the crane families. His memorable encounter with a British military officer, eager to enlist his support in the war, was translated by the *anishinaabe* interpreter Michel Cadotte. Clearly, the stories of the orator were strategic, diplomatic, and literary, evidence of native transmotion and survivance. The creation of an avian presence, and the tease of fire, heart, and mystical voice, are stories of affinity, tragic wisdom, and natural reason. Keeshkemun was an artist and diplomatic orator.

"I am a bird who rises from the earth, and flies far up, into the skies, out of human sight; but though not visible to the eye, my voice is heard from afar, and resounds over the earth," said Keeshkemun to the Englishman. "You wish to know who I am. You have never sought me, or you should have found and known me. Others have sought and found me. The old French sought and found me. He placed his heart within my breast. He told me that every morning I should look to the east and I would behold his fire, like the sun reflecting its rays towards me, to warm me and my children. He told me that if troubles assailed me, to arise in the skies and cry to him, and he would hear my voice. He told me that his fire would last forever, to warm me and my children.

Englishman, "You have put out the fire of my French father. I became cold and needy, and you sought me not. Others have sought me. Yes, the Long Knife has found me. He has placed his heart on my breast. It has entered there, and there it will remain."

Warren points out that the *anishinaabe* did not support Great Britain in the War of 1812. The Lake Superior *anishinaabe* "firmly withstood every effort made by the British to induce them to enter into the war, and it is thus they have succeeded in holding their own in numbers, and in fact, gradually increasing, while other tribes, who have foolishly mingled in the wars of the whites, have become nearly extinct."[4]

Mikhail Bakhtin observes an internal connection, a point of view in the word; here, in the sense of the crane, the *odoodemi* of the *anishinaabe*, that connection with natural reason and suave evasion, would counter the social science "discoveries" of totems and cultures in translation. "There is no aspect of language that cannot be used in a figurative sense," he writes. The "point of view contained within the word is subject to a reinterpretation, as is the modality of language and the very relationship of language to the object and to the speaker."[5]

Keeshkemun was an orator, and the crane was a connection, in a "figurative sense," to the row of his words. Surely, point of view in the words, the interpretation of those words, and the internal native connections, rather than the reversions of cultural "meaning," would be more memorable as literature.

Warren has presented these oratorical events in a historical connection as both nature and as culture; natural reason, of course, is a union of nature and language, not a separation. However, many social scientists have translated and structured native metaphors as culture and a determined performance.

"Totemism is like hysteria," asserts Claude Lévi-Strauss in *Totemism.* That totemism is a "projection outside our own universe, as though by a kind of exorcism, of mental attitudes incompatible with the exigency of a discontinuity between man and nature," a validation is possible "by making the inverse exigency an attribute of this 'second nature,' which civilized man, in the vain hope of escaping from himself as well as from nature itself, concocts from the 'primitive' or 'archaic' stages of his own development."

Lévi-Strauss points out that totemism "is an artificial unity, existing solely in the mind of the anthropologist, to which nothing specifically corresponds in reality." The comparison evades "any unifying interpretation" and "suggests a relation of another order between scientific theories and culture, one in which the mind of the scholar himself plays as large a part as the minds of the people studied."[6]

William Warren recounts the *anishinaabe* creation, *odoodemi,* and "ancient traditions" that were told by leaders of the *midewiwin,* the medicine dance, or Great Medicine Society. The *anishinaabe* lived on the shores of a great salt lake when the earth was new, and from the "deep there suddenly appeared six beings in human form, who entered their wigwams.

"One of these six strangers kept a covering over his eyes, and he dared not look" at the *anishinaabe.* "At last he could no longer restrain his curiosity," and "partially lifted his veil, and his eye fell on the form of a human being, who instantly fell dead 'as if struck by one of the thunderers.'" The intentions were friendly, "yet the glance of his eye was too strong, and inflicted certain death." He returned to the "bosom of the great water."[7] The five others remained with the *anishinaabe*, and are the original five *odoodemi*, or totems. These are *midewiwin* survivance stories.

Lévi-Strauss cites the same stories and then declares that the "myth explains that these five 'original' clans are descended from six anthropomorphic supernatural beings who emerged from the ocean to mingle with human beings." He represents the "six beings," the strangers in "human form," as supernatural, a monotheistic notion of existence outside the natural world, and anthropomorphic, the cause to attribute human motivations to animals. Moreover, he notes that the stories were "handed down" in a "mutilated form" and decides that there was "no direct relationship, based on contiguity, between man and totem." He postulates that "the myth establishes another opposition, between personal relation and collective relation. The Indian does not die just because he is looked at, but also because of the singular behavior of one of the supernatural beings, whereas the others act with more discretion, and as a group."[8] The representation of native creation stories as relational, cultural objects renounces the oneiric metaphors of "six beings" and traces of *anishinaabe* survivance. Lévi-Strauss demonstrates in his theories a structural conversion and misuse of imagination, native transmotion, the contingencies of humor in trickster stories, and the dialogic circle of literature.

Natural reason and native survivance are metaphors; more than transference, or the imaginative trace of other experiences, metaphors are the systematic concepts of absence, presence, totems, and transmotion in *anishinaabe* stories. Metaphors are crucial in the interpretation of native literature, and metaphors are comparable as native traces, totems, shamanic visions, action, and conscience of survivance.

Metaphors are persuasive in language, thought, and action. "Our ordinary conceptual system, in terms of which we both think and act, is fundamentally metaphorical in nature," and "not merely a matter of language," observe George Lakoff and Mark Johnson. "Metaphor is one of our most important tools for trying to comprehend partially what cannot be comprehended totally: our feelings, aesthetic experiences, moral practices, and spiritual awareness. These endeavors of the imagination are not devoid of rationality; since they use metaphor, they employ an imaginative rationality."[9]

Samuel Levin argues that "what matters essentially is that we bring to bear metaphoric concepts in the ordinary affairs of our lives." Levin, in *Metaphoric Worlds*, maintains that his theories of metaphor "express conceptions," compared to the expressions of "concepts" by Lakoff and Johnson. In other words, the conceptual metaphor as notion or thought compared to conceptions, or mental concepts and abstractions. *Metaphors We Live By*, he points out, takes "an 'interactional' approach, an approach that sees reality as something that happens to people and that people participate in making, rather than as some objective state of affairs which one tries to account for by means of abstraction, depersonalized theories."[10]

The native world is actuated in *anishinaabe* totems and stories of survivance. The totem is a native metaphor, a literary connection with creation, shamanic visions, and natural reason. Social science theories have reduced native myths, metaphors, and creation to the categorical representations of human development and comparative culture; these objective simulations have served dominance, not native survivance, and the perverse distinctions of savagism and civilization.

ANIMOSH TRANSMOTION

"Outside, the animals listened and the boy felt their spirits draw closer," writes Louis Owens in *Wolfsong*. "The boy listened and fasted beside the lake, and when it was time he dove seeking the vision. The wolf rose on two legs and beckoned, and for a lifetime he followed, far out into the world of men."[11]

The timber wolf, or *maiigan* in *anishinaabe*, was a totem name, but not *animosh*, the dog. The timber wolf was not named as one of the original totems, but it soon became one of the most significant *odoodemi* of the *anishinaabe*. There were more than twenty totems by the eighteenth century, including beaver, moose, hawk, and eagle; some of these totems were created in remote areas and neither mentioned in stories nor noted in translation. The coyote, or brush wolf, is not named in the *anishinaabe* language. Related to the tricky coyote, *animosh* has been more social with humans than the elusive timber wolves. Once harnessed in teams to *nabagidaabaanag*, or toboggans, in winter, and sacrificed in *midewiwin* ceremonies, *animosh* is a presence in native literature.

Now, as a metaphorical mongrel, *animosh* is a literary totem, much closer to humans than any other animal, and in that creative sense, *animosh* is human. Timber wolves are creatures of nature and totems of culture; the mythic totem teases the solace of creation and separations of evolution in survivance stories.

Dogs are named in many common expressions, such as "put on the dog," and "let sleeping dogs lie." Others are top dog, sick as a dog, tail wagging the dog, see a man about a dog, hangdog, dog in the manger, go to the dogs, and barking dogs seldom bite.[12] The dog and other domestic animals are named and ascribed to human situations more often than other creatures. The metaphors suggest both animal and human capacities. "Barking dogs seldom bite," for instance, refers to scared dogs and humans with a pose not as fierce as the manner. "Put on the dog" comments figuratively on an ostentatious manner; the origin of the expression may be a reference to the small dogs carried as pets by aristocrats.

Natives and others "put on the dog" thousands of years before the modern aristocrats. This "poses a problem for those who choose to believe that such behavior is a pointless, modern extravagance; a mere by-product of western decadence or bourgeois sentimentality," notes James Serpell. Archaeological studies provide "evidence of animal domestication," and that at least one stone-ager was buried with a domestic dog suggests an affectionate relationship between dogs and humans. "In other words, prehistoric man may have loved his dogs and his other domestic animals as pets long before he made use of them for any other purpose. Affection for pets may seem, in retrospect, trivial and unimportant."[13]

The *animosh*, put on, go to, top, sick, or in a manger, has not always been treated as a pet. Favored, at once, cursed as a "dog's life," in a "dog eat dog" culture, the canine, cur, bitch, mutt, and mongrel are teased as creatures of ambiguity and duality. The "gross bestiality" of the dog represented "all that is opposed to humanity and civilization," argues Paul Shepard. "In modern affluent societies, dogs fare well; but in times and places that far outnumber prosperity, they have been the most hated of animals. It is far worse to be called a 'dog' in this world than a 'pig' or a 'skunk.'"[14]

Charles Darwin "believed that animals have rational and moral capacities similar to our own," observes James Rachels in *Created from Animals*. "Those who continue to deny that animals have mental capacities similar to those of humans are implying that this research is fundamentally misguided. They thus join the long dismal parade of thinkers who have attempted to set aside whole fields of experimental science on a priori grounds."

Rachels considers the studies and notions of animal altruism and argues that "if anthropomorphism is a sin, we should also be wary of the companion: the similarities between ourselves and other animals may too easily be *under*estimated."[15]

The anthropomorphist ascribes and traces human emotion, the manners of civilization, and motivations to animals and nature; these modes of narration are certain to cause misconceptions in science and literature.

"The imaginary continuity between animals' lives and our own reinforces a profound and enduring metonymy, a lifelong shield against alienation," writes Shepard. The insistence on separation "denies the shared underpinnings and destroys a deeper sense of cohesion that sustains our sanity and keeps our world from disintegrating. Anthropomorphism binds our continuity with the rest of the natural world."[16]

John Stodart Kennedy names feelings, motivations, and thought the three sources of mental experiences; sources that are subjective and independent of motion or human action. Granting animals the same introspection as humans, without pretense or intentional tropes, would be "unwarranted anthropomorphism."[17]

Arguably, there are warranted anthropomorphic ascriptions of animals in narratives; literary ascriptions that are metaphorical and create a sense of creature presence, rather than attribution, causal conversions, and simulations of animal consciousness.

William James, in his consideration of consciousness and ironic assumptions of introspection, observes that "everyone assumes that we have direct introspective acquaintance with our thinking activity as such, with our consciousness as something inward and contrasted with the outer objects which it knows. Yet I must confess that for my part I cannot feel sure of this conclusion."[18] Surely, the attribution of altruism and human consciousness to animals would be contested by scientists, and by the espousers of monotheism, creationism, and the separation of animal behavior, human reason, and consciousness.

Kennedy points out in *The New Anthropomorphism* that the "most widely held scientific reason for assuming that there must be some measure of consciousness in animals is the Darwinian principle that evolution has been a continuous process."[19] Novelists and scientists, with their distinctive theories and tropes, create a sense of nature and a mode of evolution in various narratives of our creation and historical presence.

"Altogether, then, it seems likely that consciousness, feelings, thoughts, purposes . . . are unique to our species and unlikely that animals are conscious," observes Kennedy. "If we were entirely logical about it these probabilities would be enough to make us try to avoid anthropomorphic descriptions of animal behavior. But we are not entirely logical about it, and we have to ask why scientists as well as laymen should be so addicted to anthropomorphic expression."[20]

ELEPHANT TEARS

Jeffrey Moussaieff Masson asserts in the introduction to *When Elephants Weep: The Emotional Lives of Animals* that "animals cry. At least they vocalize pain or distress, and in many cases seem to call for help. Most people believe, therefore, that animals can be unhappy and also that they have such primal feelings as happiness, anger, and fear. . . . I try to show that animals of all kinds lead complex emotional lives."[21]

The novelist creates a presence of animals and nature with metaphors and lyrical descriptions that are not bound to the modes of scientific causation or objective representations. "The fundamental difficulty, however, when we wish to avoid anthropomorphism, lies in the nature of our ordinary language," argues Kennedy. "Our everyday language would be crippled without its constant use of metaphors and analogies," and anthropomorphic analogies "readily generate misunderstanding." On the other hand, "wholly objective language is almost impossible to achieve completely and attempts at it are usually clumsy and prolix because they are inevitably strained compared with our everyday speech."[22]

Nature is a narrative creation, and nature is a trope; pristine nature is untamed, unnameable, elusive, and more precarious than trickster stories. At the same time, nature, *natura*, is our creation in a lazy loan word. We trace our presence in animals, a warranted narrative creation. The memories of oral stories are revised by dominance, and deferred as mere cultural evidence in the causal discoveries and translations of the social sciences.

The nature of authored creation is silence, a written narrative of tropes, discoveries, observations, representations, comparisons, and transitive closures. Likewise, the authored animals in literature are wild tropes, fantastic creatures, and others are mundane similes of domestication and cultural dominance. Might be that the most elusive animals are in the mind of the native hunter—likewise, an evanescence in the heart of the author.

The animals created in literature are no more distinct than their animal authors, distinctions, to be sure, and causal simulations of the abstruse other in the similes of descent and evolution. The author, as the animal and unaccustomed hunter, overcomes wild animals in the authored familiarities of literature, the episteme of authored animals.

Roland Barthes observes that no one, without formalities, can "pretend to insert his freedom as a writer into the resistant medium of language because, behind the latter, the whole of History stands unified and complete in the manner of a Natural Order. Hence, for the writer, a language is nothing but a human horizon which provides a distant setting of *familiarity*, the value of which, incidentally, is entirely negative."[23]

Common sense, the outcome of causal reason, representation, speciesism, and theories of evolution are conversions of chance and the notions of pristine nature. The most inscrutable animals are tamed in the authored familiarities of human nature, the inescapable consequences of reason, iconic silence, and the philosophies of grammar; at the same time, certain animals are memorable characters with their own manners, consciousness, and points of view in literature.

Louis Owens, the novelist, created an animal with an enormous head and a thyroid condition, a giveaway dog named Custer. The presenter said, "Indians and dogs go together. . . . It's an ancient, honorable alliance. A good dog warms the lodge during those hard winters and warns when the stealthy enemy approaches. And Custer's a sweet dog; look at that face. He's just a little nervous right now."[24]

Jack London created a clever, heroic, proletarian animal character and consciousness in *The Call of the Wild*. "Buck did not read the newspapers, or he would have known that trouble was brewing, not for himself, but for every other tide-water dog." Buck, with domestic deference, "accepted the rope with quiet dignity. To be sure, it was an unwonted performance: but he had learned to trust in men he knew, and to give them credit for a wisdom that outreached his own." Buck, wise to manners, was a double canine other, a creation of competence and veneration.

London was an evolutionist and an advocate of social justice; moreover, he celebrated selective variations of heroic individualism in his stories and novels. Sometimes his animals and humans were matched to the same temperament and seasons. "It was beautiful spring weather, but neither dogs nor humans were aware of it."[25] Nature, in some of his short stories, is a superior character, and the point of view is much wider than individualism. "Nature was not kindly to the flesh. She had no concern for that concrete thing called the individual. Her interest lay in the species, the race."[26]

Buck is a totemic dog, a heroic metaphor of the wild side of civilization, and not a measure of evolution or monotheism. "Buck is perfectly at one with his self and with nature, experiencing a feeling of wholeness and completion which no civilized experience ever matched in intensity," writes Jacqueline Tavernier-Courbin. "Buck is telling us that we still have in us, below the surface, the same primitive man who existed a few hundred thousand years ago."[27]

Mary Allen observes in *Animals in American Literature* that London created "romantically realistic heroes in his dogs," an inclination that dismissed naturalism. "His dogs not only survive but they triumph. Within the realm of actual behavior, the exceptional dog is capable of deeds that humankind finds noble. Because adaptability is more important than sheer savagery, the triumphant animal is much more than the most powerful predatory beast."[28]

Such heroic and ironic animals are the encore of more than mere realism and evolutionism; rather, these are distinct creations of mutant omniscience, a marvelous punctuated equilibrium in literature. Surely some authors are punctuationalists at heart, but the contradictions of their animal characters are denatured on the "human horizon" of existential reason. Animals that are seen more in iconic silence than heard in nature are poselocked in evolution; the mutant caricatures of anthropomorphism.

Beautiful Joe is the name of a dog, a real dog who was born in a stable, and the title of an "autobiography" of that same dog, first published in 1893. Marshall Saunders created the anthropomorphic narrative based on the experiences of an abused dog who was later rescued by a generous family. Beautiful Joe, the omniscient canine, is pictured with a wise countenance in his autobiography, at ease in a decorated scene near a window. "My name is Beautiful Joe, and I am a brown dog of medium size. I am not called Beautiful Joe because I am a beauty. . . . I am only a cur," he reveals on the first page of his autobiography. "I am very unwilling to say much about my early life. I have lived so long in a family where there is never a harsh word spoken, and where no one thinks of ill-treating anybody or anything, that it seems almost wrong even to think or speak of such a matter as hurting a poor dumb beast."

Beautiful Joe is mannered, and he announces a wise deference to the readers and his human family. The common cur is obsequious and honored to say as much with no moan or protest of victimry. Human slaves, and many natives on reservations, were courageous to say otherwise in the literature of survivance at the time.

"The man that owned my mother was a milkman. He kept one horse and three cows, and he had a shaky old cart that he used to put his milk cans in," writes Beautiful Joe. "I don't think there can be a worse man in the world than that milkman. It makes me shudder now to think of him. . . . The first notice he took of me when I was a little puppy, just able to stagger about, was to give me a kick that sent me into a corner of the stable. He used to beat and starve my mother."

Beautiful Joe was published at a time of extreme cruelty to animals. Moreover, in the case of humans, the heroic adventures, captivity narratives, and other moral stories, were very popular at the turn of the last century. The autobiography ends with a hesitant but customary farewell, the mongrel ever mindful of his mythic creation in a monotheistic civilization. "Now I must really close my story. Good-bye to the boys and girls who may read it; and if it is not wrong for a dog to say it, I should like to add, 'God bless you all.' If in my feeble way I have been able to impress you with the fact that dogs and many other animals love their masters and mistresses, and live only to please them, my little story will not be written in vain."[29] Dog entreats God, and the rite of names is reversed in this ironic canine autobiography.

Even the most mannered forms of reason "are not independent of our animal nature; rather, they depend crucially on that animal nature," argues George Lakoff in *Women, Fire, and Dangerous Things*. "Imagination is not mere fancy, for it is imagination, especially metaphors and metonymy, that transforms the general schemas defined by our animal experience into forms of reason."[30]

ESCAPE DISTANCE

The barrel of my rifle was cold that autumn. Colder now in this remembrance of the death of a common red squirrel. Oak leaves rattled, and the wind hissed in the paper birch. The squirrels hunched in the trees, out of reach, at a natural escape distance, but not out of my sight. Naturally, they sensed my distance, a hunter without the honor earned in a chase. The squirrels were in cold sight; their thighs the amusement of my practiced aim. My weapon, not the bond of my imagination, was the instrument of their death; but not now, not in the silence of these words.

"Men with only hand weapons do not need to invent stern codes to insure that hunting is a challenge rather than an amusement," writes Paul Shepard in *The Tender Carnivore*. "The hunter's confrontation of the enigmas of death and animal life inspire attitudes of honor and awe expressed in ceremonial address."[31]

The sun shimmered, the leaves shivered. I waited, squeezed the trigger of my rifle, and shot a red squirrel. The bullet shattered the bones in his shoulder. He tumbled to the ground near the trunk of an oak tree, bounced once, and then reached out with one paw to climb back into the tree. The other paw was bloodied, loose, turned under, already dead. He reached with his best paw to the tree, to climb out of my sight; again and again he fell back. Blood flowed down his body. He watched me with one eye. His escape distance is eternal in my visual memory. The hunter and the author were the entire cause of his miseries, silence, and slow death.

The Boy Scouts of America and the Izaak Walton League taught me and other hunters of my generation the monomercies of the coup de grâce. We learned as hunters and later as authors never to let a wounded animal suffer. Wounded animals were put out of their miseries; at heart, our miseries of the animal other in literature.

The first mercy bullet tore the fur and flesh from his skull. The sound lasted, more than an echo in the trees. The second bullet smashed his jaw and exposed his teeth, a hideous death mask. I fired twice more to end his miseries; the bullets shattered his forehead and burst through one eye. He held onto the rough trunk of that oak tree with one paw; the blood bubbled slower and slower from his nostrils. I touched his back; my hands were warmed with his blood. At last his death was mine as a hunter that autumn.

The hunter "returns to the natural state, becomes one with the animal, and is freed from the burden of the existential split," writes Erich Fromm in *The Anatomy of Human Destructiveness*. "For modern man, with his cerebral orientation, this experience of oneness with nature is difficult to verbalize and to be aware of, but it is still alive in many human beings. . . . It is amazing how many modern authors neglect this element of skill in hunting, and focus their attention on the act of killing. After all, hunting requires a combination of many skills and wide knowledge beyond that of handling a weapon."[32]

The hunter, then, is a natural presence, and the author a secular creationist; the eternal animal, the contrarious animal other of animism and the ultramundane. The literal and simile versions of the creation of animals are traced and measured in nature, authors, and literature. Otherwise, the animals in literature are simulations, the mere poses of nature in the minds of their creative authors.

"When totemic thought, with its instinct for animal imagery, is carried forward into totemic culture, the wild animal groups are regarded as sets containing necessary secrets for human conduct, translated by myth and applied to actual human situations by speculative thought," observes Paul Shepard in *Thinking Animals*. "When it is carried forward into caste or class thought, on the other hand, the wild animals are likely to be seen as atavisms ruled by mysterious powers or mindless passions, while the domesticated animals represent puerile expressions of our civilized egos."[33]

Mary Allen notes that metaphorical animals "far outnumber the literal animals in literature," and authored animals are bestial, carnal, utilitarian, pastoral, exotic, stoical, heroic, and more, but "man's creations did not outdo the uncanny subjects in nature."

God, for instance, "created his whale easily in a day," observes Allen. Herman Melville "shows us the wrenching difficulty of the task." Gradually, the literary whaler "builds his literal whale alongside the myths of whales, later showing the view from the outside working back in. . . . Not only does he inspire a wealth of metaphysical possibilities, but as a literal animal the sperm whale is so composed as to make an extraordinary but distinctly American character."[34]

Natives and *indians* are commonly perceived as being in close association with nature and the natural, totemic presence of animals. Such nostalgic attributions, the essence of creationism over evolution, are considered as sources of native omniscience and consciousness. The native author, in this sense, would be an insinuation of a creature presence, an interpretation that presumes the notions of nativism, animism, and naturalism, over theories of evolution and modernism.

Commonsense is seldom common, as the sense of native reason has been overcome by simulations of the *indian*, notions of *mother earth*, and the attributions of natural environmentalism. Russell Means, for instance, asserts that he strongly believes "in the power of mothers" and that if "humanity keeps abusing Mother Earth, she will retaliate, and her abusers will be eliminated."[35] Native authors must be ironic and their creations a resistance in the literature of survivance; otherwise, native authors are the consumers of *indian* simulations.

N. Scott Momaday creates a sacred landscape of bears and eagles in the myths, metaphors, and traces of native ceremonies. He imagines an environment situated in memories that is twice the real, in the same sense that the references of native stories are both real and created in the sovereignty of transmotion; authored animals and seasons are the literature of survivance.

"The names at first are those of animals and of birds, of objects that have one definition in the eye, another in the hand, of forms and features on the rim of the world, or of sounds that carry on the bright wind and in the void," writes N. Scott Momaday in his memoir *The Names*. "They are old and original in the mind, like the beat of rain on the river, and intrinsic in the native tongue, failing even as those who bear them turn once in the memory, go on, and are gone forever."[36]

Joseph and Barrie Klaits observe in the introduction to *Animals and Man in Historical Perspective* that people "love and pity animals; we also use, abuse, and fear them. Animals are our companions, our amusements, and our sustenance. We pursue animals to satisfy our tastes in food and fashion or to enjoy the raw pleasure of destruction. The pursuit can also be creative, as when we seek their images through art and literature."[37]

Animals are created in nature, narratives, and economies; animals are translated, compared, and interpreted in literature and culture. The animals of literature are twice their nature: the real in visions and environments, and the authored animals of a narrative creation. The authored animals are as diverse as the real, the species of creation and evolution; animals wild, transmuted, captured, domestic, and fantastic, are healers and eternal favorites.

Language, then, is one of the real environments of the authored animals—the names, memories, manners, metaphors, and the totemic presence of animals in narratives. The totemic traces of nature are redoubled in metaphors and the creation of animal characters. Once teased by the author, the reader must conceive of a marvelous arcane animal and the wild unities of creation.

Still, authored animals are burdened by an ironic environment and by the literary styles of the authors, the very reason of their creation. The animals of stories must survive the turns of tropes, the practices of simile, metaphor, and metonymy, as necessities and contingencies of an authored nature and presence. The metaphorical bears, wolves, mongrels, totemic cranes, and other creatures, are traces of native transmotion and survivance. However, the simile animals, the mere comparison with human emotion and countenance, are caricatures in literature.

"In the language of prose, besides the regular and proper terms for things, metaphorical terms only can be used with advantage," observed Aristotle in *Rhetoric*. "Metaphor, moreover, gives style clearness, charm, and distinction as nothing else can: and it is not a thing whose use can be taught by one man to another. Metaphors, like epithets, must be fitting, which means that they must fairly correspond to the thing signified: failing this, their inappropriateness will be conspicuous; the want of harmony between two things is emphasized by their being placed side by side."[38] The difference between metaphor and simile, he noted, "is but slight." That slight of metaphor, however, mirrors a scanty comparison of simulations and presence.

Thomas McLaughlin, in his essay "Figurative Language," points out more than a "slight" divergence in the measure of tropes.

A simile is a comparison of terms. Unlike metaphor which requires the reader to do the work of constructing a logic of categories and analogies, a simile states explicitly that two terms are comparable and often presents the bases for the comparison. . . .

Metonymy accomplishes its transfer of meaning on the basis of associations that develop out of specific contexts rather than from participation in a structure of meaning." Moreover, metonymy "places us in the historical world of events and situations, whereas metaphor asserts connections on the basis of a deep logic that underlies any use of words.[39]

John Searle argues in "Metaphor" that the "relation between the sentence meaning and the metaphorical utterance meaning is systematic rather than random," and that "sentences and words have only the meaning that they have. Strictly speaking, whenever we talk about the metaphorical meaning of a word, expression, or sentence, we are talking about what a speaker might utter it to mean, in a way that departs from what the word, expression, or sentence actually means."

The "knowledge that enables people to use and understand metaphorical utterances goes beyond their knowledge of the literal meaning of words and sentences." Searle writes that a "literal simile" is a "literal statement of similarity" and that "literal simile requires no special extralinguistic knowledge for its comprehension, most of the knowledge necessary for the comprehension of metaphor is already contained in the speaker's and hearer's semantic competence, together with the general background knowledge of the world that makes literal meaning comprehensible."[40]

Native metaphors, then, may not be easily understood outside the "background knowledge" of the native, visionary world. Clearly, the metaphors of native creation, totems, natural reason, transmotion, the tease of names, and the mighty stories of animals, have been translated, more often than not, by social scientists, as evidence or romantic revisions, and with minimal comprehension of native intentions and meaning. Some native authors write into the general knowledge of the social sciences, and serve their readers the very similatives of dominance rather than ironic narratives of *indian* simulations or the tropes of transmotion and survivance.

Philip Wheelwright declares that metaphor is an "element of tensive language."[41] Donald Davidson explains "metaphor as a kind of ambiguity: in the context of metaphor, certain words have either a new or an original meaning, and the force of the metaphor depends on our uncertainty as we waver between the two meanings."[42] Robert Rogers, in a psychoanalytic exploration of figurative language, notes that one "puzzling aspect of the expressive capaciousness of metaphor takes the form of an image's potential for focusing both thought and emotion in a particularly intense, economical way."[43]

Janet Martin Soskice, in *Metaphor and Religious Language*, defines metaphor as that "figure of speech whereby we speak about one thing in terms which are seen to be suggestive of another." She notes that the "greatest rival of metaphor, simile, in its most powerful instances does compel possibilities. Simile is usually regarded as the trope of comparison and identifiable within speech by the presence of a 'like,' or an 'as,' or the occasional 'not unlike.'"

Still, "to regard simile as necessarily mere 'same-saying' of the trivial sort is greatly to misrepresent that trope. Simile may be the means of making comparisons of two kinds, the comparison of similars and dissimilars, and in the latter case, simile shares much of the imaginative life and cognitive function of its metaphorical counterparts. For this reason, we can say that metaphor and simile share the same function and differ primarily in their grammatical form."[44]

Soskice would, it seems, summon the more classical view that the difference between metaphor and simile "is but slight." However, the author notes, a simile cannot "be used in catachresis." Simile cannot create the lexicon, as does "dead end" or the "leaf of a book."

George Lakoff and Mark Johnson provide one of the most accessible descriptions of metaphor in *Metaphors We Live By*.

Metaphor is for most people a device of the poetic imagination and the rhetorical flourish—a matter of extraordinary rather than ordinary language.

Moreover, metaphor is typically viewed as characteristic of language alone, a matter of words rather than thought or action. For this reason, most people think they can get along perfectly well without metaphor. We have found, on the contrary, that metaphor is pervasive in everyday life, not just in language but in thought and action. Our ordinary conceptual system, in terms of which we both think and act, is fundamentally metaphorical in nature.[45]

Authored animals are the tropes of human severance, an environment of iconic silence. Metaphor and simile are the traces of creations, memories, and narrative conversions, the nature and presence of animals in the literature of survivance. Tropes are the associations of naturalism, and the traces of animal consciousness. Likewise, there are many epistemic tropes, literary styles, and critical interpretations of authored animals in literature. The native animals created in the literature of survivance are the figures of transmotion, not dominance.

The literal similes of brute consciousness and bestiality are similar to speciesism and comparable to manifest manners and the monotheistic separation of animals and humans. Native stories must create a natural union of authored animals on a tricky landscape of human and animal survivance—the survivance of humans in the literature of animals.

N. Scott Momaday, Leslie Silko, Louise Erdrich, Louis Owens, and Gordon Henry Jr. are native novelists with diverse cultural experiences and distinctive literary styles. The authored animals in their novels are mythic and mundane, creatures of native survivance. Surely, the tropes and metaphors of animal creations are as diverse as the authors.

Grey, the main character in *The Ancient Child* by Momaday, is a metaphor of native identities. "Her father was Kiowa and her mother Navajo, and the two cultures came together in her easily, more or less." Grey imagined the death of Billy the Kid, and she "dreamed of sleeping with a bear. The bear drew her into his massive arms and licked her body and her hair. It hunched over her, curving its spine like a cat, until its huge body seemed to have absorbed her own. Its breath which bore a deep, guttural rhythm like language, touched her skin with low, persistent heat."[46]

The authored bear is a totem, an oneiric creation, and a mythic character in the novel. The motion of the bear is a presence and transcendence at the same time. The heat of the authored animal is natural, human, and mythic. Foremost, the bear is the mighty healer of human separation in a narrative. That monotheistic severance of men over women, humans over animals, civilization over savagism, is never closure; bears endure in nature, and in the stories of humans, as bears must as authors.

"Living beyond civilized life, sexually and boldly aggressive, the bear gives vent to a massive and uncontrolled appetite, upsetting rule and restriction," write Paul Shepard and Barry Sanders in *The Sacred Paw*. "But in its display of maternal care and concern, the bear is the very essence of civility and order. Standing for both male and female characteristics, the bear would appear to have no gender."[47]

Set, an artist in *The Ancient Child*, was an orphan separated from a sense of a native presence. He raised a medicine bundle and returned in stories to the spiritual power of his ancestors. The return is eternal, a shared occurrence in the sovenance of bears; a metaphor of transmotion, survivance, and native sovereignty.

"Set took the medicine bundle in his hands and opened it. The smell of it permeated the whole interior. When he drew on the great paw, there grew up in him a terrible restlessness, wholly urgent, and his heart began to race. He felt the power of the bear pervade his being, and the awful compulsion to release it. Grey, sitting away in the invisible dark, heard the grandmother's voice in her mouth. When Set raised the paw, as if to bring it down like a club, she saw it against the window, huge and phallic on the stars, each great yellow claw like the horn of the moon."[48] The metaphor of the bear and the medicine bundle are obscure and unnameable powers, but the simile of the "horn of the moon" is direct and abates the uncertainties and shadows of the totemic medicine.

Momaday told Charles Woodard in *Ancestral Voices* that he was "serious about the bear" and "identified with the bear" because he is "intimately connected with that story. And so I have this bear power. I turn into a bear every so often. I feel myself becoming a bear, and that's a struggle I have to face now and then."[49] Momaday became a bear in his own stories.

Momaday turns the metaphors of authored animals into an unrevealed presence, the tensive myths of creation and native solace in *House Made of Dawn*. The mere mention of the bear is traced in sound, motion, and the memories of the characters.

Abel was paid three dollars to cut wood. Angela "watched, full of wonder, taking his motion apart." The sound of the ax was incessant. "Once she had seen an animal slap at the water, a badger or a bear. She would have liked to touch the soft muzzle of a bear, the thin black lips, the great flat head. She would have liked to cup her hand to the wet black snout, to hold for a moment the hot blowing of the bear's life. She went out of the house and sat down on the stone steps of the porch. He was there, rearing above the wood." Later, they came together, the tease of creation in the bear heat of the narrative. "He was dark and massive above her, poised and tinged with pale blue light. And in that split second she thought again of the badger at the water, and the great bear, blue-black and blowing."[50]

Susan Scarberry-Garcia observes, in her study of *House Made of Dawn*, that this "sensual image which depicts Abel's bear-like physique and presence has been dismissed in the criticism as a forlorn white woman's fantasy about having a dark elemental man as her ideal lover."[51]

Momaday told Charles Woodard that many "things happen in *House Made of Dawn* that I can't explain in a logical way. They are based upon insights which I think are valid, but those insights are not fully conscious. That is, they weren't consciously developed. They exist beneath the level of everyday consciousness, but they are nonetheless real."[52]

Metaphors are intentions and motivations, and the metaphors of the bear are an ancient presence in the novel; the motivations of natural reason, the inscriptions of native realism, transmotion, and native survivance. "The elements constituting a work obey an internal logic, not an external one," observe Oswald Ducrot and Tzvetan Todorov in the *Encyclopedic Dictionary of the Sciences of Language.* "Motivation is thus a variant of realism. It is not conformity to the genre, but a cloak that the text casts prudently over the rules of the genre."[53]

Leslie Silko encircles the reader with mythic witches, an ironic metaphor of motivation in the creation stories of *Ceremony.* Alas, the hardhearted witches invented white people in a competition, a distinctive metaphor that overcame the similative temptations of a mere comparison of natives with the extremes of dominance.

"The old man shook his head. 'That is the trickery of the witchcraft,' he said. 'They want us to believe all evil resides with white people. Then we will look no further to see what is really happening. They want us to separate ourselves from white people, to be ignorant and helpless as we watch our own destruction. But white people are only tools that the witchery manipulates; and I tell you, we can deal with white people, with their machines and their beliefs. We can because we invented white people; it was Indian witchery that made white people in the first place."

> *Long time ago*
> *in the beginning*
> *there were no white people in this world*
> *there was nothing European*
> *And this world might have gone on like that*
> *except for one thing:*
> *witchery.*
> *This world was already complete*
> *even without white people.*

*There was everything
including witchery.*[54]

Louis Owens points out that "Betonie's words and the story of witchery underscore an element central to Native American oral tradition and worldview: responsibility." This sense of responsibility, of course, is a metaphor that denies closure; the actions, connections, and intentions, are not causal, but obscure ceremonies. "To shirk that responsibility and blame whites, or any external phenomenon, is to buy into the role of helpless victim."[55]

The authored animals are connected to the environment, not to the similes of human consciousness. Silko creates animals with a natural character; the metaphors are their motivation and presence. Simile is used in the novel to describe motion and to compare animals to the environment, not to assay human characteristics. For instance, the "mountain lion came out from a grove of oak trees in the middle of the clearing. He did not walk or leap or run; his motions were like the shimmering of tall grass in the wind. . . . Relentless motion was the lion's greatest beauty, moving like mountain clouds with the wind, changing substance and color in rhythm with the contours of the mountain peaks: dark as lava rock, and suddenly as bright as a field of snow."[56]

VISIONARY MONGRELS

Momaday, Silko, and Owens are authors of memorable animals; the metaphors of their creations are characters, some with names and consciousness. The motivations are natural reason, and a native sense of presence.

These authors use simile as motion, comparisons, to be sure, but not as mere attributions of animal and human characteristics. The simile is more than the signature of "like" and "as" or "mere 'same-saying' " as noted by Janet Martin Soskice. However, the style of simile is a common comparative mode in narratives; the most limited or direct is the "literal simile" described by John Searle.

Louise Erdrich uses a style of tropes in her novel *Tracks* that is closer to the literal or prosaic simile than to the obscure metaphors of motivation and animal presence; the other authors mentioned here seldom used the literal style of simile. For instance, "she shivered all over like a dog," and he's "hiding from you like a dog," and "I'd go off in the bush like a sick dog first, alone," and his "head shaggy and low as a bison bull," and she "leaned over the water, sucking it like a heifer," and the "bear followed, heeling her like a puppy," and the "man was bearded, huge, clumsy-looking like a weak-sighted bear," and more.[57]

Erdrich names moose, pigs, bears, cats, and other animals, but the most common authored animal in *Tracks* is the dog. The animals in her novel are more often than not generic creations, and few dogs or other animals are characters in a natural environment. The generic animal is a generic and literal simile.

"I think like animals, have perfect understanding for where they hide," said Nanapush. The generic animal is structural, a binary beast in a prosaic simile. "Moses, who had defeated the sickness by turning half animal and living in a den," is an authored human as the beast. "He said the animals understood what was happening, how they were dwindling," is an instance in the novel of generic animal consciousness.[58]

Tracks has more dogs on the page than other animals. One unnamed authored animal has character and is more memorable than the other generic dogs in the novel. "Lily had a dog, a stumpy mean little bull of a thing with a belly drum-tight from eating pork rinds. The dog was as fond of the cards as Lily, and straddled his barrel thighs through games of stud, rum poker, *vingt-un*. The dog snapped at Fleur's arm that first night, but cringed back, its snarl frozen, when she took her place."[59]

Custer, the authored animal in *Bone Game* by Louis Owens, is a memorable character in the tensive metaphor of his name. The names of some animals are ironic, and other authored animals have a sense of presence and character without a name. In another scene a character in the novel recommends a guard dog: "I mean it. You should get a dog. . . . A big, mean one. And remember, dogs don't like ghosts or witches. We keep them around the hogans at home just for that."[60]

Owens, in *The Sharpest Sight*, creates a tricky bond between a rabbit and hunter. "Cherokee rabbits were smart. They lived by tricks in a world of words and had a good time doing it." Cole "raised the rifle and aimed the notched sight at a spot just below the rabbit's ear. 'Time for a trick,' he whispered to the rabbit. He pulled back the hammer and shouted."

Then, at "the shout, the cottontail leaped and spun and disappeared into the brush."[61] Good dogs have been ruined by rabbits, and the presence and motivation of the literary rabbit is not lost in a prosaic simile.

Gordon Henry Jr. created a wild and comic scene of two dogs stuck together in a natural, sexual, totemic dance, a white dog, a brown dog, and in the end, one dead dog, in his novel *The Light People.*

Boozhoo tried to separate the dogs, and then he turned to his own magic, "my sideline vocation, my years of training. First I tried mental magic: I attempted to project the image of a piece of meat into the mind of the dancing white dog. For a minute I thought it worked, since I heard the white dog give off a low growl and I thought I saw his mouth water. But the dogs remained stuck together."

LaVerve was drunk; he arrived with his rifle and shot the white dog. "But the only thing that changed was the dog dance; the white dog whimpered as he remained fast to the brown female, following behind her in a more frantic dance that still failed to separate them." LaVerve tried again to pull the dogs apart and bloodied his hands before he took another drink and drove away drunk in his pickup.

Boozhoo carried the dogs "back to Seed's place. . . . Seed studied the dogs. He spoke without looking up at me. 'We've got to get this dead one off before he stiffens up.' Seed slid out of his chair then and leaned over the dead white dog. He whispered into the dog's ear. I didn't hear the words or the language, but when he settled back into his chair he told me to take the white dog out and bury it. I did as he told me, and I expected the white dog to remain fast to the brown, but when I lifted the dead dog the two dogs separated and the brown dog ran off into the darkness."[62]

The presence of authored animals in these selected novels are real as tropes of creation in the literature of survivance. The creatures in native literature are seldom mere representations of animals in nature or culture, wild, domestic, generic, or otherwise; however, there is an unnameable presence, the traces of a familiar nature, comic motivation, native reason, and the introspection of authors.

Owens, Momaday, Silko, Erdrich, and Henry use metaphor as motivation, the pleasurable conversions of an unnameable creation into animal characters, and some with omniscience, consciousness, and names. Momaday creates a mythic landscape, a transcendence of bears as humans, and the heat of mortality. Erdrich uses literal and prosaic similes in her novel more than the other authors. Owens and Henry create a comic and ironic presence of native mongrels.

Monotheistic creation is a separation of animals and humans in nature and literature; the common unions since then have been both domestic and aesthetic. Literal simile is a familiar disseverance of authored animals on a human horizon. The more obscure tropes in literature must be closer to nature and animal consciousness than a literal simile. The authors are animals, the readers are animals, the animals are humans, and the authored hunters are the animals in their own novels.

Georges Bataille envisions a "tableau of eroticism," at once the "pure negation" of animals created at a human border. The animal in a word is a tensive union, but that unnameable sense of presence is no obvious evolution of eroticism, no natural desire in literature. The treeline is a metaphor, and bears rush the word there, a human in each hand; cranes are the storiers, our ancestors; tricksters wear out the seasons; and *animosh* runs a car wash on the reservation. There, at the treeline is a "tableau of eroticism" in the motion of names and pronouns. The author hies the animals in season, and the narrator becomes the animal in a pronoun, however slight the name. The animal of *me* is elusive, and so *our* presence in a narrative. Who is the pronoun of the bear, crane, and others in totemic creation? We trace the *me*, and *you*, in the metaphors of bears, cranes, wolves, the avian turn and totemic sleeve at the treelines.

"The animal might in a sense but cannot actually say 'I am.' The same is true, moreover, of the sleeping man: the animal is perhaps a man asleep, man an animal that rouses itself from the sleep of nature," muses Bataille in *The Accursed Share*. "More often than not, we don't know what to make of an animality to which, for very deep reasons, the earliest men attributed a divine life. But we easily treat animals as things. From the beginning they were at once things and beings similar to us, at times even undefinable aspects of the divine."[63]

Meanwhile, those dogs who move behind the wheel as drivers when their masters park the car are very close to the real tropes of consciousness; those dogs waiting behind the wheel are certain to be seen as human. The dogs are either ready to be seen as humans or to drive automobiles into our consciousness and prove that punctuated equilibrium, or punctuationalism, is not hindered by prosaic similes, domestic loyalties, or learned critiques of anthropomorphism.

The animals in native narratives must tease creation and mediate the memories of that divine shimmer at the treeline. The simulations of our separation are scriptual; causal and comparative abstractions that are otherwise undone by nature. Even the wise narratives on evolution are more chance than closure.

CHAPTER FOUR

Fugitive Poses

PICTURE ARCHIVES

G eorge Steiner, the literary essayist, observes that it "is not the literal past that rules us, save, possibly, in a biological sense. It is images of the past. These are often as highly structured and selective as myths. Images and symbolic constructs of the past are imprinted, almost in the manner of genetic information, on our sensibility. Each new historical era mirrors itself in the picture and active mythology of its past or of a past borrowed from other cultures."[1]

The *indian* is an imprinted picture, the pose of a continental fugitive. The simulation of the other is the absence of the native; the *indian* is an imprimatur of a theistic civilization. Native resistance was abstracted as a fugitive pose in national histories; at the same time, the *indian* was a cultural concoction of bourgeois nostalgia and social sciences evidence. Cultural pageantry, dioramas, and museum presentations pictured the fugitive *indian* in the archives of dominance.

The *indian* is an ascribed name, and the noun is not native; the ascriptive simulations are the creases of inconceivable discoveries, ethnographic surveillance, and fugitive poses in the pageantry and portraiture of dominance. Clearly, the stories of these circumstantial simulations, in the cause of savagism and civilization, score the unbidden interimages of the *indian* as a native.

W. J. T. Mitchell mentions a "pictorial turn" in the academic discourse on pictures, an anxiety over "visual representation" and modernity. "What makes for the sense of a pictorial turn, then, is not that we have some powerful account of visual representation that is dictating the terms of cultural theory, but that pictures form a point of peculiar friction and discomfort across a broad range of intellectual inquiry." He cites the connections of "spectacle" by Guy Debord and "surveillance" by Michel Foucault, and argues that "we still do not know exactly what pictures are, what their relation to language is, how they operate on observers and on the world, how their history is to be understood, and what is to be done with or about them."[2]

Foremost, native creation stories, trickster transmotion, and totemic survivance are that "pictorial turn." Later, the interimage conversions of the *indian* are the postmodern "simulacra turn" of entertainment and commodity.

Roland Barthes argues that "all images are polysemous." The interimage of the *indian* is the absence of the unnameable native. The *indian* is not a connection to the real, a sense of presence, or crease of natural reason. Underlying the semiotic signifiers of the image, or the actual perception, are "a 'floating chain' of signifieds," or the concepts, and the reader is "able to choose some and ignore others. Polysemy poses a question of meaning and this question always comes through as a dysfunction, even if this dysfunction is recuperated by society as a tragic" or poetic game.[3] The interimage is polysemous, a dysfunction of meaning; the *indian* is a polyseme of tragic victimry.

The *indian* is poselocked in portraiture, intaglio, photogravure, captivity narratives, and other interimage simulation of dominance; the poselocked fugitives of ethnocentric discoveries, not the traces of heard stories, or the tease of natural reason, transmotion, and native survivance.

The generative interimages of "discovered" natives are cutout simulations, without a substantive connection or reference; *one simulation is the specious evidence of another.* Simulations, in this sense, are not mimicry, imitations, or reduplications, not even ironic extremes or parodies, but rather, "substituting signs of the real for the real itself," as Jean Baudrillard observes in *Simulations*. That *indian* simulations are named the real is derisory. The authentic *indians* are oxymora, and the absence of natives. "For ethnology to live, its object must die."[4]

The interimage portraiture, photographic and iconic enactments of the other, are seen with no sense of a native presence or referent; interimage simulations are monocausal and, in certain instances of translation, ethnographic evidence of culture. However, the rhetoric of surveillance transposes a native presence, as one circumstantial simulation subserves another in the course of interimage spectacles and dominance.

The dominance of interimage simulations could be overturned by the pleasures of tricky virtual images rather than by cultural piety, pretensions, or substantive evidence. For instance, the technologies of virtual reality create, by choice and interaction, situations that are their own essence. Those fugitive poses of *indians* could be roused once more from the very ruins of interimage simulations, even rescued as ethnographic evidence; a computer generation, evermore in the interactive world of electronic contrivance and virtual realities. Such motion, the virtual transmotion, creates a native presence out of the burdens of representations.

The recent digital manipulations of photographic images, however, are comparable to the interimage simulations of *indians* as engraved images based on earlier drawings. Computer "software can generate completely synthetic photorealistic pictures," writes William Mitchell in "When Is Seeing Believing?". He points out that synthetic pictures, unlike "drawings and paintings, which we regard as inherently trustworthy products of human intention . . . can easily trick us into false beliefs."[5]

The title character in *Forrest Gump*, for instance, is seen in the cinematic presence of three presidents at the White House. John Kennedy is heard in a conversation on screen with the artless hero. This, however, is interactive entertainment, not an interimage simulation named to represent the real. Industrial Light and Magic created the scenes by the digital manipulations of archival newsreel footage.[6]

Photographs are poselocked in silence, to be sure, but not "totally passive." Elizabeth Edwards points out in the introduction to *Anthropology and Photography* that photographs "suggest meaning through the way in which they are structured, for representational form makes an image accessible and comprehensible to the mind, informing and informed by a whole hidden corpus of knowledge that is called on through the signifiers in the image."[7] The fugitive poses of the native, and latent interimage simulations, serve the no-nos of reductive evidence and the "hidden corpus" of dominance.

"Jean Baudrillard has suggested that simulation is the ultimate telos of the postmodern esthetic," writes Eric Gans in *Originary Thinking*. Gans touches on the notion that the production of simulations is an esthetic representation of scarce realities. "Here 'form' has ideally no concrete expression at all; the perfect simulation is indistinguishable from the original. Presumably we know it to be a simulation only because we have paid to experience it. . . . The esthetic of the age of simulation would seek to create a utopia of plenty not merely in material but in interactive terms, as though human beings were finally able to forget the deferred violence of the originary event."[8]

Baudrillard observes that "representation tries to absorb simulation by interpreting it as false representation" and that "simulation envelops the whole edifice of representation as itself a simulacrum." He outlines four "successive phases of the image." The first is the "reflection of a basic reality," the second "masks and perverts a basic reality," the third, "masks the absence of a basic reality." The last phase "bears no relation to any reality," the image is "its own pure simulacrum." Baudrillard notes that in the "first case, the image is a *good* appearance: the representation is of the order of sacrament. In the second, it is an *evil* appearance: of the order of malefic." The third "*plays at being* an appearance: it is of the order of sorcery. In the fourth, it is no longer in the order of appearances at all, but of simulation."[9] The interimage *indian* "masks the absence" of the real, the unnameable native, and in many narratives and motion pictures the *indian* "bears no relation to any reality." The *indian* named in treaties was a perversion of native transmotion; the federal agents were an "evil appearance." Commonly, notice of the *indian* is "pure simulacrum," the shelf life of a commodity.

"Culture is now dominated by simulations, Baudrillard contends, objects and discourses that have no firm origin, no referent, no ground or foundation," notes Mark Poster. "In a commodity the relation of word, image or meaning and referent is broken and restructured so that its force is directed, not to the referent of use value or utility, but to desire."[10]

Ethnographic interimages are the narrative closures of the seen over the heard, the simulation of icons over chance, emblems over totemic names, manners over the native tease, and the desire of the scriptural over the performance of oral narratives.

"Writing puts a distance between man and his verbal acts," writes Jack Goody in *The Domestication of the Savage Mind.* Writing, "and more especially alphabetic literacy, made it possible to scrutinize discourse in a different way by giving oral communication a semi-permanent form; this scrutiny favoured the increase in scope of critical activity, and hence of rationality, scepticism, and logic to resurrect memories of those questionable dichotomies."[11]

Théodor de Bry, Russell Means, and Joan Halifax, to name three contrivers of *indians*, contributed their nonce overtures and curious turns to interimage simulations; the common contrivance of a native absence. The artist and engraver, the radical actor, and the humane author have in common the generation of interimage simulations and narrative polysemy.

Théodor de Bry never encountered more than a gruesome simulation of the natives he depicted in his engravings. Published in the late sixteenth century, his engraved pictures have been used as ethnographic portraiture. He heightened previous simulations and created an interimage savagism for an international audience. "Europeans had always known that cannibals and other monstrous races inhabited the fringes of the known and ipso facto civilized world," writes Anthony Grafton in *New Worlds, Ancient Texts*. "European publishers, illustrators, writers of firsthand accounts, and compilers of compendiums made cannibalistic images virtually emblematic of America."[12]

Théodor de Bry created new engravings for the republication of the *True History of His Captivity* by Hans Staden, which first appeared in Germany in 1557. "The account contains much ethnographic detail, including a complete and horrifying account of the cannibalistic acts he witnessed." De Bry's "much more elaborate versions" and "masterly reworking" of the original crude woodblock prints in his 1592 edition of *America* "heightens the horrors of scenes in which Staden himself appears, often in an attitude of prayer."[13]

De Bry collected ethnographic pictures by many artists and adventurers. "Very often he or his other engravers were better artists than those who produced his models," notes William Sturtevant in *First Images of America*. "The results give a homogenized impression: the figures are all 'neoclassical,' the compositions artificial and European. But more careful examination shows that in his own way he was faithful to his sources, for the transfer of clothing, houses, and other artifacts from one culture to another occurs infrequently."

Hans Staden reported that he was captured by natives and held for "about ten months" in a coastal area of Brazil. Three years later he published "an account of his adventures." The woodcuts picture *indian* artifacts, writes Sturtevant. "Small and crudely done, they are nevertheless extremely important ethnohistorical evidence, for they vividly depict varied activities and were clearly drawn by Staden or under his direct supervision. Perhaps because of the focus on cannibalism (and the ritual surrounding it), these woodcuts became the basis for more skillfully elaborated versions, especially by de Bry."[14]

De Bry's other engraved interimage simulations of *indians* were based on the watercolors by John White who, in turn, used "images of Virginia Indians as the models for his depiction of the ancient Picts and Britons." De Bry depicted a "female warrior of the ancient Picts" in *America*. Grafton points out that, in the introduction to this first volume, Théodor de Bry "writes that he was directed to append these illustrations based on a 'certain old English history' to those of the Virginians 'to demonstrate that the inhabitants of Britain had been no less forest dwellers than these Virginians.' "[15]

Grafton writes that the "tendency of Europeans to equate the alleged barbarism of the American populations they encountered with the cultural life of their own ancestors would eventually lead some people to believe that human societies, rather than inevitably deteriorating, progressed through increasingly sophisticated stages of civilization."[16]

The narratives of discoveries included, in most instances, the drawings of natives, new territories, and other documents. Later, at the end of the voyages, some of the drawings were reproduced as engravings in various publications. These engraved pictures are the source of interimage simulations.

Paul Hulton, in his essay "Images of the New World: Jacques Le Moyne de Morgues and John White," observes that "it is doubtful whether professional artists were ever employed on these voyages. Graphic records might have been made by the captain of the ship or by the pilot, if the ship carried one, who would have a rudimentary knowledge of draughtsmanship, enough to enable him to draw his landmarks, harbours, or coastal profiles." The value of "pictorial evidence" was recognized by the late sixteenth century, and artists were employed on "voyages of exploration." Jacques Le Moyne "sailed with Laudonnière to Florida in 1564." John White was with Walter Raleigh in Virginia, and he worked with the surveyor Thomas Harriot.[17]

The New World was represented first in drawings and then in engravings. The extant "graphic records" of the earliest explorations and colonial possessions are mostly Spanish and Portuguese. "The earliest French discoveries in North America are very sparsely illustrated, with almost no element of scientific realism."[18] These drawings were the first images and representations of natives. Once the marvelous savages, the *indians* were pictured for the first time with some sense of artifact accuracy; however, the countenance of the native women, in particular, was more occidental than native. Later, the engraved figures, based on the original drawings, became the first interimage simulations. Since then, many new interimages of the *indian* are based on that first simulation.

"Jacques Le Moyne and John White were familiar with the growing volume of graphic material emerging from the new discoveries. What so distinguishes their contributions from those of their predecessors is the extensiveness of their records and the new and vivid way they were published by Théodor de Bry in large-scale, expertly (and accurately) engraved illustrations with explanatory notes," writes Hulton. "The image had at last become as important as the text and more memorable."[19] The interimage of the *indian* became more important because the simulations took the place of natives.

De Bry made some changes in the *indian* figures he engraved, compared to the drawings by White. These changes are "precisely known because of the existing originals. The engraver keeps closely to his models, though the features are often Europeanized and the poses somewhat modified to accord more with the fashion of European Mannerism; the hair length is not altered and for the women made only slightly more wavy. Thus the changes may be said to be minor, perhaps the minimum thought necessary to make these exotic beings acceptable to De Bry's European readership."[20] Hulton observed the want of the "exotic" other, the interimage simulation of the *indian* as a commodity.

These exotic interimage simulations were secured in museums, in academic service, and as historical evidence. The *indian* sustains the other, the creases of savagism and civilization; at the same time, the ravenous natives were erased, and crown simulations of the rustic, reservation *indian* were used in national pageants and continental promotions. "Booster images are ubiquitous in western art, so much so that they occur at every stage of the frontier process and often reflect promotional expectations far more accurately than they record historical landscapes," observes William Cronon in *Discovered Lands, Invented Pasts.* John White's watercolors, a turn to "a vision of abundance," were "first encounter" promotions. "White's images, after being turned into woodcuts by Théodor de Bry and printed with a glowing text by Thomas Harriot, became the models for an endless parade of booster tracts for centuries to come, in which well-watered woodlands, fertile soils, tame wildlife, and peaceable natives all beckoned to the would-be settler and investor."[21] Obviously, *indians* were captured in fugitive poses by brush and camera, and then cast as boosters, the poster *indians* of the landscape. The simulation of the *indian* is the absence of the native, and the *indian* in booster art is the absence of native memories and the actual landscape.

EXOTIC EXCLAVES

At the same time that colonial nations dominated much of the world and many native communities were removed to federal exclaves, the new technologies of photography captured the fugitive other in the structural representations of savagism and civilization. The "pictorial turn" of cultural surveillance, the desires of objectivism in the new social sciences, became the manifest manners of the time. "In encountering countries that were being transformed through the impact of social change, the photographer paradoxically chose to focus on unchanging representations of peoples and cultures," writes Iskander Mydin in "Historical Images—Changing Audiences." "For it was the 'exotic', the culturally different, which fascinated, in both scientific and popular terms." Christopher Pinney points out in "The Parallel Histories of Anthropology and Photography" that "photography appears as the final culmination of a Western quest for visibility and scrutiny. It stands at the technological, semiotic and perceptual apex of 'vision', which itself serves as the emulative metaphor for all other ways of knowing."[22]

Russell Means posed in photographs with the new interimage warriors of the American Indian Movement during the occupation of Wounded Knee in South Dakota. A decade later, he moved into movies and a laudable postindian interimage simulation by a celebrated artist—namely, a studio production of a silk screen portrait by Andy Warhol. The fugitive poses of the postindian, the poses that come after the discoveries and interimages of the *indian* and the portraiture of dominance, are, paradoxically, the simulations of survivance that undermine ethnographic evidence and manifest manners.[23]

"How about the *American Indian* series?" asked Patrick Smith in *Warhol: Conversations about the Artist.* "Was that any particular Indian?"

"Yeah. That was Russell Means," said Ronnie Cultrone who was, at the time, a studio production assistant to Andy Warhol. "He was involved with the Wounded Knee Massacre, which I don't really know too much about, to tell you the truth. But I think he's still in court. I don't know. Something like that."[24]

Andy Warhol pictured the narrative closures of the obvious and the most noticeable simulation of an *indian*. Indeed, the studio production of Russell Means is an artistic, kitschy ethnographic, interimage simulation in several obscure dimensions: the absence of the other at a massacre, the pasticcio warrior, and the postindian poses of the American Indian Movement.

Means has demonstrated notable ambitions as a speechmaker and radical politician. He was a candidate for the presidency of the Oglala Sioux Tribal Council in South Dakota and later he aspired, with Larry Flynt, the hustler publisher of *Hustler,* to become the presidential executives of the United States. Means lost both elections, but his desires to bear uncommon simulations were heartened as Chingachgook in the film *The Last of the Mohicans.*

"When we sever ourselves from society in a rite of change, there is an invisible door that we pass through that has no words on the other side," writes Joan Halifax in *The Fruitful Darkness.* "I believe it is through stillness and silence that the door opens. Inside the secret room, we weave the threads of understanding into the cloth of culture."[25]

Halifax celebrates an aesthetic metashamanism, a paradise that would be heard in silence, an oxymoronic nostalgia, and then woven into the "cloth of culture." Once more natives are burdened with aesthetic silence and the simulations of a lonesome civilization; the romantic interimages in the literature of dominance. "Tribal peoples are natural experts in interspecies communication," she writes. "Many times I have found myself sitting with an elder who speaks for hours in a language totally unfamiliar to me, and yet the pictures come, and the energy of Presence holds the time together like a well-woven blanket."[26] The burdens of translation from the oral to the scriptural, the contingencies of nature, and the cast of the sacred are not heard in these simulations of the passive presence of the other. Silence and a "pictorial turn" are mundane simulations of dominance.

Thich Nhat Hanh "invited people to put photos of their deceased relatives in a book placed on the altar," writes Halifax about her Buddhist teacher in Plum Village, France. "Practicing Buddhism is about discovering ourselves to be in a great flowing river of continuities. . . . It was in Plum Village that I began to question our relationship to the dead. I wondered if we can see beyond personal histories of loss and grief to an autobiography that includes the loss of forests and rivers."[27] The interimage simulations and pictures of the native dead have been on the altar of dominance for several centuries.

OCCIDENTAL SURVEILLANCE

The notion that a photograph is worth a thousand words is untrue in any language. Native stories create a sense of presence, a tease of memories, and a resistance to pictures of victimry. Yet, the simulations of the *indian* serve the manifest manners of unbidden dominance. Photographs are specious representations of the other, the treacheries of racialism. Pictures are possessory, neither cultural evidence nor the shadows of lost traditions.

Cameras are the instruments of institutive discoveries and predatory surveillance; photographs are cultural commodities and class representations that reduce a sense of native presence to an aesthetic silence and dominance. Some good people mount their photographs as the common narratives of cultural remembrance, but the fugitive poses of the *indian* other, outside the case of technologies and social functions of photographic representations, are simulations of severance, not the pictures or stories of native survivance.

Pierre Bourdieu observes that there are uncertain and ambiguous class distinctions in the cultural and domestic values of photographs. "The realization of the artistic intention is particularly difficult in photography," he writes in *Photography: A Middle-brow Art*, "probably because, fundamentally, it is only with difficulty that photographic practice can escape the functions to which it owes its existence." Moreover, "photography can only provoke an institutional piety, sustained by its social function; the desire to progress to a more intense practice aimed at properly and exclusively artistic ends is most likely to become lost in an apophatic aesthetic or, at most, to be accomplished (by negating itself) in the total renunciation of any practice, because the different social classes can only distinguish themselves in this regard by distancing themselves, in different ways, from ordinary practice."[28]

The apophasis of the native other in ethnographic portraiture, or the allusions by denial and negation of the fugitive pose as an "aesthetic intention," is, nonetheless, a simulation of dominance by controversion.

Photographs were the new conceptions and simulations of the real, a common choice by the end of the nineteenth century. Painting and other forms of representation had been the foundations of visual consciousness, but the camera captured countenance and action, the acutance of motion. Capturable native motion is aesthetic servitude, an eternal *indian* simulation. The portraiture of natives became a transposed desire and ornamentation of interimage dominance.

"Photographic information made people more aware of speed and time," writes Donald Lowe in *History of Bourgeois Perception*. "Such perceptual interpretation would have been incomprehensible to people from other cultures. They would have had to acquire the bourgeois perceptual emphasis on visual information in discontinuous, mechanical time, before they could have translated static traces into motion."[29]

Roland Barthes observes in *Camera Lucida* that "whatever it grants to vision and whatever its manner, a photograph is always invisible: it is not it that we see." The photograph is the "advent of myself as other: a cunning dissociation of consciousness from identity." He notes that "photography transformed subject into object, and even, one might say, into museum object."[30]

Natives bear the solace and mythic chance of traditions and memories in narratives, *not* cameras. Natives posed in silence at the obscure borders of the camera, fugitive poses that were secured as ethnographic evidence and mounted in museums. That silence could have been resistance to the mummers of camera dominance. Eternal poses are not without humor, but the photographic representations became the evidence of a vanishing race, the assurance of dominance and victimry.

The bourgeois sanctions of interimage simulations serve the cultural nostalgia of representations. Persistently, the possession of fugitive *indian* poses is a desire to maintain institutive dominance. Obviously, the "wonder and illusion of representation is different from the wonder and illusions of reality. In this respect representation is exactly the opposite of what it has always been supposed to be. Representation is miraculous because it deceives us into thinking it is realist, but it is only miraculous because it is something other than what it represents," writes David Freedberg in *The Power of Images.*[31]

"The photographic semblance of eternal, universal Truth and innocent, uncomplicated pleasure is what always potentially links the medium to institutional power; it seems to reproduce so easily those grand narratives of our culture," writes Linda Hutcheon in *The Politics of Postmodernism.*[32]

What can we see in the photographic representations of the racial other that is not dominance? Portraiture as evidence, or even postindian pasticcio, must be more than the eternal silence of a fugitive pose; there, in the stare of the shadows, is an elusive native presence. The crucial stories of natives in photographs are in the eyes and hands, not in the costumes or simulations of culture; the eyes are a tacit presence, the costumes are the racial enactments of the other, an ethnographic commodity. Costumery, masks, and decorations are changeable, and borrowed *indian* clothes are prosaic interimage simulations, neither cultural codes nor ironic stories of conversion. The eyes that meet in the aperture are the assurance of narratives and a sense of native presence.

"What is the content of the photographic message? What does the photograph transmit?" asks Roland Barthes in *Image—Music —Text.* "Certainly the image is not the reality but at least it is its perfect *analogon* and it is exactly this analogical perfection which, to common sense, defines the photograph. Thus can be seen the special status of the photographic image: *it is a message without a code*; from which proposition an important corollary must immediately be drawn: the photographic message is a continuous message."[33]

What could the absence of a code and a continuous message of cultural dominance mean in portraiture? The histories of the nation are creases of interimage simulations and the captious warrants of civilization; at the same time, the evidence of the actual removal and termination of real natives is incontrovertible. The camera was one more new weapon in the course of discoveries and cultural dominance. The fugitives of manifest manners learned how to pose in silence as an act of survivance.

John Tagg points out in *The Burden of Representation* that the camera has the power of surveillance and representation. "Like the state, the camera is never neutral. The representations it produces are highly coded, and the power it wields is never its own."[34]

The simultaneous cuts of time and motion are the counts of surveillance, the causal simulations of manifest manners and dominance. Those natives captured as *indians* in ethnographic photographs, the stoical poses of the other, are the cultural fugitives of desire and dominance.

"The human sciences are a surveillance; the exact sciences are an observation," writes Michel Serres in *The Limits of Theory*. "The first are as old as our myths; the others, new, were born with us, and are only as old as our history. Myth, theater, representation, and politics do not teach us how to observe; they commit us to a surveillance."[35] The observation of the native is not the same course as surveillance and dominance. Likewise, native consciousness, natural reason, and a clever sense of native survivance were not the same as terminal monotheism. The natives were observers, more mature in their humor, tease of causes, and tragic wisdom, than were the "discoverers." Occidental surveillance, not observation, generated the fugitive poses, interimage simulations, and the ominous notions of savagism and civilization.

"The systematic study of societies different from one's own has been undertaken only within the Western tradition," writes Eric Gans. "But this quest for diversity is also, despite itself, a reduction of diversity. The fascination with the ethnological Other only hastens the revelation that the Other is just more of the Same."[36]

Photographs are never worth the absence of narratives because languages are imagination and photographs are the simulations of culture and closure. Natives are the eternal fugitives of the camera; the decorated poses, captured and compared, are the public evidence of dominance, not the private stories of survivance, not the tease of creation, or the clever turns of the seasons.

"When we are afraid, we shoot. But when we are nostalgic, we take pictures," writes Susan Sontag in *On Photography*. "Still, there is something predatory in the act of taking a picture. To photograph people is to violate them, by seeing them as they never see themselves, by having knowledge of them they can never have; it turns people into objects that can be symbolically possessed."[37]

The pictures of *indians* as the other, the wounded fugitives of the camera, are not the same as those nostalgic photographs of homesteaders and their families in a new constitutional democracy. The manifest camera created interimage fragments of fugitive poses that separated natives from their communities and ancestral land; the simulations of the other as the *indian* turned the real into the unreal with no obvious presence in time or nature. For these reasons, and more, the *indian* in photographs should be seen in the shadows of the eyes and hands, an honorable invitation to underived narratives rather than public representations and closure.

Natives have been eye to eye with occidental predation and the ironies of civilization for more than five centuries. The same nations that celebrated political and religious liberties embraced racialism, constitutional treasons, master objectivism, and institutive evidence over the stories of creation, natural reason, and the tease of native tricksters.

The eyes and hands of wounded fugitives in photographs are the sources of stories, the traces of native survivance; all the rest is ascribed evidence, surveillance, and the interimage simulations of dominance. The eyes and hands have never been procured in colonial poses, never contrived as cultural evidence to serve the fever of institutional power.

The eyes are the narrative presence of natives, and the poses are the simulations of the other, the unreal representations of the other as causal evidence of *indianness*, the state, conditions, and instance of simulations as the real; at the same time, the simulations are ironies because even the fugitive poses of the other are overcome by the wicked closure of savagism and civilization.

"Closure" is another name for the nescient representations of the other, and in this sense, the extreme closure of the interimage *indian* in photographs. "Representation is what determines itself by its own limit. It is the delimitation for a subject, and by this subject, of what 'in itself' would be neither represented nor representable," writes Jean-Luc Nancy in *The Birth to Presence*. "But the irrepresentable, pure presence and pure absence, is also an effect of representation."[38]

The eyes and hands are the narratives not the ruins of native bodies. "Photographs in themselves do not narrate. Photographs preserve instant appearances," writes John Berger in *About Looking*. "No painting or drawing, however naturalist, belongs to its subject in the way that a photograph does."[39] The eyes in a photograph are the secret mirrors of a private presence, not the closure of performance, or public representations; indeed, the eyes hold the presence of the photographer on the other side of the aperture. The instances of native eyes in the aperture are continuous narratives that counter the closure of discoveries and cultural evidence in photographs.

Jean-Luc Nancy argues that the "body first was thought *from the inside*, as buried darkness into which light only penetrates in the form of reflections, and reality only in the form of shadows." Literature mimes bodies, and bodies are shadows, and the shadows become representations in photographs. "The body is but a wound," he writes in *The Birth to Presence*.[40]

The eyes are the secret stories of our wounded bodies, and the poses are the absence of the other, an ironic exposure because the representation of bodies as cultural evidence is the certain death of the other, death by continuous photographic exposure.

"Whatever it grants to vision and whatever its manner, a photograph is always invisible: it is not it that we see," writes Roland Barthes in *Camera Lucida*. The eyes, in this sense, are the presence we see in photographs. "Every photograph is a certificate of presence. This certificate is the new embarrassment which its invention has introduced into the family of images."[41]

Quanah Parker, for instance, is pictured in both tribal clothes and in a morning coat with an umbrella, pocket watch chain, and derby. He is supported by a rustic wall in the first photograph and in the second by a classical stucco simulation. He is posed near the same ornate column in both photographs. These could be fashion pictures of an *indian* fugitive; indeed, the obscurities of modes and costumes could be a much better interpretation of native histories than the rush to cultural evidence.

The costumes in photographs are not the same as real clothes, ceremonial vestments, or the languages of clothes and fashions, because the stories of each appearance are never the same as the *indian* simulations. Costumes are the seasons, the fashions, and the measures of time; the species of costumes in pictures are not the monotheistic closure of creations.

Parker was Comanche, an eminent leader at the turn of the last century who defended the use of peyote as a religious freedom. The narratives of his religious inspiration, his crossblood contingencies, are not obvious in either of the photographs. His hair is braided in both pictures, but the poses seem to be the causal representations of then and now, tradition and transition, or variations on the nostalgic themes of savagism or civilization. His eyes, not the costumes, are the narratives, his presence in the pictures;

his eyes are the sources of imagination, not the mere notice of an umbrella, a derby, or bound braids. His eyes are the presence of the pictures; the stories of resistance, and traces of native survivance. His eyes dare the very closure of his own fugitive poses.

Quanah Parker was an inspiration to the native people of the plains. "The great warrior established his bravery when he and a group of Comanches refused to accept the dictates of the Treaty of Medicine Lodge and battled to the end at Adobe Wells in Texas in 1874," writes Rennard Strickland in *The Indians of Oklahoma*. "Parker then led his people down the new road, became a famous tribal judge, and as a member in the Native American Church was a widely identified peyote figure. While willing to adjust to farming and the new economic ways, Parker continued to practice the old Comanche family way of having a number of wives. Ironically, while Parker remains to the present a controversial figure in his own tribe, the Parker pattern of selective adaptation and resistance became the one Oklahoma's Indians generally followed."[42]

The decorative feathers, beads, leathers, woven costumes, silver, turquoise, bone, native vesture, and *indian* simulations have turned humans into the mere objects that bear material culture in photographs. Moreover, peace pipes, medals, trade axes, bows and arrows, rifles, and other weapons are the obscure simulations of *indianness*. Natives are seldom pictured with families or children, in situations of humor, or other contingencies. Most photographers of *indians* focused on the fugitive warrior pose and decorative costumes as traditional, the occidental simulations of the *indian*; these interimage closures of presence would be mimicked several generations later by postindian leaders as the actual sources of traditions and identities. These postindian "traditions" are the ironic interimage simulations in the ruins of representations. The imitations of the fugitive poses are the double closures of presence, an ironic separation with no wisdom or sense of the real: the fugitive remains of cultural dominance and kitschy victimry.

Edward Curtis, for instance, one of the most dedicated pictorial photographers of natives and *indians*, actually altered some of his photographs to preserve the fugitive poses of *indian* traditions. Some of these poses have become the evidence of traditions in the new simulations of urban *indianness* and postindian identities.[43]

Curtis removed umbrellas, suspenders, the many tracks of civilization, and any traces of written languages. This was unfortunate because at the turn of the last century thousands of native scholars had studied at federal and mission schools and were teachers on the same federal exclaves that photographers visited with their costumes and cameras. Curtis was the best of the portrait photographers; nevertheless, his portraits enhanced the interimage of the noble savage as the antithesis of civilization. He visited hundreds of native communities and processed more than forty thousand pictures, the simulation of *indians* in fugitive poses. Alas, his dedication proved that ethnographic photography is an oxymoron. The last aversions, however, are overturned once more with the evidence of new interimage simulations.

Edward Curtis created *indian* images that "would often perform the graphic equivalent of riding into the darkness of an unknown future," notes Mick Gidley in *Representing Others*. "Curtis concentrated on representing 'traditional' ways, even to the extent of issuing wigs to cover shorn hair, providing costumes, and removing signs of the mechanistic twentieth century."[44]

Natives were simulated in portraiture generations before the invention of photography. George Catlin, Karl Bodmer, Charles Bird King, and other painters have been praised for their exotic and ethnographic portraits of natives. King recorded personal native names with most of his portraits, but the eyes, hands, noses, and costumes were ethnic interimage simulations and homogeneous.[45] "Not all of the Indian portraits executed by King were painted from life," notes Andrew Cosentino in *The Paintings of Charles Bird King*. "At times, when the number of delegates to the capital abated, he was asked to paint oil versions of portrait sketches made by others in the field." Painted "entirely in his studio," his portraits "lack the sense of natural vitality evident in the words of such an artist as George Catlin."[46]

George Catlin, the celebrated nineteenth-century artist and author, was not bound to a studio. He painted hundreds of *indian* portraits, and, concerned that his work be seen as accurate, rather than aesthetic, he "attached certificates of authenticity to the backs of his Indian portraits." The signatures of "authenticity" were by *indian* agents, army officers, and others in government service. These sanctions of *indian* portraiture, similar to those published with *indian* captivity narratives, are ironic, compared with the recent federal laws that protect *indian* artists. The endorsements of "authenticity," then and now, *indian* as subject to *indian* as artist, are evidence of a "pictorial turn" in consciousness and consumer protection.

"Catlin gives us portraits and landscapes, epic rituals and candid camp scenes, but he never quite ties them together," observes William Cronon in *Discovered Lands, Invented Pasts*. "His brush is too broad, his palette too bold, and his eye for detail too weak to carry us very far into this Indian world." What natives "do with their hands, how they use their tools, what they eat and how they prepare it, why they inhabit the land as they do: such things we cannot easily learn from him."[47]

Catlin and other painters created fugitive poses, ethnographic simulations of *indians* with vacuous eyes and barren hands. The *indians* in most portraits were interimage simulations. The stories of native survivance were erased in portraiture; silenced on a landscape without names or narratives. The portraits were the coincidence of discoveries in the cause of dominance.

The portraiture of natives mustered an interimage simulation of *indians* that featured an exotic countenance and concentrated more on costumes as artifacts than on the inimitable gestures of eyes and hands. "The human hand, as well as being the principal vehicle of motor activity, is the chief organ of the fifth sense, touch," writes John Napier in *Hands*. "With the eye, the hand is our main source of contact with the physical environment." Pictures of native hands are at rest, and the "hand at rest is beautiful in its tranquillity, but it is infinitely more appealing in the flow of action." Photographs capture the motion of eyes and hands. "When the hand is at rest, the face is at rest; but a lively hand is the product of a lively mind."[48]

Robert Brilliant points out in *Portraiture* that the notion of ethnographic portraits "seems to cause some critical difficulty in assessing their worth as portraits because the subjects are so often ignored as subjects of portraiture or they are strongly subordinated to other agendas of representation." The *indian* is the simulation of ethnographic portraiture. "Of course, portrait artists working in their own culture rarely think like ethnographers, nor is it customary to apply anthropological techniques to the portraits of those with whom one shares a common culture."[49] Again, ethnographic portraiture is an oxymoron of dominance.

"The photograph both loots and preserves, denounces and consecrates. Photography expresses the American impatience with reality," Sontag argues in *On Photography*. "After the opening of the West in 1869 by the completion of the transcontinental railroad came the colonization through photography. The case of the American Indians is the most brutal." Tourists invaded the privacy of natives, "photographing holy objects and the sacred dances and places, if necessary paying the Indians to pose and getting them to revise their ceremonies to provide more photogenic material."[50]

The public at the time was more interested in the exotic warriors who had fought the soldiers than in the native historians, artists, and medical doctors. The first photographers worked for the railroads, the military, or government surveys; their pictures of the plains tribes, the Sioux and Comanche in particular, "helped create the image of an Indian in a long headdress, made so familiar later by Hollywood films," write Dorothy and Thomas Hoobler in *Photographing the Frontier.* "Studio photographers went so far as to keep on hand what was regarded as 'typical' Indian dress to supply to Indians who might otherwise come to be photographed in nondescript, more practical attire."[51]

What might have been the watchwords of the entrepreneurs on the other side of the camera? Hundreds of photographers created simulations that would amuse and menace natives for more than a century, but the men and women armed with cameras were seldom abused in native communities. The natives were the *observers*; the others with cameras were the agents of surveillance. The lonesome ones waited to be seen behind their cameras.

How were the native *observers* in the aperture to know that the pictures of them would be obtained by surveillance, possessed as cultural evidence, sold as postcards, and then established in new museums of desire and dominance as the representations of *indian* traditions? Only mythic ironies and an incredible watchword could touch the obvious contradictions, the occidental obsession to render the natives unreal as *indians* in their own natural observations of time and place.

How would these photographers of the *indian*, the patrons of *idiofacient* commodities, explain the distinctions between public and private simulations of the other? There are more serious troubles to consider, but remember the eyes and hands, and the stories that the loss of privacy is the loss of motion and freedom. Photographers abused the native sense of privacy to capture an image and then either sold or distributed the pictures to various agencies. How should we now respond to the photographs that have violated the privacy of the natives? Cover the eyes? Whose eyes should be covered?

How could aesthetic simulations absolve those who inherited their dominance in the celebration of the arts? Digital manipulations of photographs could overturn the fugitive poses and create an ironic aesthetic of surveillance. Namely, virtual realities are interactive entertainment, new situational observations and stories, but the noble savages of past discoveries have become the noble and romantic victims of television and motion picture simulations. Nonetheless, the eyes are the shadow presence, and the eyes of the photographer in the aperture are forever in the narratives of the pictures.

"Privacy is usually considered a moral interest of paramount importance. Its loss provokes talk of violation, harm, and loss of agency," writes Julie Inness in *Privacy, Intimacy, and Isolation.* "Privacy is defined as a variety of freedom, a freedom that functions by granting the individual control over the division between the public and the private with respect to certain aspects of life."[52] Native privacy, transmotion, and freedom were seldom considered in the photographic simulations of the *indian* other. The camera captured native transmotion, and that silence of the picture was the closure of native rights and privacy. The prurient pictures of nude native women reproduced as postcards were the ironic teases in a nation that associated natural bodies with savagism.

Those who discover the other in pictures, the *indian* as the absence of the real, have denied the native observation of their own presence in the histories of representations; moreover, natives must bear the treacherous interimage simulations of cultural dominance. Otherwise, the lonesome, curious other with the camera could be seen as an ironic absence in the new stories of a native presence.

"The only thing left for me to do is to find a refuge in the other and to assemble—out of the other," writes Mikhail Bakhtin in *Art and Answerability*, "the scattered pieces of my own givenness, in order to produce from them a parasitically consummated unity in the other's soul using the other's resources. Thus, the spirit breaks up the soul from within myself."[53]

The most obvious search for the other is in the simulations of the *indian*; the eyes and hands are narratives in the same aperture, and the capture of native transmotion is the evidence of the other. Edward Curtis and other photographers are seen in the camera, and in native stories, but not in the picture. The other in the camera, the lonesome agent of interimages, is the absence in the picture; the eyes and hands of natives are secured as an ironic presence of motion and observation.

"The *I* hides in the other and in others, it wants to be only an other for others, to enter completely into the world of others as an other, and to cast from itself the burden of being the only *I* (*I-for-myself*) in the world," writes Bakhtin in *Speech Genres and Other Late Essays*.[54]

Natives had practiced medicine, composed music, published histories, novels, and poetry, won national elections, and traveled around the world before the turn of the century, but their experiences were obscured by the interimage simulations of the *indian*, the antithesis of civilization in photographs and motion pictures. The simulations of the *indian* other in the cinema, in fact, continue to be the bourgeois source of notions about *indians*. The interimage simulations of the real as the absence of natives, have become the historical evidence of the *indian*; ersatz cultures over the actual presence of natives.

"More than any other medium, photography is able to express the values of the dominant social class and to interpret events from that class's point of view, for photography, although strictly linked with nature, has only illusory objectivity," writes Gisèle Freund in *Photography and Society*. "First catering to the intellectual elite, photography next reached out to the bourgeois middle class. But when commercial photographers made pictures to please an uneducated public, even the initial supporters of photography became vehement critics."[55]

The interimage simulations and fugitive poses are the eternal contradictions of *indian* portraiture, photography, and narratives of dominance; the *presence* of the *indian* is the absence of the native, the more of the one, is the decline of the other. These contradictions are transmutable in trickster stories, shamanic visions, virtual realities, and the ironies of postindian literature. Watch the eyes and hands in fugitive poses to see the motion of natives, and hear the apophatic narratives of a continuous presence.

CHAPTER FIVE

Native Transmotion

C harles Aubid was a sworn witness in federal court that autumn more than thirty years ago; he raised his hand, heard the oath for the first time in *anishinaabemowin*, the language of the *anishinaabe*, and then waved at United States District Judge Miles Lord.

Aubid was a witness in a dispute with the federal government over the right to regulate the wild rice harvest on the Rice Lake National Wildlife Refuge near the East Lake Reservation in northern Minnesota.

The *anishinaabe* natives have harvested *manoomin*, wild rice, for more than three centuries. This nutritious native cereal, referred to as "fool's oats" by early explorers, is a trickster creation and sustenance to the *anishinaabe*; the traditional autumn harvest has been observed since the early fur trade in the territory. Today, *manoomin* is both a native tradition and a commodity.

Federal agents had assumed the authority to announce the wild rice season and regulate the harvest, a bureaucratic action that decried a native sense of transmotion, survivance, and sovereignty.

Aubid, and many other *anishinaabe* witnesses, were in federal court to convince the judge to restrain the government from regulating the *manoomin* harvest on the national refuge. A century after the area had been ceded in treaties, the refuge was established by the government. William Falvey, the federal attorney, argued that control of the refuge was legal and that the natives in court were not elected to represent the interests of the reservation. Most of the native witnesses testified in *anishinaabemowin*, and their testimony was translated by two *anishinaabe* interpreters.

Sam Yankee, then an elected member of the Minnesota Chippewa Tribal Executive Committee, a federation of reservations in the state, explained that the *anishinaabe* had been granted the right to continue the wild rice harvest. Actually, the *anishinaabe* had neither lost the rights of a traditional harvest, nor the transmotion of native sovereignty. These rights are inherent in most treaties.

Francis Paul Prucha points out in *American Indian Treaties* that in three early treaties the *anishinaabe* "retained hunting and fishing rights." The 1837 treaty, for instance, provided that the "privilege of hunting, fishing, and gathering wild rice, upon the lands, the rivers and the lakes included in the territory ceded, is guarantied to the Indians, during the pleasure of the President of the United States."[1]

Aubid, who was eighty-six years old at the time, testified in *anishinaabemowin* that he was present as a young man when the government agents told Old John Squirrel that the *anishinaabe* would always have control of the *manoomin* harvest. Aubid told the judge that there once was a document, but the *anishinaabe* always understood their rights in stories, not hearsay. John Squirrel was there in memories, a storied presence, and he could have been heard by the court as a visual trace of a parol agreement.

Falvey, the federal attorney, objected to the testimony, as he heard it in translation, as hearsay, and therefore not admissible as evidence. The judge agreed with the objection and explained to the witness that the court cannot hear as evidence what a dead man said, only the actual experiences of the witness.

"John Squirrel is dead," said Judge Miles Lord. "And you can't say what a dead man said." The judge waited for his words to be translated and then invited the witness to continue his story.

Aubid turned brusquely in the witness chair, bothered by what the judge said about John Squirrel. English was his second language, but he told his stories in *anishinaabemowin*, the language of his visual memories and native sovenance. Aubid wore spectacles with thick lenses; he squinted, and leaned into the line of sight, closer to the judge. He pointed at legal books on the bench and then shouted that those books contained the stories of dead white men.

"Why should I believe what a white man says, when you don't believe John Squirrel?" Aubid turned twice more in the witness chair and waited for the translation.

Judge Lord was deferentially amused by the analogy of native stories to court testimony, judicial decisions, precedent, and hearsay. "You've got me there," he said, and then considered the testimony of other *anishinaabe* witnesses.

Lord was humorous, generous, perceptive, and might have encouraged native resistance, but he did not seem to understand the precise reference to the presence of a fourth person in the story, "when you don't believe John Squirrel." Aubid named the storied *anishinaabe* as a presence, not as an absence; as the virtual evidence, not as mere hearsay.[2]

The regulation of the wild rice harvest was not decided then and there; later, in other cases, federal courts acknowledged the inherent rights of natives to regulate natural resources on treaty reservations. Francis Paul Prucha observed that the "treaties, which reformers at the end of the nineteenth century considered an obstacle to the progress of the Indians, have turned out, in the late twentieth century, to be one of the principal bastions of protection for the lands, the political autonomy, and the hunting and fishing rights of present-day reservation Indians."[3]

Aubid, in his testy testimony in *anishinaabemowin*, presented at least four distinctive creases of native reason and sovereignty. The first crease was native evidence in the *anishinaabe* language; second, the mien of a chancer, the native tease of moral pieties and the procedural course of evidence; third, native sovenance, and the stories of survivance as testimony in court. The last crease of native reason was that sense of *anishinaabe* presence by resistance, storied transmotion, and assertive sovereignty.

Aubid, in his *anishinaabe* stories about that meeting with the government men, created a presence of John Squirrel. That sense of presence, as sworn testimony in court, was the obviative, the fourth person in the poses of evidence. Monotheism is hearsay, the care of creation, the concern of weak memories, and the curse of deceivers. The rules of evidence are selective, and sanction cozenage over native sovenance, boundaries over stories of sovereignty; however, evidence is never ultimatory. Squirrel was twice the tease of native evidence; the sense of his presence in stories, an actual presence in the memories of others, and an obviative presence as semantic evidence. These stories and creases of native reason are evidence, a dialogic circle. John Squirrel is a virtual criterion of evidence in native sovenance; the stories of survivance and sovereignty.

Aubid created an *anishinaabe* presence of others in his stories and testimony, and, in a sense, he was a virtual cartographer, because he mapped a visual representation, a native criterion of transmotion and sovereignty.

VIRTUAL CARTOGRAPHY

"The map is not the territory," but the territory is the map, and that chiastic inversion, an elusive connotation of semantics, secreted but never erased virtual cartography. Alfred Korzybski was the wise mapper and the chiastic mete of mental mappery. Surely, he would never retract natural reason, sovenance, totemic stories, and dream songs, the native transmotion that creates a sense of presence, only to carry out that mean promise of semantics and modernity.

Maps are pictures, and some native pictures are stories, visual memories, the source of directions, and a virtual sense of presence; others are simulations and not a trace of the actual territory. Maps are references, not counterfeits; the memories of the actual territory are not transposed by simulations. Mappery is virtual, the creation of base line representations.

"Silence a people's stories and you erase a culture," said Louis Owens, the novelist and essayist. "To have graphic evidence of this phenomenon, all we have to do is look at a map. Mapping is, of course, an intensely political enterprise, an essential step toward appropriation and possession. Maps write the conquerors' stories over the stories of the conquered."[4]

Native memories, stories of totemic creation, shamanic visions, burial markers, medicine pictures, the hunt, love, war, and songs, are the transmotion of virtual cartography. Tricky creation stories, totemic pictures, and mental mappery are the embodiment of native transmotion and sovereignty. Native mappers are storiers and visionaries.

The *anishinaabe* song pictures, for instance, are the cues of the virtual memories of music. The pictures animate the memories of the melody and the wavering voice of a native singer. The song pictures, incised on birch bark, are virtual cartography. These pictures are the creation of hundreds of distinctive songs and stories about dreams, love, war, animals, birds, motion, and ceremonial music of the *midewiwin*, the great society of healers, or the Grand Medicine Society.

Henry Rowe Schoolcraft, the geologist, ethnologist, moralist, and *indian* agent, observed that "pictographic scrolls and devices, rudely cut or painted on wood, rocks, or the scarified trunks of trees, and even songs recorded by this method, are well known traits of our aboriginal tribes." Moreover, the practice of "drawing pictures on skins, trees, and various other substances, has been noticed by travelers and writers from the earliest times. Among the more northerly tribes, these figures are often observed on that common substitute for the ancient papyrus among these nations, the bark of the *betula papyracea*, or white birch: a substance possessing a smooth surface, easily impressed, very flexible, and capable of being preserved in rolls."[5]

Frances Densmore recorded, transcribed, translated, and then interpreted *anishinaabe* music on reservations at the turn of the last century. "We are particularly indebted to her for collecting the oldest songs of the tribe, thereby rescuing them from certain oblivion," notes Thomas Vennum in his introduction to *Chippewa Music*. Densmore would eschew, no doubt, the notion that her studies of *anishinaabe* music were rescue transcriptions.

Most of the songs were presented with stories and pictures. One song picture shows a human figure with a walking stick. The story of the picture is that "through the power" of the *midewiwin*, "a man lives to be so old that he leans on a staff as he walks," and the song is very old.

> *those who are spirits*
> *are making me old*
> *where I am sitting*

"Many of the songs are taught only to those who pay for the privilege of learning them, and all the songs are recorded in mnemonics on strips of birch bark," writes Densmore. "This record serves as a reminder of the essential idea of the song and is different in its nature from our system of printing. The Indian picture preserves the idea of the song, while our printed page preserves the words which are supposed to express the idea but which often express it very imperfectly."[6] Song pictures are the creations and the memories of the music, a virtual cartography.

The *anishinaabe* picture of the *midewiwin* "path of life" is a representation of the transmotion of life from creation to old age. Mainans, the *midewiwin* healer, created the picture and told stories about the transmotion of the "path of life."

The tangent lines at the turn of each angle are representations of the seven temptations, a virtual cartography. Densmore pointed out that the sense of temptation in this connection "implies primarily a trial of strength and motive." The first and second tangent lines of temptation are resistance and the chance of life; the third, a spiritual initiation of the *midewiwin*; fourth, the temptation of middle age; fifth, the temptation and reflection of old age; and sixth, a return to a spiritual presence, the temptations of the visionary. The seventh and last temptation is the endurance of old age, at a time when *maji manidoo*, or the evil spirit, comes to mind.[7]

Figure 1

The *anishinaabe* song pictures, stories, and the *midewiwin* scrolls, or the sacred documents of the great healers, were incised on birch bark, and cedar; other pictomyths were painted on cragged rocks. The virtual cartography of the *midewiwin*, incised on birch bark, is the depiction of animals and water spirits in a ceremonial center.

"The purpose of the picture writing" in the *midewiwin* "is to assist the memory and to afford a means of record which is intelligible only to initiates of the society," observes Densmore in *Chippewa Customs*. "The principal symbol is the straight or wavy lines which proceed from figures of men or animals, usually indicating 'spirit power.' If these lines proceed from the mouth they indicate song or speech, if from the ear, they indicate sounds which are heard." The "sky, earth, lakes, and hills, as well as sounds" were pictured in *midewiwin* documents. The virtual cartography of the *anishinaabe* includes messages, casual records, and representations of action, "days, direction, and duplication of numbers."[8]

Messages were incised on cedar and birch bark and placed in obvious locations. Animals, children, and totemic histories were represented by the virtual mappers. For instance, two families were pictured in canoes. The father in one canoe is a totemic bear and the mother is of the catfish totem; their three children sit with them in the canoe. Pictured in the second canoe is a totemic eagle, a mother of the bear totem, and their children.[9]

Figure 2

Native virtual cartography is much more than the base lines and cardinal directions of territory. The pictures of totemic bears, catfish, and eagles, are creative connections of *anishinaabe* stories, totemic sovenance, natural reason, and a tricky sense of native presence. That presence is transmotion, the tease of creation in pictures, memories, and stories; totemic names are visionary, the document is possessory.

"I am a bird who rises from the earth, and flies far up, into the skies, out of human sight; but though not visible to the eye, my voice is heard from afar, and resounds over the earth," said Keeshkumun, the *anishinaabe* orator of the crane totem, to the Englishman.[10]

Richard Kearney points out in *The Wake of Imagination* that one of the "greatest paradoxes of contemporary culture is that at a time when the image reigns supreme the very notion of a creative human imagination seems under mounting threat. We no longer appear to know who exactly produces or controls the images which condition our consciousness. We are at an impasse where the very rapport between imagination and reality seems not only inverted but subverted altogether."[11]

The monotheistic dominance of creation, nature and natives, and the pious separation of animals and humans, has persisted in the diplomatic mode of treaties with natives, the *whereas* diction of *fee simple patents*, and the *metes and bounds* of tenure mappery.

Alice Beaulieu, my grandmother, was born January 3, 1886, on the White Earth Reservation in Minnesota, in the same year that the Statue of Liberty was dedicated in New York. That same year, Geronimo, the leader of the Chiricahua Apache, was exiled as a war prisoner at Fort Pickens, Florida, and later at Fort Sill, Oklahoma. He appeared at international exhibitions and attended by invitation the inauguration of President Theodore Roosevelt.

President Roosevelt signed a fee simple patent, in the name of my grandmother, on May 21, 1908, an issue of subdivided land on the reservation under provisions of the General Allotment Act of 1887. The act provided "for the allotment of lands in severalty to Indians on the various reservations, and to extend the protection of the laws of the United States and the Territories over the Indians, and for other purposes."[12] Those "other purposes" were trustee warrants of dominance, and natives were so encumbered on reservations that thousands moved to urban areas.

The General Allotment Act "resulted in the reduction of the total tribal land base from 140 million acres to 50 million acres over a period of five decades," notes Charles Wilkinson in *The Eagle Bird*. "On its face the law did not provide that any land would pass from Indian hands. Instead, it dictated that each tribal member would receive a fixed amount of tribal land—80 acres of farmland or 160 acres of grazing land." Mistaken and devious, the government reasoned that "Indians would benefit from private enterprise rather than collective ownership. Allotment would make Indians into farmers."[13]

My grandmother never saw the actual area of the patent in her name; she was curious, but had no reason or the means to locate the land because, like most natives, she leased the allotment to a lumber company. Moreover, she would not have been able to understand the patent description without some general knowledge of surveys. Alice probably did not know, at the time, that the reservation and most of the nation was measured and subdivided in a systematic cadastral survey.

The United States Public Land Survey progressed westward and subdivided the nation into sections, each a square mile, and thirty-six sections comprised a township. The survey lines were "oriented predominantly in cardinal directions. This system stands in sharp contrast to the metes and bounds survey of the eastern seaboard of the United States."[14]

The General Land Office of the United States issued a fee simple patent, based on a cadastral survey, to "Alice Beaulieu, a White Earth Mississippi Chippewa Indian, for the east half of the southeast quarter of Section twenty-four in Township one hundred forty-two north of Range thirty-seven west of the Fifth Principal Meridian, Minnesota, containing eighty acres."[15] The document is historical, enured by the trustees of dominance, and possessory. Eighty acres and a trustee is never the same as that sense of native presence in virtual cartography.

The Hereford Cathedral *mappamundi*, that thirteenth-century map of the world, pictures trade routes, sacred and secular histories, myths, place names, and other information. Norman Thrower noted in *Maps and Civilization* that the *mappamundi* seems to have been used as an altarpiece, as an aid to travelers, and as "inspirational pictures like the stained glass windows of the cathedrals."[16]

There is no commensurate *mappamundi* of the native world; however, the native stories of creation, totemic visions, and sacred documents, are comparable to the spiritual inspiration of cathedral windows. The sacred *midewiwin* documents and other native stories were active creations, not passive representations; the visions and sacred songs of the *midewiwin* were once secreted in evasive and tricky stories by native healers. To reveal the stories and visions of this great society of healers to outsiders, at a time when native communions were menaced by agents of church and state, was worrisome to elders and unanswerable, an incoherence in the traditions of the *anishinaabe*. Yet, not to bear that credence as a *midewiwin* healer, and not to nurture and tease native stories of survivance, would have been an unendurable absence to the new native storiers and visionaries. That was a testy time in native stories, since the visual and aural were transcribed as the scriptural; and the transmotion of native memories, that sense of a presence in stories, was courted in the social sciences as cultural evidence. The *anishinaabe* and other natives have endured in virtual cartography, the certain mete of native sovereignty.

Henry Rowe Schoolcraft, the author of *algic* cultures, derived from the word *algonquin*, reports in the *Archives of Aboriginal Knowledge* that eleven *anishinaabe* leaders presented a visual land claim on five birch bark scrolls to the federal government in January 1849. Martell, an adventurer, and opportunistic interpreter, was the "prime mover of the visit, and the motions of the entire party." The natives arrived with their petition and no accreditation by the local *indian* agent; clearly, the subscription of an agent was evidence of dominance. "The plan of a retrocession of territory, on which some of the natives expressed a wish to settle and adopt the modes of civilized life, appeared to want the sanction of the several states in which the lands asked for lie. No action upon it could therefore be well had, until the legislatures of these states could be consulted." The party resorted "to the native pictorial art, which furnishes the subject of this notice."

That visual claim is an *anishinaabe* totemic narrative; there are seven creatures pictured on the foremost secular document. The totemic crane on the right of the birch bark scroll is followed on a path by three totemic martens, a totemic bear, a trickster, and on the left of the document, at the end, a totemic catfish. These seven totemic pictures are connected to the crane by direct lines, eye to eye, and heart to heart.

Oshkabawis, the *anishinaabe* leader, is represented as the totemic crane on the document and "has a line drawn from his eye forward, to denote the course of his journey, and another line drawn backward to the series of small rice lakes," notes Schoolcraft. "The entire object is thus symbolized in a manner which is very clear to the tribes, and to all who have studied the simple elements of this mode of communicating ideas." Oshkabawis, "who headed the party," was named a crane warrior by Schoolcraft. "To the eye of the bird standing for this chief, the eyes of each of the other totemic animals are directed as denoted by lines, to symbolize union of views. The heart of each animal is also connected by lines with the heart of the Crane chief, to denote unity of feeling and purpose."[17] The report does not clearly indicate that the author was present at the time of the totemic petition to the government. The picture was drawn by Seth Eastman, the soldier, surveyor, and painter. The totemic crane was not the creation of a native artist. The word *oshkaabewis* means a "ceremonial attendant."[18]

Keeshkemun, the crane orator, was an *anishinaabe* leader at the time. Oshkabawis was a noted pipe bearer, "who officiated in all public councils, making known the wishes of his chief, and distributing amongst his fellows, the presents which the traders occasionally gave to the chief," observes William Warren in *History of the Ojibway Nation*. Keeshkemun was a leader by "hereditary descent, but he made himself truly such, through the wisdom and firmness of his conduct, both to his people and the whites. During his lifetime, he possessed an unbounded influence over the division of his tribe with whom he resided, and generally over the Lake Superior bands and villages."[19]

Warren does not mention the presentation of the totemic map and visual land claim to the federal government. The *anishinaabe* historian talked to many native leaders, considered both oral and written documents, and never noted the party or the claim in his native history, completed in 1853. Schoolcraft indicated that the birch bark petition was presented to the U.S. Congress in 1849. Keeshkemun, and his pipe bearer Oshkabawis, were crane leaders in the eighteenth century. Oshkabawis was recorded in the *Atlas of Great Lakes Indian History* by Helen Tanner as a native village in 1810 and 1830, located near Lac du Flambeau.[20]

Schoolcraft reports that the native document "commences with the totem of the chief," the leader of the crane totem named Oshkabawis, "who headed the party." Schoolcraft was either not present, at the time of the petition, and constructed a narrative of misconceptions, or he was mistaken about the characters and dates, or there were two *anishinaabe* crane leaders with the same names, or he inadvertently misrepresented the name of the totemic crane in the birch bark document as the actual leader of the petition. The pictures and visual stories in the document are common *anishinaabe* totems, and the interpretive notes are exotic and comparable, but the significance of this picture entreaty, as a native political document, is obscure and arguable.

The visual stories of the totemic cranes, and other creatures eye to eye, and heart to heart, set as a union of views, are native scenes in virtual cartography. Schoolcraft, however, subscribed the totemic creation to serve as a historical document, a literal petition that traduced a native sense of presence, and the tease of creation in the pictures. Surely, he was a conversionist and misconceived the scenes of *anishinaabe* creation. Totemic pictures are visionary and storied creases of native sovenance, not casuistic or semantic conversions in the name of archive dominance.

"Picture-writing is indeed the literature of the Indians," writes Schoolcraft. "It shows the Red Man, in all periods of our history, both as he was and as he is; for there is nothing more true than that, save and except the comparatively few instances where they have truly embraced experimental Christianity, there has not been, beyond a few customs, such as dress and other externals, any appreciable and permanent change in the Indian character since Columbus first dropped anchor at the Island of Guanahan."[21]

David Turnbull reasoned in *Maps Are Territories* that the to-temic pictures on the birch bark document is a map, "but the information it conveys can only be understood within the cultural specifics of the circumstances that it portrays and cannot be generalized beyond that context." Moreover, the "power of maps lies not merely in their accuracy or their correspondence with reality. It lies in their having incorporated a set of conventions that make them combinable in one central place, enabling the accumulation of both power and knowledge at that centre."[22] Clearly, *anishinaabe* visual stories, totemic creations, and other pictures are mappery, the virtual cartography of native survivance and sovereignty.

Native sovereignty is sovenance, the immanence of visions, and transmotion in artistic creations. Sovereignty, moreover, is practical, reciprocal, and theoretical, but there is no such word in the *anishinaabe* language; however, the native sense of motion and use of the land in the northern woodlands does not embrace inheritance or tenure of territory. The criteria of transmotion are in the stories of trickster creation, the birch bark documents of the *midewiwin*, song pictures, beaded patterns, winter counts, painted hides, ledger art, and other creases of motion in virtual cartography.

BLUE HORSES

Howling Wolf Honanistto was a political prisoner for three years at Fort Marion in Saint Augustine, Florida. The Southern Cheyenne warrior and artist created active native scenes in rich colors, and the style of his painting was named ledger art at the end of the nineteenth.

Ledger art is the continuance of a new warrior tradition, the memories of "personal exploits and tribal histories" that became a "representational style through generations of artists," observes Joyce Szabo in *Howling Wolf and the History of Ledger Art*.[23]

"Howling Wolf emerges as a careful planner of line and color. His draughstmanship is confident and precise whether in pen or pencil," and his "compositions stress the interplay between curving, arabesque forms and firm, straight lines." With crayons, pencils, and watercolors, he created brilliant scenes of ceremonial warriors and bright horses in rich hues. "Blue and green horses appear on the same page with brown and black ones. Costume elements and brilliant textiles were rendered in as many colors as apparently possible."

Szabo points out that the history of the ledger art style, paintings on the lined pages of ledger account books in prison, is "one of gradual abandonment of many traditionally dictated conventions, development of new approaches to old subjects, and investigation of new images. Ledger art is above all art produced by Plains men who lived in societies that encouraged them to achieve as individuals," and that "individuality did not have to be imposed or suggested from outside forces."

The warriors and their horses are pictured in motion, the artistic transmotion of native sovereignty. The scenes and motion were of memories and consciousness, not poses and simulations. The transmotion of ledger art is a creative connection to the motion of horses depicted in winter counts and heraldic hide paintings. The hides and shields are visionary.

Native transmotion is seen in the raised hooves of horses, the voice lines, traces of arrows, the curve of feathers, footprints, and the trail of buffalo blood in a hunt. "The frenzy of the battle is conveyed through twisting, turning men and horses moving in all directions," and the pictographic representation and conventions of "flying arrows, bullets, and a variety of prints heighten the tension of the action," notes Szabo. "Figures racing across the page with action, beginning or ending at some point beyond the confines of the piece of paper, frequently ignoring the limitations of the edge of the page. Horses, humans, and objects are cut off midway thus adding to the dynamic sweep of the action, a movement of forces too monumental to be contained within the arbitrary boundaries of the page."[24] Native transmotion races as a horse across the page, and the action is a sense of sovereignty.

Howling Wolf, a native expressionist, created blue, red, and green horses, the transmotion of memories as a political prisoner. He painted his bright horses several years before the birth of the artist Franz Marc. The German expressionist, at the turn of the last century, painted many animals in several colors; his most notable creations are sensuous horses in rich chromatic hues of blue, the spiritual tease of blue horses. The artistic visions of these two expressionist were not the same, but their horses are comparable creations. The Cheyenne artist painted the horses of his memories as a warrior, the blue transmotion of native survivance. The German artist painted the blue horses of his mythical liberation, the presence of creation.

Franz Marc was "probably the best animal painter since the prehistoric men who painted caves," asserts art historian Frederick Hartt. "His romantic, poetic art sought liberation from the conventions of human existence in the world of animals."[25]

Marc declared his "enthusiasm for the arts of primitive people and children," observes George Heard Hamilton in *Painting and Sculpture in Europe, 1880–1940*. Marc, a member of the Blaue Reiter circle of artists, wrote that the new expressionist "movement was 'trying to get back by another road to the mysterious and abstract images of inner life, which is governed by laws different from those science discloses in nature.' "[26]

Vassily Kandinsky and Marc established and edited *Almanach Der Blaue Reiter*. The Blue Rider Alamanac "featured contributions from a wide range of artists," and one issue pictured a "chief's collar from Alaska." Marc "intended to study theology, but changed his mind and turned to painting." He "made several trips to Paris, where he came into contact with all the latest developments in modern art."[27] Marc may have seen hide paintings and other native artistic creations in museums and at Wild West Shows in Europe.

The Musée de l'Homme in Paris conserves a treasure of ornamental robes that are painted by unknown native artists. These painted hides were collected in the eighteenth century for the monarchy in France. George Horse Capture, curator of the Plains Indian Museum, examined the robes and notes in *Robes of Splendor* that they "are the earliest remaining examples of painted hides."

"I carefully touched each robe four times, and their power reached out, leaving me humble and grateful," writes Horse Capture. He studied one robe with red and black horses in motion, and a circle of hooves at a battle site. One warrior, on a horse in motion, wore a ceremonial headdress.

"Several clusters of images tell of individual heroics, and the field of action is divided by a gold strip of porcupine quillwork," he observes. "I was startled to find a gallant chief, bedecked in red and black garments, astride his galloping pony. His magnificent war bonnet captivated me. It was made of a circle of long, thin diamonds divided by different colors. Instantly, I was engulfed in memories of lying on my grandmother's star quilt and wondering about its design. I realized that the answer to that mystery was at hand. The star quilt's design was nearly identical to this warrior's war bonnet; the elongated diamonds represent the feathers of the golden eagle."

Horse Capture notes that the star design on the bonnet has remained as a native style. "This discovery was very important to me, and I felt grateful to the robe, the warrior, and the artist. To me, this joining was a sign that we would meet again and influence each other somewhere down the road."[28]

COLONIAL INVERSIONS

"One of the marks of colonialism is that it bends traditional diplomatic structures to exploitive ends," asserts Dorothy Jones in *License for Empire: Colonialism by Treaty in Early America.* "This can happen because accountability is not built into the diplomatic system. The only check is the assumption of countervailing force. When that is absent, as it invariably is in situations of colonialism, the whole treaty system becomes a weapon in the arsenal of the stronger power."[29]

Colonialism, nationalism, and theocentrism are variations on narratives of dominance; these political, economic, and causal powers are not obvious historical instances of natural reason, rights of motion, or entitlements of native sovereignty. At the same time, the establishment of constitutional democracies in the past two centuries has secured new and diverse narratives of governance: the diplomatic narratives of treaties, executive documents, and court decisions that acknowledge the rights and distinctive sovereignty of native communities.

"Native American claims to aboriginal land within what is now the United States is not a story of broken treaties, amended statutes, or breach of the sacred duty of guardianship," asserts Michael Kaplan in *Irredeemable America.* "Rather, it is the story of the unbridled, unabashed, and undisguised power of the conqueror over the conquered." The conqueror assumed the exclusive right to "grant title," and the "native occupant was totally devoid of any power to dispose of the soil. Hence, a grant of Indian lands by Indians could not convey a title paramount to the title granted by the United States to other parties." Kaplan argues that the "doctrine of aboriginal title in the courts" seems to provide some sense of political leverage. "Aboriginal title is a political issue, for the most part, not a legal one."[30]

The presence of natives on this continent is obvious, a natural right of motion, or transmotion, and continuous sovereignty; in other words, natives are neither exiles nor separatists from other nations or territories. The presence of natives on this continent is an obvious narrative on sovereignty—that is, natural reason and the sovenance of motion, and survivance. The onset is transmotion, and later, in a constitutional democracy, the legal entitlements of native sovereignty.

Regrettably, the discussions of natural reason and power, the sovereignty of native transmotion in a constitutional democracy, have been reduced to the metes of territoriality, and mere victimry, by many contemporary scholars.

Native sovereignty is the right of motion, and transmotion is personal, reciprocal, the source of survivance, but not territorial. The notions of native sovereignty are present in the earliest oral stories and presentations, in creation stories, totemic and trickster visions, in native trade languages, and they are even heard in translations; moreover, a commensurate sense of transmotion and sovereignty is patent in contemporary native autobiographies, creative literature, histories, letters, and government documents.

"Individuals were created or constructed at the same time as nations," notes David Elkins in *Beyond Sovereignty*. He argues that if "modernity created the autonomous individual, the postmodern condition will take us 'beyond individuals' as well as 'beyond nations' as units of analysis." Native sovereignty, in this sense, would have a natural ethical and historical presence in the notions and theories of transnational survivance. "Rights and the concept of the individual were parts of the same interdependent process of creating a sharper line between public and private realms," he observes. "The creation of the individual and the assumption that a private realm deserves sanctuary from public authority occurred concurrently with the building of authority on territorial lines."[31]

Sovereignty as motion and transmotion is heard and seen in oral presentations, the pleasures of native memories and stories, and understood in the values of human and spiritual motion in languages. Sovereignty is transmotion and used here in most senses of the word motion; likewise, the ideas and conditions of motion have a deferred meaning that reach, naturally, to other contexts of action, resistance, dissent, and political controversy. The sovereignty of motion means the ability and the vision to move in imagination and the substantive rights of motion in native communities.

Native transmotion is an instance of natural reason, and an aesthetic creation, to be sure, but not a literal simile of nature as a resistance to civilization; transmotion is motion and native memories, and not mere comparatives or performative acts. The sovereignty of motion is survivance, shared power, and performative transmotion is an ethical presence of nature, native stories, and natural reason.

The sovereignty of motion is mythic, material, and visionary, not mere territoriality, in the sense of colonialism and nationalism. Native transmotion is an original natural union in the stories of emergence and migration that relate humans to an environment and to the spiritual and political significance of animals and other creations. Monotheism is dominance over nature; transmotion is natural reason, and native creation with other creatures.

Max Oelschlaeger argues that natural history is a connection of wilderness and civilization, not a separation: how could nature be so cruel and sustain humans at the same time? He deconstructs the modernist view that "prehistoric people longed to escape the wilderness condition" and presents the "natural world" as a home, not an enemy. The magna mater metaphor is a myth of hunters, a world of humans and animals. The mother earth metaphor has an agricultural connection, the earth as a mythic mother, the center of fertility and nurturance.

"Clearly, the agricultural revolution provided the material precondition for the emergence of identifiably modern civilization by necessitating permanent settlement, producing an agricultural surplus, and starting a rippling process of social and technological change; ideological restructuring was inevitable," observes Oelschlaeger in *The Idea of Wilderness*. "No absolute measure of humanization exists, but before the agricultural revolution humankind minimally altered the natural world, while afterward it became a relentless agent of ecological change. The cultivation of cereals and the domestication of animals are clearly positive accomplishments in the face of environmental crisis: the only apparent alternative was starvation."[32]

Natural reason is a native tease of the seasons, the myths and metaphors of human and animal connections to the environment —shamanic visions, transmotion, and territorial reciprocity, but not monotheistic separations or colonial environmental dominance. William Cronon observes that to the colonists land became a "form of capital" and source of wealth. New England ecological practices were "inherently antithetical to earlier Indian economies." Native transmotion was connatural with the environment; natives altered the land, but their ecological practices as hunters, and as agriculturists, were not based on economies of abundance, and the environment was not a commodity. "Indian communities had learned to exploit the seasonal diversity of their environment by practicing mobility: their communities characteristically refused to stay put," writes Cronon in *Changes in the Land*. "English fixity sought to replace Indian mobility; here was the central conflict in the ways Indians and colonists interacted with their environments." Natives moved from "habitat to habitat to find maximum abundance through minimal work, and so reduce the impact on the land." The English lived in permanent settlements and "improved" the land. "The struggle was over two ways of living and using the seasons of the year, and it expressed itself in how two peoples conceived of property, wealth, and boundaries on the landscape."[33]

Native stories sustain the reason of survivance and traces of transmotion endure in contemporary native literature. N. Scott Momaday, for instance, wrote about his grandmother, who "lived out her long life in the shadow of Rainy Mountain, the immense landscape of the continental interior lay like memory in her blood." He "wanted to see in reality what she had seen more perfectly in the minds eye." His journey, several centuries later, was another story of native transmotion, a pilgrimage.

"There is a perfect freedom in the mountains, but it belongs to the eagle and the elk, the badger and the bear. The Kiowas reckoned their stature by the distance they could see, and they were bent and blind in the wilderness," he writes in *The Way to Rainy Mountain*.[34] "The names at first are those of animals and of birds, of objects that have one definition in the eye, another in the hand, of forms and features on the rim of the world, or of sounds that carry on the bright wind and in the void," writes N. Scott Momaday in his memoir *The Names*. "They are old and original in the mind, like the beat of rain on the river, and intrinsic in the native tongue, failing even as those who bear them turn once in the memory, go on, and are gone forever."[35]

Sovereignty is in the visions of transformation: the humor of motion as survivance over dominance; the communal movement to traditional food sources; dreams and memories as sources of shared consciousness; the stories of reincarnation, out of body travel; the myths and metaphors of flying; communal nicknames and memories of migration; the spiritual and herbal powers to heal and locate lost souls. These are evidence of natural reason and the personal power of creation; the native names and remembrance of motion and sovereignty.

Native North American "reincarnation is an expansion of continuity, or survival," observes Richard Slobodin in *Amerindian Rebirth.* "The great moralists do seem to share a predilection for the ethic of the closed, stable community, which is the type in which reincarnation beliefs flourish." Reincarnation, of course, is a new incarnation of native presence, and that transmotion, animalistic, avian, or human, even in secure urban communities, is survivance and the natural reason of sovereignty.[36]

CROSSOVER SOVEREIGNTY

The Bering Strait migration theory has been established by the social sciences and embraced in popular culture as the original move of natives in the Western Hemisphere. There is no decisive evidence to show the actual direction of this mythic migration. The scientific theories are ironic evidence; migration in either direction is native transmotion and sovereignty. Other observers have documented the motion of native cultures by language groups, by the use of trade languages, and by various theories and racialist notions of animism, nomadism, and savagism.

Native sovereignty as transmotion and natural reason is never the same in monotheistic civilizations; the discoveries, cues of dominance, covenants, and territorial boundaries are the means and declarations of separatism and nationalism. "Rousseau envisages men converting natural rights into civil rights and keeping sovereignty in their own hands," notes Maurice Cranston in *The Noble Savage.* "Rousseau argues that sovereignty cannot be delegated; it can only be exercised in person."[37] Native transmotion, then, has been converted into the provisions of inherent rights in treaties, and these conversions of transmotion are the distinctions of native sovereignty.

Native sovereignty is documented in oral histories, treaties, and other literary sources by native scholars and contemporary authors. However, many of these stories and documents have been reduced by objectivism, positivism, and the methodologies of the social sciences; collectors have stolen ceremonial material and distorted by translation and comparative interpretations the transmotion of sovereignty in ways that serve the mere commercial interests of cultural dominance and the romance of native victimry.

Rousseau "adored liberty and could endure no constraint, no discomfort and no subjugation whatever," notes Judith Shklar in *Men and Citizens.* "Moreover, all society was a form of enslavement for him, since it inevitably forced him to do something he did not feel like doing. At all times it afflicted and discomfited him." Rousseau adored his liberty in natives, and so he romanced the nature of noble savages.[38]

"The true forms of government," observed Aristotle, "are those in which the one, or the few, or the many, govern with a view to the common interest; but governments which rule with a view to the private interest, whether of the one, or of the few, or of the many, are perversions. For the members of a state, if they are truly citizens, ought to participate in its advantages." He wrote that it is "clearly better that property should be private, but the use of it common."[39]

Native transmotion and permanence are contingencies of governance and sovereignty. The native distinctions of public and private, in the course of names, nature, and possessions, are ceremonial, situational, and visionary. The *anishinaabe* once buried the dead with their treasures. William Warren notes that the *anishinaabe* buried their dead with "the articles needed in life for a journey. If a man, his gun, blanket, kettle, fire steel, flint and moccasins; if a woman, her moccasins, axe, portage collar, blanket, and kettle." Death is transmotion, a common "road of souls" to the west.[40]

The translation of *daniwin,* an inanimate noun in the language of the *anishinaabe,* means property, riches, treasure, and wealth; that one word once cued common interests more than a private and avidious tenure. Native names, estates of nature, and the uses of land and resources were stories of survivance and reciprocity.

Jean Bodin, the sixteenth-century French political philosopher, defined political sovereignty in terms of power. The ruler and the community, he theorized, were bound by natural laws and principles of justice; sovereignty, then, was not determined by supernatural or monotheistic sanctions alone. His concepts of sovereignty became an ethical foundation, as the class separations in communities were bound to mediate conscience and reason. Sovereignty is the nature of communities, and the modernist conceit is "limited sovereignty." The limitation of sovereignty is not sovereignty.

"Bodin himself preferred the monarchical body politic which was ruled legitimately," observes F. H. Hinsley in *Sovereignty.*

The "sovereign power" that "resided in a king but in which the royal wielder of sovereignty would give proper recognition" to the common "rights of his subjects and to the customary rules and basic laws of the body politic." Royal power would be limited and "exercised through institutions." As Hinsley notes, "Although the word 'sovereignty' had gained currency by the beginning of that century, Bodin in his *Six livres de la république* of 1576 was perhaps the first man to state the theory behind the word."

The "origin and history of the concept of sovereignty are closely linked with the nature, the origin and the history of the state," writes Hinsley. He would argue, it seems, that natives have neither a state nor sovereignty. The authority in stateless societies, he asserted, "relies on psychological and moral coercion rather than on force; if it resorts to force it does so because the rules and customs of the society demand this."[41]

Jean Bodin "is indeed among the first to stress the indivisibility of sovereignty and its function as a mark of the individuality of a state in legal terms, as 'the most high, absolute and perpetual power over the citizens and subjects of a Commonweale.' Sovereignty stands in a relation of mutual implication to the state; to be sovereign is to be sovereign *over* a state, and the state is dependent on a 'powerful sovereignty' as to its existence," writes Jens Bartelson in *A Genealogy of Sovereignty*.[42]

CONSTITUTIONAL PRONOUNS

Natives or *indians* are mentioned, and otherwise a presence named in consideration of territorial sovereignty, three times in the Constitution of the United States. Article I relates to taxes and excises and empowers the Congress "To regulate Commerce with foreign Nations, and among the several States, and with the Indian Tribes." And the two other notices refer to natives not being taxed on treaty land.

The Fourteenth Amendment provides that "Representatives shall be apportioned among the several States according to their respective numbers, counting the whole number of persons in each State, excluding Indians not taxed." That exclusion, in a sense, would become a measure of native sovereignty.

Constitutional theories are the manners of state dominance, a causal enervation of natural reason and native survivance; at the same time, however, treaties and the mention of a native presence in the nation have been the sources of conscience, ethics, and the recognition of inherent rights in later court decisions.

Native natural reason is not the same as the notion of natural laws; natural reason is transmotion, the stories of survivance and sovereignty. Native stories and the tease of creation are natural reason; the laws of nature suggest a creator, and that notion turns on monotheism and dominance.

The United States and native communities have entered into more than 380 treaties in the nineteenth century. Since then more than four thousand federal statutes have been enacted in the name of natives and their communities; these, and an uncertain number of judicial decisions, executive orders, institutive policies, and agency practices, are the intractable documents that overburden native memories, associations, and communities. At the same time, the treaties and other documents are the assurance of a native historical presence in a constitutional democracy.

The myths, ceremonies, treaties, narratives, documents, and statutes that have contributed to an obscure description of inherent sovereignty, and the concept of transmotion, are diverse and touch on the tragic wisdom of native survivance. At the same time, even the relatively mundane considerations of native stories in national histories are diminished by the practices of metes and bounds and cadastral boundaries.

The theoretical considerations of native sovereignty are derived from many sources: treaties, natural reason, international law, constitutionalism, federal jurisdiction, common law principles of intergovernmental immunities, trusts, taxation, and reservation casinos. Moreover, court evidence, testimonies, and native stories, are crucial to the understanding and meaning of transmotion as sovereignty.

"References to sovereignty are multiplying today precisely because the concept is on the whole a useful and largely positive feature of modern international life," note Michael Fowler and Julie Bunck. "A cardinal virtual of the concept is that it allocates responsibility as well as authority. The concept of sovereignty helps to create stable expectations that distinguish the business of one state from that of another."[43]

Sovereignty as transmotion is not the same as the notions of indigenous treaty sovereignty; transmotion can be scorned and denied, but motion is never granted by a government. Motion is a natural human right that is not bound by borders. Sovereignty as transmotion is tacit, inherent, and not the common provisions of treaties with other governments. Treaties with natives were strategic, national documents, of course, and most treaties were transacted to remove natives at the close of colonial dominance, and the new conversions of a constitutional democracy. The "treaties had certain characteristics or elements that, although appearing paradoxical or even incompatible, did not cancel each other out but existed together in an anomalous whole," notes Francis Paul Prucha. "In their actions, whites frequently enough disregarded Indian rights, but both theoretically and in practice the treaties gave the Indians a protected existence."[44]

The notions of tacit sovereignty, and the political significance of treaties, are decided in courts as the contracts and documents of a constitutional democracy. The Constitution of the United States provides that the Congress shall have power to "regulate commerce with foreign nations, and among the several states, and with the Indian tribes." The President "shall have power, by and with the advice and consent of the Senate, to make treaties." Treaties, then, are not an absolute assurance of native sovereignty. For instance, the 1837 treaty stated that the *anishinaabe* would have the "privilege of hunting, fishing, and gathering the wild rice," but these provisions were "guaranteed to the Indians, during the pleasure of the President of the United States." That reserved constitutional power over the treaties with natives is a statement of treaty sovereignty. The power is over both people and territory. Sovereignty as transmotion is visionary. The motion is in natural reason, totemic stories, and other associations with humans and the earth; transmotion is survivance, not an absolute power over people or territories.

"Most Indian rights are lodged in promises made in treaties, agreements, executive orders, and federal statutes," writes Charles Wilkinson. "The Supreme Court made it clear in *Lone Wolf* v. *Hitchcock* in 1903 that Congress has the power unilaterally to break Indian treaties. It cannot be seriously questioned that the *Lone Wolf* rule is the law today and that it will remain the law. International treaties can be broken, and it is unlikely that Indian treaties would be placed on a higher plane."[45]

The Treaty of Medicine Lodge Creek provided that the Kiowa and Comanche Reservation could not be ceded without native approval as specified in the treaty. Congress, however, sold excess native land in violation of the treaty. Lone Wolf, a Kiowa, sued Ethan Allen Hitchcock, the Secretary of the Interior. "The Supreme Court declared that Congress had plenary authority over Indian relations and that it had power to pass laws abrogating treaty stipulations."[46] Prucha pointed out that after the "*Lone Wolf* decision the idea of requiring Indian consent for the disposition of their lands was largely discarded in regard to statutes as well as to agreements, and Congress unilaterally provided for the sale of surplus lands remaining after allotments had been completed."[47]

Prucha argued that the recognition and independence of the treaties "meant more to Indian groups than did their lands, and tribes eagerly sought treaties in order to gain political recognition and not just acquire the economic benefits that came from presents and from annuities paid for land."[48] Timewise, his observations are contestable; many native governments and organizations have acted to restore treaty land and to acquire new native property. Prucha, however, has touched on the critical and theoretical distinctions of native sovereignty as political recognition and power over territory.

"Historically, the tie between sovereignty and territory is undeniable, except perhaps among nomadic peoples. Yet there was a time when sovereignty was divided, when secular sovereignty and religious sovereignty, for example, were in different hands," writes Gidon Gottlieb in *Nation against State*. He considered sovereignty as two components: "sovereignty as power over people" and "as power over territory. A new space for nations would develop the concept of sovereignty over a people. Sovereignty over territory means final authority within a given territory." He points out that the "alternative to a territorially organized world is one in which there is no final authority of a territorial character or one in which there are no clear territorial boundaries."[49]

Clearly, the notions of native sovereignty must embrace more than mere reservation territory. Sovereignty as transmotion is tacit and visionary; these notions and other theories of sovereignty are critical in the consideration of native rights, and the recognition of those rights outside of reservations, and in urban area. "Mobility is built into the very essence of our nation," observes Alan Dowty. He argues that a "freer flow of people, goods, and ideas would increase pressure for changes within closed societies."[50] Moreover, these theories and practices of sovereignty, and the assertion of human rights as more than territorial representations, are critical concerns in international politics.

David Jacobson asserts that human rights are universal. "Every human being in every society is a carrier of such rights. They do not change with geography, culture, or stage of development, and they do not distinguish between race, class, sex, religion, or national origins," he writes in *Rights across Borders.*[51] Human rights are positive rights.

"The rise of collective humanitarian intervention and the shrinking of traditional conceptions of sovereignty and domestic jurisdiction are essential for the preservation of peace in the new international order," writes Fernando Tesón in *Beyond Sovereignty.* The critical connections are human rights, the "concept of exclusive domestic jurisdiction," and the "collective intervention" of the United Nations Security Council. These are suitable considerations of native human rights, treaties, and sovereignty.

Tesón points out that "if we lose the battle for democracy and human rights, we necessarily lose the battle for peace and security. The lesson is, perhaps, that the gradual dilution of state sovereignty is not just one more historic phenomenon, one more stage in the unfolding of the blind laws of history over which we lack control. It is, rather, a moral imperative."[52]

The United States Supreme Court ruled in *Cherokee Nation* v. *Georgia,* 1831: "Though the Indians are acknowledged to have an unquestionable, and, heretofore, unquestioned right to the lands they occupy, until that right shall be extinguished by a voluntary cession to our government; yet it may well be doubted whether those tribes which reside within the acknowledged boundaries of the United States can, with strict accuracy, be denominated foreign nations. They may, more correctly, perhaps, be denominated domestic dependent nations." This opinion is consideration of a native sovereignty that has never been surrendered by treaty or statute. Chief Justice John Marshall wrote that "the relations of the Indians to the United States is marked by peculiar and cardinal distinctions which exist no where else." Moreover, the relation of natives "to the United States resembles that of a ward to his guardian."[53]

Most of the treaties with natives were executed by the federal government as a consequence of the resolution of the contention over state and federal sovereignty. There were serious debates over the future sovereignty of each state during the Constitutional

Convention. How would the sovereignty of the states be reserved in a confederation by form, but with no substance? "We the People of the United States," and other themes of indivisible federal sovereignty, were received in some editorials at the time as the certain end of state sovereignty.

On October 17, 1787, Noah Webster, "A Citizen of America," wrote that if the "federal constitution has collected into the federal legislature no more power than is necessary for the *common defence and interest,* it should be recognized by the states." Webster asserted that the "states have very high ideas of their separate sovereignty; altho' it is certain, that while each exists in its full latitude, we can have no *Federal Sovereignty.* However flattered each state may be by its independent sovereignty, we can have no union, no respectability, no national character, and what is more, no national justice, till the states resign to one *supreme head* the exclusive power of *legislating, judging* and *executing,* in all matters of a general nature."[54] His examination of the proposed constitution would, in the oblique traces of histories, embrace native sovereignty as a measure of national justice. A federation of sovereign states might not have negotiated treaties with natives. The federal treaties, in spite of treacheries, are the undeniable documents of a native presence in a constitutional democracy. At the same time, however, the federal government established a military to *control* natives on the frontiers.

Natives were the others, outside of monotheistic civilization and the national debates over state and federal sovereignty; despite the manifest of dominance, the notion of inherent native rights has continued as a sense of treaty sovereignty. This, of course, was an unintended consequence of national justice in a constitutional democracy.

"The assertion of national sovereignty by the theory of the extended republic gave a new normative status to the exercise of the powers of the federal government, freeing these powers from any state veto and making them superior to any contravention by state action," writes Samuel Beer in *To Make a Nation.* He points out that national "sovereignty also legitimated the exercise of these powers directly over individuals."[55] National sovereignty, not the care of the states, would determine the exercise of authority over natives and their treaties.

Benjamin Franklin, at the conclusion of the Constitutional Convention in Philadelphia on September 17, 1787, wrote that he agreed to the "Constitution, with all its Faults, if they are such, because I think a General Government necessary for us, and there is no *Form* of Government but what may be a Blessing to the People if well administered; and I believe farther that this is likely to be well administered for a Course of Years, and can only end in Despotism as other Forms have done before it, when the People shall become so corrupted as to need Despotic Government, being incapable of any other."[56]

Natives might have heard, twelve years earlier, the stories of his clever overtures of constitutional unanimity. The Continental Congress created three regional departments of *indian* affairs on July 12, 1775, and named several commissioners to represent the united colonies. The "commissioners were to work to preserve peace and friendship with the Indians and, in a quaint understatement, 'to prevent their taking any part in the present commotions.' The appointment of Benjamin Franklin, Patrick Henry, and James Wilson for the middle department indicates the importance attached to the matter." The commissioners held numerous councils with native nations, "tested the attitude" of natives, "picked suitable spots for meetings, called the chiefs and warriors to the councils, arranged for presents," and other duties. Franklin proposed to the confederation that "no colony could engage in offensive war against the Indians without the consent of Congress," and, "a perpetual alliance, both offensive and defensive, should be made with the Six Nations. For them, as well as for all other tribes, boundaries should be drawn, their land protected against encroachments, and no purchases of land made except by contract drawn between the great council of the Indians and the Congress." Federal agents were named to "prevent injustices in the trade." However, this "centralized control of Indian affairs did not appeal to all the states," asserts Prucha. There was native resistance, but the necessity of a federal authority prevailed.[57]

James Madison, the political theorist, observed contradictions in the "regulation of commerce" with native communities, "and how the trade with Indians, though not members of a State, yet residing within its legislative jurisdiction, can be regulated by an external authority, without so far intruding on the internal rights of legislation, is absolutely incomprehensible. This is not the only case in which the articles of confederation have inconsiderately endeavored to accomplish impossibilities; to reconcile a partial sovereignty in the Union, with compleat sovereignty in the States;

to subvert a mathematical axiom, by taking away a part, and letting the whole remain."[58] Madison anticipated, in a sense, the current constitutional debates over federal, state, and native sovereignty in connection with reservation casinos and many other controversial issues of native and state jurisdiction.

The deliberations at the convention over the power to make treaties "did not mention Indian treaties specifically, but the power of states to make any treaties was repeatedly denied," notes Prucha. "As a further protection against state usurpation, the convention declared federal laws and treaties superior to those of the states."[59]

Madison wrote to George Nichols that the new government "will be able to take the requisite measures for getting into our hands the Western posts which will not cease to instigate the Savages, as long as they remain in British hands. It is said that the Southern Indians are encouraged and armed by the Spaniards for like incursions on that side. A respectable Government would have equal effect in putting an end to that evil."[60]

President James Madison, two decades later, named Albert Gallatin, Henry Clay, and John Quincy Adams as special peace commissioners to negotiate an end to the War of 1812. The British, as an early strategy, "made it a sine qua non that its Indian allies be parties to the peace and have their boundaries recognized. It might be best, the instructions added, to create an independent Indian state between Canada and the United States," writes Bradford Perkins in *The Cambridge History of American Foreign Relations*. The "British commissioners at Ghent elevated the buffer state proposal into a sine qua non, even led their superiors to believe the Americans might accept it. When London came to realize that the Americans would break off negotiations rather than agree, the ministry backed off." Gallatin learned that the "buffer state idea was only a proposal for discussion—which of course meant that it was no longer discussed."[61] The negotiators were strategic and evermore devious in their cause of peace. The natives were never "parties to the peace" and would never realize an autonomous state; even the sense of aboriginal title to native territory was uncertain by dominance.

The Treaty of Ghent provided for the restoration of captured territories, and the United States promised to restore the same to natives. Many natives were destitute, abandoned to the maneuvers and wiles of war, peace, and territorial politics. Native resistance, and later the negotiation over treaties, would become the stories of survivance.

Native sovereignty, the notion of transmotion, and the sense of territorial reciprocity are not powers that were delegated by the federal government or by any other agency; rather, the sovereignty of transmotion is a native presence. This tacit sovereignty has been described as a doctrine of limited sovereignty, or the "reserved rights" doctrine, and has never been surrendered or extinguished by natives in treaties.

"Indian Affairs were at first seen as a domestic problem, equal to and linked with the problems of war debts, western land claims, orderly expansion, and so on," writes Dorothy Jones in *License for Empire*. "It was only after the repeated failure of attempts to handle Indian affairs as a domestic problem that United States officials were forced to consider relations *with* the Indians, rather than a unilateral policy *for* the Indians."[62] The basis of the relations with natives shifted from the "domestic to the diplomatic," and the treaty system became a new social order in native histories.

Indian Tribes as Sovereign Governments, a sourcebook on tribal laws and policy, notes that the "Supreme Court has found that tribal governments are 'unique aggregations possessing attributes of sovereignty over both their members and their territory.' Powers not limited by federal statute, by treaty, by restraints implicit in the protectorate relationship or by inconsistency with their status remain with tribal governments or reservation communities." Felix Cohen points out in the *Handbook of Federal Indian Law* that the powers of Indian tribes are, in general, "inherent powers of a limited sovereignty which has never been extinguished."[63] Certain powers over jurisdiction, however, have been limited by federal statutes, and agency policies in the past century.

This doctrine, a recognition of native sovereignty and power was first stated by Chief Justice John Marshall in *Worcester v. Georgia*, 1832. The argument was over the authority of the state to impose state laws on the Cherokee Nation.

The Indian nations had always been considered as distinct, independent political communities, retaining their original rights, as the undisputed possessors of the soil, from time immemorial, with the single exception of that imposed by irresistible power, which excluded them from intercourse with any other European potentate than the first discoverer of the coast of the particular region claimed. . . . The words "treaty" and "nation" are words of our own language, selected in our diplomatic and legislative proceedings, by ourselves, having each a definite and well understood meaning. We have applied them to Indians, as we have applied them to the other nations of the earth. They are applied to all in the same sense. . . .

The treaties and laws of the United States contemplate the Indian territory as completely separated from that of the states; and provide that all intercourse with them shall be carried on exclusively by the government of the union.[64]

President Andrew Jackson held to the conception of unitary sovereignty and state authority over natives, observed Robert Burt in *The Constitution in Conflict.* "Jackson's predecessors in office had a markedly different conception of the relationship of states and Indian tribes; this conception was the basis for John Marshall's ruling in *Worcester* v. *Georgia,* that states had no authority to extend their jurisdiction over Indian tribes and that such measures were inconsistent with federal treaties. Jackson's avowal that he 'has not the authority to prevent' state exercise of territorial jurisdiction was thus apparently disingenuous."[65]

The notions of unitary sovereignty, the practical and political powers of the states, indivisible national sovereignty, and federal authority, native sovereignty, and treaty rights have motivated the consideration of many theories on political power, and the rights of territorial dominion, but the contention over state jurisdiction and native sovereignty can never be decisively resolved in theories or court decisions.

The Eleventh Amendment to the Constitution, for instance, restricts the right to initiate suits against the states. Recently, a native government sued the state to negotiate an agreement to establish a casino in Florida. The Supreme Court ruled in *Seminole Tribe* v. *Florida* that a provision of the "Indian Gaming Regulatory Act was an unconstitutional incursion on state sovereignty."

Justice David Souter "attacked the majority opinion on both broad theoretical grounds and specific legal analysis," reported Linda Greenhouse in the *New York Times.* The Constitution, he said, "demonstrated that state governments were subject to a superior regime of law in a judicial system established, not by the state, but by the people through a specific delegation of their sovereign power to a national government that was paramount within its delegated sphere."[66]

Jurisdictional issues and state immunities to lawsuits are continuous contentions of state and native sovereignty; in this case
the issues are casino gambling on a reservation and the provisions
of federal legislation. The Indian Gaming Regulatory Act recog-
nizes that native governments have the "exclusive right to regulate
gaming" on reservations if such activities are not prohibited or in
violation of state or federal laws. The new law established three
classes of native gaming: the first, traditional native games; the
second, games such as bingo, lotto, and pulltabs; the third and
most controversial of the three includes lotteries, slot machines,
blackjack, and other casino games. The new regulations require
that natives negotiate an agreement with the state government to
present the third class of casino games. Florida refused to negotiate
with the Seminoles.

The Indian Gaming Regulatory Act is an invitation to casino
riches and the enervation of native sovereignty in competition
with the constitutional sovereignty of the states. The Red Lake
Band of Chippewa Indians in Minnesota and the Mescalero
Apache Tribe in New Mexico have sued agencies of the federal
government to declare the new gaming laws unconstitutional
and to prohibit the appointment of the National Indian Gaming
Commission. The essential issues in these suits are native rights
and sovereignty.

The contention over state and native sovereignty is historical
and constitutional; the case of jurisdiction is state, native, and
federal. The first states, had there been a fedcration of unitary
sovereignty, might not have sustained the cause or national diplomatic nature to negotiate treaties with natives. Treaties with natives
would not have had the same political value to the states, since
natives might have been removed without treaties.

Native casinos, state immunities to lawsuits, taxation, probate
on reservations, and other recent court actions on federal, state,
and native jurisdiction demonstrate the eternal contention over
the notions, statements, courses, and practices of sovereignty, as
constitutional matters; contention that must be considered and
decided in the Supreme Court.

The "We" in "We, the people of the United States," is not the
foremost pronoun of a native presence on this continent. The
measure of that national pronoun would not cover natives as
constitutional citizens for more than a century.

The Fourteenth Amendment to the Constitution provides that "All persons born or naturalized in the United States, and subject to the jurisdiction thereof, are citizens of the United States and of the State wherein they reside. No State shall make or enforce any law which shall abridge the privileges or immunities of citizens of the United States; nor shall any State deprive any person of life, liberty, or property, without due process of law; nor deny to any person within its jurisdiction the equal protection of the laws." Natives in traditional communities and on reservations were not embraced by this constitutional provision for more than a century; moreover, as natives were not respected as citizens, their constitutional rights were denied by state governments.

Citizens are so at birth, and others "achieve citizenship" by naturalization. Edward Corwin points out in *The Constitution* that the category of citizens at birth "derives from the principle of *jus soli* ("the law of the soil") of the English common law." The second notion of citizens at birth, "owe their citizenship to Congressional legislation which applies the *jus sanguinis* ("the law of blood relationship") of the Roman civil law, and embraces with certain qualifications persons born outside the United States and its outlying possessions to parents one or both of whom are citizens of the United States."[67] Clearly, natives are the embodiment of the common law principle of jus soli, and jus sanguinis, as the foundational family histories of the continent. Yet, natives were not named citizens of the nation until the twentieth century.

Article IV of the Constitution provides that the "Citizens of each State shall be entitled to all privileges and immunities of citizens in the several States." Most natives on reservations were denied this provision; federal *indian* agents authorized natives to travel outside the reservations.

The Indian Citizenship Act of 1924 provided that "Indians born within the territorial limits of the United States be, and they are hereby, declared to be citizens of the United States."[68] Some natives had been granted citizenship earlier in connection with devious land allotments, military service, residence outside of the reservation, marriage, and by other means; however, the enactment of a distinct citizenship act reveals the previous separation and the absence of constitutional rights on reservations.

The Preamble is not constitutional, and by "itself alone it can afford no basis for a claim either of governmental power or of private right."[69] That pronoun, however, is a source of justice and unity in a constitutional democracy. "We, the people," is a generous, common pronoun, and a mighty promise.

The promise of that plural pronoun is not passive, but an active obligation to be *the* people of this nation; the *we*, as natives of this continent, are the presence, transmotion, and stories of survivance.

We, the natives of this continent, are the storiers of presence, and we actuate the observance of natural reason and transmotion in this constitutional democracy.

Notes

1. The Chinese Monkey King, or mind monkey, is a tricky character in traditional stories. The *anishinaabe* trickster *naanabozho* is an elusive, native conversion in ironic oral stories. The Chippewa, Ojibway, and variations on those names, are the *anishinaabe*. The mind monkey and the mind trickster are related in their tease of creation.
2. Anthony C. Yu, trans. and ed., *The Journey to the West* (Chicago: Univ. of Chicago Press, 1977). *Hsi-yu Chi*, one of the classics of Chinese literature, was first published in 1592. See also *Monkey*, trans. Arthur Waley (New York: Grove, 1958). *Journey to the West*, translated by W. J. F. Jenner, was published by the People's Republic of China (Beijing: Foreign Languages Press, 1982).
3. James J. Y. Liu, *Essentials of Chinese Literary Art* (Belmont CA: Duxbury Press, 1979), 85, 86, 88. "Chinese dramatists do not think in terms of 'tragedy' and 'comedy,' but, like Chinese novelists, often mixed the serious with the lighthearted, the happy with the sad, the high with the low. This has caused some embarrassment to modern scholars and critics. In particular, much ink has been spilled over the questions whether there is true tragedy in Chinese, and if not, why not." Similar questions have been asked about whether there is a true sense of tragedy in native stories. Tragedy, of course, is a monotheistic creation; tragedy, in this sense, is a paradox, because salvation is tragedy deferred, and that must be the greatest of tragedies because there is never closure but rather the promise of a truer, wiser moment of eternal solace. The "characters in nonrepresentational drama are embodiments of human experience or qualities, rather than portraits of individuals." Similarly, native trickster stories are the embodiment, not the reality, of a character.
4. Bonnie S. McDougall, author and ed., "Writers and Performers, Their Work, and Their Audiences in the First Three Decades," *Popular Chinese Literature and Performing Arts in the People's Republic of China, 1949–1979* (Berkeley: Univ. of California Press, 1984), 271, 272, 273, 300, 302.
5. Merle Goldman, *Literary Dissent in Communist China* (New York: Atheneum, 1971), 278.

6. Feng Jicai, *Chrysanthemums and Other Stories* (New York: Harcourt Brace Jovanovich, 1985), 4, 5, 12, 13. Susan Wilf Chen translated the stories and wrote the introduction. Chen observes that the "controls on Chinese literature may be tightened without warning at any time. In the fall of 1983, a campaign was launched to purify Party ranks and to 'eradicate spiritual pollution.' Yang Hansheng, vice-chairman of the China Federation of Literary and Art Circles, stated this campaign's implications for the arts as follows: 'All our literary and art workers should adhere to the slogan of literature and art in the service of the people and of socialism, and to the socialist orientation of literature and art. But some writers and artists have shown themselves apathetic by their manifest lack of interest in writing about revolutionary history or the Four Modernizations; or by their fondness for love stories and the fabrication of bizarre, preposterous plots; or by concentrating on depressing, negative things; or by playing up abstract notions of 'the value of the human, humanism, or universal human nature,' and calling for a 'return of human nature,' etc.; or even by writing pornographic descriptions or propagating religion and feudalism." Chen noted that this statement appeared in *Renmin ribao*, Nov. 11, 1983.

Communist Party censors recently banned several authors in a "spiritual civilization" campaign. The *San Francisco Chronicle* reported on Feb. 4, 1997, that the novels of Wang Shou and Mo Yan were banned by the government. "Wang's sardonic works feature rogues, robbers, the disaffected on the margins of Chinese society who don't fit the conservative Communist ideal. Mo Yan, author of *Ample Breasts, Fat Buttocks*, also has been singled out for criticism." President Jiang Zemin and Ding Guangen, the head of propaganda, "ordered artists and writers to demonstrate their loyalty by adhering to the party line." The Communist Party "would not relax its control over the arts."

7. Gerald Vizenor, *Griever: An American Monkey King in China* (Normal: Illinois State University/Fictive Collective, 1987; reprint, Minneapolis: Univ. of Minnesota Press, 1990), 109, 110 (page citations are to the reprint edition). *Griever* won the Fiction Collective Award in 1986, the American Book Award in 1988, and was first published by Illinois State University Press, Normal, 1987. References to the Lazarist Sisters of Saint Vincent de Paul are from the *New Yorker*, May 17, 1982, a four-part article on Tianjin by John Hersey.

8. Tianjin is a city of more than seven million people, a port city on the Hai He River east of Beijing in the People's Republic of China. Tianjin, or Tientsin, was a colonial concessions city at the turn of the last century. John Hersey, who was born there, wrote about the city in the *New Yorker*, May 17, 1982. Laura Hall, my wife, and I were teachers at Tianjin University for one semester in 1983. That same year, we were present for the opening of Maxim's de Beijing on the same day as the thirty-fourth anniversary

of the founding of the People's Republic of China. Such experiences and contradictions were not uncommon in the nation. Tianjin, at the time we taught there, had invited only about fifty foreigners to work in the city. Communist Party officials would not allow me to contact the author Feng Jicai, who lived in Tianjin.

9. Jerzy Kosinski, *Being There* (New York: Bantam, 1972), 64, 90, 91, 92. Several of my colleagues, the other foreign teachers, were not surprised by the response of the censor. The cadre must have missed, or misread, page 64. "Though Chance prodded and massaged his organ, he felt nothing· even in the early morning, when he woke up and often found it somewhat enlarged, his organ refused to stiffen out: it gave him no pleasure at all." The censor must have read "organ" as a musical instrument.

10. Gerald Vizenor, *Bearheart: The Heirship Chronicles* (Minneapolis: Univ. of Minnesota Press, 1990), vii, 247.

11. Gerald Vizenor, *Darkness in Saint Louis Bearheart* (Saint Paul: Truck Press, 1978).

12. K. C. Chang, ed., *Food in Chinese Culture* (New Haven: Yale Univ. Press, 1977), 373.

13. Vizenor, *Bearheart*, xiii.

14. Louis Owens, afterword, *Bearheart*, 247, 248.

15. Gerald Vizenor, *Shadow Distance: A Gerald Vizenor Reader* (Hanover NH: Univ. Press of New England, Wesleyan Univ. Press, 1994).

16. Claudine Aguilera, "Freedom of Expression or Public Obscenity?" *Daily Californian*, University of California, Berkeley, Nov. 11, 1996.

17. Thomas Jefferson, "Letters," in *Thomas Jefferson* (New York: Library of America, 1984), 777, 778, 779, 915, 916.

18. Thomas Jefferson, "Notes on the State of Virginia," in *Thomas Jefferson*, 264, 265, 266.

19. I. Bernard Cohen, *Science and the Founding Fathers: Science in the Political Thought of Jefferson, Franklin, Adams, and Madison* (New York: W. W. Norton, 1995), 297, 298, 299.

20. Ernesto Che Guevara, *The Motorcycle Diaries*, trans. Ann Wright (London: Verso, 1995), 87, 88, 97, 119, 131, 148, 149.

21. Robert Burchfield, *Unlocking the English Language* (New York: Hill & Wang, 1991), 110, 111.

22. Gerald Vizenor, *The Everlasting Sky: New Voices of the People Named the Chippewa* (New York: Crowell-Collier, 1972). "Before you begin listening to the *oshki anishinaabe* speaking in this book, please write down a short definition of the word *indian*," I wrote in the introduction. "Your brief organization of thoughts about the word *indian* will help you understand the problems of identity among tribal people who are burdened with names invented by the dominant society."

23. John Nichols and Earl Nyholm, *A Concise Dictionary of Minnesota Ojibwe*

(Minneapolis: Univ. of Minnesota Press, 1995). The word *manidookaazo* means to "take on spiritual power by one's own authority."

24. R. R. Bishop Baraga, *A Dictionary of the Otchipwe Language* (Minneapolis: Ross & Haines, 1966; First published 1878).

25. Gerald Vizenor, *Manifest Manners* (Hanover NH: Univ. Press of New England, Wesleyan Univ. Press, 1994), 145.

26. Georges Bataille, *The Accursed Share*, 3 vols. (New York: Zone Books, 1991), book 2, 198, 202, 240, 241.

27. Charles A. Eastman, *Indian Boyhood* (New York: McClure, Phillips, 1902; reprint, with an introduction by David Reed Miller, Lincoln: Univ. of Nebraska Press, 1991), 3, 280, 288, 289. "What boy would not be an Indian for a while when he thinks of the freest life in the world? This life was mine. Every day there was a real hunt. There was real game," writes Eastman. "We were not only good mimics but we were close students of nature. We studied the habits of animals just as you study your books."

28. Frances Karttunen, *Between Worlds: Interpreters, Guides, and Survivors* (New Brunswick: Rutgers Univ. Press, 1994), 143.

29. Karttunen, *Between Worlds*, 151.

30. Mark Warren, *Nietzsche and Political Thought* (Cambridge: MIT Press, 1991), 196, 197.

31. Walter Kaufmann, ed. and trans., *Basic Writings of Nietzsche* (New York: Modern Library, 1992), 727, 728, 729.

32. Eastman, *Indian Boyhood*, 13, 14, 16, 17.

33. Anthony Paul Kerby, *Narrative and the Self* (Bloomington: Indiana Univ. Press, 1991), 4, 5, 45.

34. Francis Jacques, *Difference and Subjectivity* (New Haven: Yale Univ. Press, 1991), 175, 187. "The result is that we have begun to situate the self, which the whole Cartesian tradition has always regarded as an extralinguistic reality, within discourse."

35. Karttunen, *Between Worlds*, 139, 150.

36. Erik H. Erikson, *Identity: Youth and Crisis* (New York: W. W. Norton, 1968), 16, 17, 67.

37. Gerald Vizenor, *Crossbloods: Bone Courts, Bingo, and Other Reports* (Minneapolis: Univ. of Minnesota Press, 1990), 199, 200, 202, 203. "Senator Mondale at Rough Rock" was first published in the *Twin Citian* magazine, July 1969, and reprinted in the *Congressional Record*, Aug. 7, 1969.

38. Charles Taylor, *Multiculturalism and "The Politics of Recognition"* (Princeton: Princeton Univ. Press, 1992), 25, 32, 34.

CHAPTER 1. PENENATIVE RUMORS

1. Theodor W. Adorno, "The Essay as Form," in *Notes to Literature* (New York: Columbia Univ. Press, 1991), 1:11, 19, 20.

2. Richard Rorty, *Contingency, Irony, and Solidarity* (New York: Cambridge Univ. Press, 1989), 73.

3. Adorno, "The Essay as Form," 1:18, 19.

4. Michel Serres, "Panoptic Theory," in *The Limits of Theory*, ed. Thomas Kavanagh (Stanford: Stanford Univ. Press, 1989), 27, 44, 46. "Will the human sciences reabsorb the exact sciences as they did in antiquity?" asks Serres. "As they tell us of it in myth?" The same question could be asked about the "regressive burden" of mythic *indians*, those who have lived into the simulation of an absence as the real and now the "traditional" *indians* oppose both science and discourse, and the dialogic act of a second presence. How ironic that the *indian* could absorb the absence and presence, the very cause of surveillance, simulation, and dominance. The terminal myths of the "true" *indians* will be realized, no doubt, in an urban sweat lodge.

5. Hayden White, *The Content of the Form* (Baltimore: Johns Hopkins Univ. Press, 1987), 55, 57.

6. Mikhail Bakhtin, *Speech Genres and Other Late Essays*, ed. Caryl Emerson and Michael Holquist, trans. Vern W. McGee (Austin: Univ. of Texas Press, 1986), 170. See also Gary Saul Morson and Caryl Emerson, *Mikhail Bakhtin: Creation of a Prosaics* (Stanford: Stanford Univ. Press, 1990), 46.

7. Adorno, "The Essay as Form," 1:4, 5, 23.

8. Mikhail Bakhtin, *Art and Answerability*, ed. Michael Holquist and Vadim Liapunov (Austin: Univ. of Texas Press, 1990), 2, 126, 208.

9. Eric Gans, *Originary Thinking: Elements of Generative Anthropology* (Stanford: Stanford Univ. Press, 1993), 10, 218.

10. David Carroll, *Paraesthetics* (New York: Methuen, 1987), 159.

11. John Pizer, *Toward a Theory of Radical Origin: Essays on Modern German Thought* (Lincoln: Univ. of Nebraska Press, 1995), 3, 14, 15.

12. Jean Baudrillard, *Simulacra and Simulation* (Ann Arbor: Univ. of Michigan Press, 1994), 1, 2, 3. The condition is complicated "because simulating is not pretending: 'Whoever fakes an illness can simply stay in bed and make everyone believe he is ill. Whoever simulates an illness produces in himself some of the symptoms.' " Simulation is an irreference, while "dissimulating leaves the principle of reality intact: the difference is always clear, it is simply masked, whereas simulation threatens the difference between the 'true' and the 'false,' the 'real' and the 'imaginary.' " Indians are simulations, the symptoms of the real, but not a mask. Indian posers are the irreferences of a double other.

13. René Girard, *Job: The Victim of His People* (Stanford: Stanford Univ. Press, 1987), 102, 103.

14. Vizenor, *Manifest Manners*, 168.

15. René Girard, *The Scapegoat* (Baltimore: Johns Hopkins Univ. Press, 1986), 84, 85. The trickster is a transformational character that teases representations and liberates the mind in stories.

16. Jarold Ramsey, *Reading the Fire* (Lincoln: Univ. of Nebraska Press, 1983), 27, 42. Tricksters "are overcharged with biological energy." They try anything, as the "casual supererogatory transformations of parts of their bodies into foodstuffs for the sustenance of the people to come." Tricksters are "unkillable. They may suffer bad luck or just retribution in the form of starvation, poisoning, dismemberment, ingestion by monsters, incineration, drowning, fatal falls, and so on," but "they revive. . . . and go blithely on their way. They are mythic survivors."

17. Gerald Vizenor, *Dead Voices* (Norman: Univ. of Oklahoma Press, 1992), 136, 137.

18. Will Wright, *Wild Knowledge* (Minneapolis: Univ. of Minnesota Press, 1992), 3, 5, 15, 21.

19. René Girard, *Violence and the Sacred* (Baltimore: Johns Hopkins Univ. Press, 1977), 51.

20. Girard, *Scapegoat*, 21.

21. René Girard, *A Theater of Envy* (New York: Oxford Univ. Press, 1991), 209.

22. Andrew J. McKenna, *Violence and Difference* (Urbana: Univ. of Illinois Press, 1992), 30, 53.

23. René Girard, "Generative Scapegoating," in *Violent Origins: Ritual Killing and Cultural Formation*, ed. Robert Hamerton-Kelly (Stanford: Stanford Univ. Press, 1987), 74.

"The *pars pro toto* principle, accepting the small loss in order to save the whole, is even more efficacious in group dynamics," writes Walter Burkert in *Creation of the Sacred* (Cambridge: Harvard Univ. Press, 1996), 51.

24. Girard, *Job*, 62, 63, 75, 112. "The system consists of whitening the community by blackening the scapegoat; to consolidate it, the belief in this mythic blackness must be strengthened. The most effective means, obviously, is the victim's confession, in due and proper form." Job, and in other narratives and historical contexts, *indians*, must announce their "infamy, proclaiming it loudly and convincingly." Such public statements were made at mission schools, at treaty conferences, and in many government documents.

25. Aristotle, *Poetics*, vol. 12 of *The Complete Works of Aristotle*, ed. Jonathan Barnes, Bollingen Series (Princeton: Princeton Univ. Press, 1984), 2320, 2323, 2325 (1450a16, 1452a2, 1452b31–1453a11).

26. Tobin Siebers, *The Ethics of Criticism* (Ithaca: Cornell Univ. Press, 1988), 21.

27. Paul Woodruff, "Aristotle on *Mimesis*," in *Essays on Aristotle's Poetics*, ed. Amélie Oksenberg Rorty (Princeton: Princeton Univ. Press, 1992), 82, 88.

28. George Steiner, "The Art of Criticism 2," interview, *Paris Review* (winter 1995): 58.

29. Jacques Derrida, "*Différance*," in *A Derrida Reader: Between the Lines*, ed. Peggy Kamuf (New York: Columbia Univ. Press, 1991), 70, 74. In *Positions* (Chicago: Univ. of Chicago Press, 1981), 27, Derrida defines "*différance*"

as the "systematic play of differences, of the traces of differences, of the *spacing* by means of which elements are related to each other."

30. Tobin Siebers, *The Ethics of Criticism* (Ithaca: Cornell Univ. Press, 1988), 71, 82, 83, 98.

31. Brook Thomas, *The New Historicism* (Princeton: Princeton Univ. Press, 1991), 10, 12, 13.

32. Noam Chomsky, *Language and Thought* (Wakefield RI: Moyer Bell, 1993), 45.

33. Leonard Bloomfield, *Eastern Ojibwa* (Ann Arbor: Univ. of Michigan Press, 1957), 32, 34, 130. Ojibwa, Ojibway, Ojibwe, Chippewa, *anishinaabe*, and *anishinaabeg*, the plural, are names of the same language. Bloomfield based his studies on *anishinaabe* spoken on Walpole Island, Ontario. "When both actor and object are animate third persons, one of the two is obviative. There is at least one form where both actor and object are obviative: *waùpemaùnit* 'if the other sees still another.' " David Crystal notes the obviative in *The Encyclopedic Dictionary of Language and Languages* (Oxford: Blackwell, 1992), and in *The Cambridge Encyclopedia of Language* (New York: Cambridge Univ. Press, 1987). There is no reference to the obviative or fourth person in Nichols and Nyholm, *A Concise Dictionary of Minnesota Ojibwe*.

34. Vladimir Nabokov, *Speak, Memory: An Autobiography Revisited*, in *Vladimir Nabokov: Novels and Memoirs, 1941–1951* (New York: Library of America, 1996), 503.

35. Vladimir Alexandrov, *Nabokov's Otherworlds* (Princeton: Princeton Univ. Press, 1991), 32, 33.

36. Carol Vogel, "Americana (and Some Surprises) at Winter Antiques Show," *New York Times*, Jan. 17, 1996. Two dealers presented native artifacts for sale at the Winter Antiques Show. A ghost dance dress from 1890, "made from deer hide colored with yellow ocher and decorated with vermillion stars, half-moons and pipes," was offered at $250,000. The blanket on display was from "the collection of John Wesley Powell, founder of the Smithsonian: a Ute-style Navajo chief's blanket circa 1820–1840 made of hand-spun wool." The blanket was priced at $550,000.

37. Jürgen Habermas, *The Philosophical Discourse of Modernity* (Cambridge: MIT Press, 1987), 114, 115, 322.

38. Danilo Kis, *Homo Poeticus: Essays and Interviews* (New York: Farrar, Straus & Giroux, 1995), 17, 18. See also Seamus Deane, introduction, *Nationalism, Colonialism, and Literature* (Minneapolis: Univ. of Minnesota Press, 1990), 8.

39. David Couzens Hoy, *The Critical Circle: Literature, History, and Philosophical Hermeneutics* (Berkeley: Univ. of California Press, 1978), 38, 39, 40, 41.

40. Maurice Blanchot, *The Work of Fire* (Stanford: Stanford Univ. Press, 1995), 22, 23.

41. D. H. Lawrence, *Studies in Classic American Literature* (New York: Penguin, 1923), 40, 41, 42.
42. Vizenor, *Manifest Manners*, 25.
43. Jean Baudrillard, *Fatal Strategies*, in *Jean Baudrillard: Selected Writings*, ed. Mark Poster (Stanford: Stanford Univ. Press, 1988), 187, 200.
44. Gerald Vizenor, "Departing from the Present," editorial essay, *Minneapolis Tribune*, April 1974; reprinted in Gerald Vizenor, *Crossbloods: Bone Courts, Bingo, and Other Reports*, (Minneapolis: Univ. of Minnesota Press, 1990), 275–78. McGaa and Harkins lectured at a public forum sponsored by the Minnesota Humanities Commission.
45. Vizenor, *Crossbloods*, xiv, xv, 193, 194, 195. The *St. Paul Pioneer Press Dispatch* reported on Jan. 4, 1987, that Banks borrowed money from the tribal council on Pine Ridge to establish his company, Loneman Industries. Recently his autobiography was published in Japan.
46. Baudrillard, *Jean Baudrillard*, ed. Poster, 198, 201, 202.
47. John E. Mack, *Abduction: Human Encounters with Aliens* (New York: Charles Scribner's Sons, 1994), 2, 4, 5.
48. Mack, *Abduction*, 396, 398, 399.
49. Fanny Kelly, *My Captivity among the Sioux Indians* (1871 with original illustrations; reprint, New York: Carol Publishing Group, 1993), v, 52, 53, 212. Kelly was captured on July 12, 1864, two years after the "horrible massacres in Minnesota in 1862." She was released five months later at Fort Sully in Dakota Territory.
50. Richard VanDerBeets, *The Indian Captivity Narrative* (Lanham MD: Univ. Press of America, 1984), x, 50. The archetypal journey—abduction and separation, ordeal and transformation, and escape, return, or redemption —is structural.
51. C. G. Jung, *Flying Saucers: A Modern Myth of Things Seen in the Skies* (London: Routledge & Kegan Paul, 1959), 1, 2, 5.
52. C. D. B. Bryan, *Close Encounters of the Fourth Kind* (New York: Penguin Arkana, 1996), 9, 28, 446.
53. Mack, *Abduction*, 43.
54. Budd Hopkins, *Intruders* (New York: Random House, 1987), 105, 202. See also David Jacobs, *Secret Life* (New York: Simon & Schuster, 1992).
55. William Jones cited in Ruth Landes, *Ojibwa Religion and the Midewiwin* (Madison: Univ. of Wisconsin Press, 1968), 227, 228. See also Selwyn Dewdney and Kenneth Kidd, *Indian Rock Paintings of the Great Lakes* (Toronto: Univ. of Toronto Press, 1962), 20.
56. Hopkins, *Intruders*, 194.
57. Jules Zanger, introduction to Kelly, *My Captivity among the Sioux Indians*, v, vi.
58. Jung, *Flying Saucers*, 14, 16, 21, 22.
59. Marlita A. Reddy, ed., *Statistical Record of Native North Americans* (Detroit: Gale Research, 1993), 5. The U.S. Census of 1890 asked "American

Indians" about native languages, whether the "tribe is increasing or decreasing," the number of "Negroes, mulattos, quadroons, octoroons with the tribe," the tribe of the individual and parents, and the "proportions of Indian or other blood." The census of 1900 and 1910 asked nearly the same questions about the tribe of the individual, parents, and proportions of blood as the past enumeration. However, these questions were not asked again on the census until 1950. The census of 1950 also asked about the ability to read, write, and speak English, and the "ability to read any language other than English."

60. Jacques Derrida, *Archive Fever* (Chicago: Univ. of Chicago Press, 1996), 2, 3, 7, 80, 89, 90.

61. Reddy, *Statistical Record*, 5, 13, 233. The 1930 census reported 332,397 *indians* in the nation; the actual number was higher, since many natives were not counted in native communities. My father and his generation were the beginning of a White Earth Reservation diaspora.

62. Michel Foucault, *The Archaeology of Knowledge* (New York: Pantheon, 1972), 216, 218, 219.

63. Georges Bataille, *The Accursed Share* (New York: Zone Books, 1988), 1:67, 68, 72, 73.

64. Georges Bataille, *Visions of Excess* (Minneapolis: Univ. of Minnesota Press, 1985), 122, 123.

65. Gloria Cranmer Webster, "Kwakiutl," in *Encyclopedia of North American Indians*, ed. Frederick Hoxie (New York: Houghton Mifflin, 1996), 320, 321, 322. Webster is director of the U'mista Cultural Centre, Alert Bay, British Columbia.

66. Gerald Vizenor, *The People Named the Chippewa: Narrative Histories* (Minneapolis: Univ. of Minnesota Press, 1984), 75, 77.

67. David Patterson, *Literature and Spirit* (Lexington: Univ. Press of Kentucky, 1988), 22, 23.

68. Mikhail Bakhtin, *The Dialogic Imagination*, ed. Michael Holquist (Austin: Univ. of Texas Press, 1981) 236, 237.

69. Louis Owens, "Louis Owens," in *Contemporary Authors*, Autobiography Series, vol. 24 (New York: Gale Research, 1996), 288, 298; Louis Owens, "Motion of Fire and Form," in *Native American Literature*, ed. Gerald Vizenor (New York: HarperCollins College, 1995), 83.

70. Bataille, *Accursed Share*, 1:70, 76, 77.

71. Pierre Bourdieu, *The Logic of Practice* (Stanford: Stanford Univ. Press, 1990), 125, 126.

72. Michel Foucault, "The Subject and Power," in *Michel Foucault: Beyond Structuralism and Hermeneutics*, ed. Hubert Dreyfus and Paul Rabinow (Chicago: Univ. of Chicago Press, 1982), 30, 210, 211.

73. Marc Simmons, introduction, Robert Silverberg, *The Pueblo Revolt* (Lincoln: Univ. of Nebraska Press, 1970), v, 5. The Spanish returned to power in 1692.

74. Alvin H. Wilcox, *A Pioneer History of Becker County Minnesota* (St. Paul: Pioneer Press, 1907), 272, 273, 274; U.S. Congress, *Testimony in Relation to Affairs at the White Earth Reservation*, Senate Committee on Indian Affairs, March 8, 1887.

75. Gary Gutting, ed., *The Cambridge Companion to Foucault* (New York: Cambridge Univ. Press, 1994), 11, 12.

CHAPTER 2. WISTFUL ENVIES

1. Franz Kafka, *The Complete Stories* (New York: Schocken Books, 1983), xxi, 390. The story "The Wish to Be a Red Indian" was first published in *Meditation, Betrachtung* (Leipzig: Rowohlt Verlag, 1913). John Updike noted in the foreword, "Fantasy, for Kafka even more than for most writers of fiction, was the way out of his skin, so he could get back in." The Indian is the absence, the transcendence; simulations of the *other* are common sources of identities, even the causes of many native posers and impostors. "Kafka needs, and hopes for, too much from awareness," writes Paul Goodman in *Kafka's Prayer* (New York: Hillstone, 1947), 24. "Let us turn off that fierce light and go into good daylight." Thomas Mann, in "Homage" to *The Castle* (New York: Knopf, 1968), x, wrote that Kafka was "a religious humorist."

2. Maurice Blanchot, *The Work of Fire* (Stanford: Stanford Univ. Press, 1995), 13, 14, 17, 18, 25. Kafka trusted literature; for him, the right word, that sense of the right image, is a mythic presence in literature.

3. Edmond Jabès, *The Little Book of Unsuspected Subversions* (Stanford: Stanford Univ. Press, 1996), 48, 51, 66, 83. "Our absence from the world is perhaps nothing but our presence in the void," writes Jabès. "Identity is not so much apprehending a face as winning it over."

4. Jacques Derrida, *Writing and Difference* (Chicago: Univ. of Chicago Press, 1978), 64, 65, 68.

5. Edmond Jabès, *The Book of Questions* (Hanover NH: Univ. Press of New England, Wesleyan Univ. Press, 1991), 1:31, 32. Natives are the absence outside the book; the absence in the silence and separation of the social sciences. Natives are a presence in the book. Natives are the book, otherwise natives are without touch, "neither doubles nor opposites."

6. Derrida, *Writing and Difference*, 75, 76, 77. Jews and natives are the question, the presence of a question in the book, "that everything *belongs to the book*," as the book is first. The first natives, in this poetic sense, are in the book, and there are no other visions but the creation of the world in the book. The absence of the native is pronounced in the methods of cultural anthropology, and that is measured in the book, as the presence of natives and the other is in the book.

7. Kamuf, ed., *A Derrida Reader*, 19, 21.

8. Walter J. Ong, *Orality and Literacy* (New York: Methuen, 1982), 14, 15, 45, 46, 74, 75, 132, 133. See also Jacques Derrida, *Of Grammatology* (Baltimore: Johns Hopkins Univ. Press, 1976); Jack Goody, *The Domestication of the Savage Mind* (New York: Cambridge Univ. Press, 1977).

9. Jacques Derrida, *The Post Card* (Chicago: Univ. of Chicago Press, 1987), 469, 470, 472, 473.

10. John William Miller, *The Paradox of Cause and Other Essays* (New York: W. W. Norton, 1978), 15, 16. Natives would consider chance an element in the mysteries of nature. The Navajo would structure chance and cause differently in their language.

11. Kamuf, ed., *Derrida Reader*, 26, 27. In Derrida's interpretation, the trace of native oral stories is not absolute in the motion of survivance and sovereignty.

12. Jacques Derrida, *Positions* (Chicago: Univ. of Chicago Press, 1981), 8, 27.

13. Colin G. Calloway, ed., *Our Hearts Fell to the Ground: Plains Indian Views of How the West Was Lost* (Boston: Bedford Books, 1996), 196, 199. "The promise of a rejuvenated world had tremendous appeal to people who looked about them and saw poverty, chaos, and confusion. . . . As it had done with the Sun Dance and other religious ceremonies, the government moved to suppress the Ghost Dance." Casper Edson, like Luther Standing Bear, attended the Carlisle Indian School and returned to his native community. Many other native scholars returned as teachers, translators, and writers, the first generation of natives who had learned how to read and write English. Standing Bear wrote two books. The Ghost Dance vision was told in translation to thousands of natives by this first distinctive generation of scholars who had studied at mission and federal schools. Wovoka's message, transcribed by Edson in broken, boarding school English, was first published in James Mooney, *The Ghost-Dance Religion and the Sioux Outbreak of 1890* (Chicago: Univ. of Chicago Press, 1965).

14. John William Miller, *In Defense of the Psychological* (New York: W. W. Norton, 1983), 143.

15. Bakhtin, *Speech Genres*, 150. Contrary to the sense of victory in rhetoric, the destruction of the opponent in dialogue "also destroys that very dialogic sphere where the word lives," writes Bakhtin. Gary Saul Morson and Caryl Emerson point out in their introduction to *Rethinking Bakhtin* that "Bakhtin was to rethink this concept in dialogic terms as 'creative understanding.'" Tzvetan Todorov, in *Mikhail Bakhtin: The Dialogical Principle* (Minneapolis: Univ. of Minnesota Press, 1984), considers *dialogism* to be "loaded" with a "multiplicity of meanings" and therefore he uses the term "intertextuality," borrowed from Julia Kristeva. "Intertextuality belongs to discourse and not language, and therefore falls within the sphere of competence of translinguistics and not that of linguistics. However, not all relations between utterances are necessarily intertextual."

16. Bakhtin, *Speech Genres*, 141, 142.
17. Jamake Highwater, *The Primal Mind: Vision and Reality in Indian America* (New York: Harper & Row, 1981), xvi, xvii.
18. Jamake Highwater, "Second-Class Indians," *American Indian Journal* (July 1980): 9.
19. Jane Katz, ed., *This Song Remembers: Self-Portraits of Native Americans in the Arts* (Boston: Houghton Mifflin, 1980), 171, 176.
20. Vizenor, *Manifest Manners*, 13, 61, 62. See also Jack Anderson, "A Fabricated Indian?" (Universal Press Syndicate, 1984).
21. Jamake Highwater, *Shadow Show: An Autobiographical Insinuation* (New York: Alfred Van Der Marck Editions, 1986), 10, 11. "We must not feel guilty if we are among those who have managed to survive," writes Highwater. "I begin to think that our borrowed lives are necessities in a world filled with hostility and pain, a confusing world largely devoid of credible social truths. . . . The light by which we see is a mythic lantern." The trope is not magic, as the author simulated the lantern and the light. We "see" the ironies of his borrowed survival.
22. David Nyberg, *The Varnished Truth: Truth Telling and Deceiving in Ordinary Life* (Chicago: Univ. of Chicago Press, 1993), 220.
23. Terry Goldie, *Fear and Temptation: The Image of the Indigene in Canadian, Australian, and New Zealand Literatures* (Montreal: McGill-Queen's Univ. Press, 1989), 14, 37. The *indigène* is an indigenous native of a continent.
24. Russell Means, *Where White Men Fear to Tread* (New York: St. Martin's, 1995), 538, 539. Means, without any apparent sense of irony, points out that "Powwow Indians are Plains Indian wanna-bes, no different from New Agers who appropriate what is comfortable for them but won't live the lifestyle that created the trappings."
25. Richard White, "The Return of the Natives," review of *Where White Men Fear to Tread*, by Russell Means, the *New Republic*, July 8, 1996, 37, 38. Means "dreams of a treatment center on Pine Ridge, where therapy will be based on his people's traditional values. There he will help them overcome what he regards as one of their central problems: 'they think they don't deserve success, so each time they create circumstances to fail.'"
26. Michel Foucault, *The Archaeology of Knowledge and the Discourse on Language* (New York: Pantheon, 1972), 15, 183, 184.
27. Ian Hacking, *Rewriting the Soul: Multiple Personality and the Sciences of Memory* (Princeton: Princeton Univ. Press, 1995), 198, 199, 210, 211, 258, 259.
28. Daniel Schacter, *Searching for Memory* (New York: Basic, 1996), 52.
29. Christopher Shea, "A New Book Explores the Fragility of Memory," *Chronicle of Higher Education*, July 26, 1996. Schacter said artists "know something about memory that scientists have only recently taken seriously: It is not an objective record of lived experiences, but a delicate and malleable system, highly attuned to emotion."

30. Philip Hilts, "In Research Scans, Telltale Signs Sort False Memories from True," *New York Times*, July 2, 1996, B10. See also Sharon Begley, "You Must Remember This," *Newsweek*, July 15, 1996, 64.

31. Schacter, *Searching for Memory*, 17.

32. Jean Baudrillard, *Simulations* (New York: Semiotext(e), 1983), 2, 38.

33. Schacter, *Searching for Memory*, 252, 308.

34. Frank Stringfellow Jr., *The Meaning of Irony* (Albany: State Univ. of New York Press, 1994), 151.

35. Joseph Notterman, *Forms of Psychological Inquiry* (New York: Columbia Univ. Press, 1985), 169, 170.

36. Keith Jenkins, *On 'What Is History?'* (New York: Routledge, 1995), 6, 9, 15.

37. Hayden White, *Tropics of Discourse: Essays in Cultural Criticism* (Baltimore: Johns Hopkins Univ. Press, 1978), 81, 82. "What authority can historical accounts claim as contributions to a secured knowledge of reality in general and to the human sciences in particular?"

38. Vizenor, *Manifest Manners*, 64, 68, 72, 73.

39. Otto Rank, "Life and Creation," in *Literature and Psychoanalysis*, ed. Edith Kurzweil and William Phillips (New York: Columbia Univ. Press, 1983), 40, 41.

40. Tzvetan Todorov, *On Human Diversity* (Cambridge: Harvard Univ. Press, 1993), 91, 92, 93, 94, 96, 114.

41. John William Miller, *In Defense of the Psychological*, 159.

42. Charles Dickens, *American Notes* (New York: Random House, Modern Library Edition, 1966), 327.

43. Dickens, *American Notes*, 218.

44. Dickens, *American Notes*, 257, 258.

45. V. S. Pritchett, *Complete Collected Essays* (New York: Random House, 1991), 208.

46. Aleksandr Borisovich Lakier, *A Russian Looks at America* (Chicago: Univ. of Chicago Press, 1979), 192, 193, 194. Lakier explained that the "white man threw himself upon the books and therein lies the answer as to why he rules the world. The red man seized the hunting weapons and the black man was left with the agricultural tools. That is why the Indian considers the white higher than himself and thinks that he degrades himself in adopting agriculture and being like the Negro. To an Indian's way of thinking, to bind his labor to a lump of earth would mean to deprive himself of freedom." He traveled in the United States in 1857. His journal was published in Russia in 1859.

47. Dickens, *American Notes*, 211.

48. Giacomo Constantino Beltrami, *A Pilgrimage in Europe and America Leading to the Discovery of the Sources of the Mississippi and Bloody River* (London: Hunt & Clarke, 1828), 123, 124, 298, 299, 300. "I saw some of the Indians land yesterday from their canoes; I was surprised at their grotesque appearance; for being a little given to pyrrhonism, I had always

doubted the accounts I had read of them." However, he wrote, "I hope soon to see them more closely, and to observe the workings of their minds and the habits of their lives, and I shall then be able to judge better of them than by books." Indeed, and later he observed that on "viewing their various qualities, physical and moral in combination, they present a mass of contradictions sufficient, I conceive, to embarrass the judgment of the profoundest observer." Doubtless, he was very embarrassed, but not to the extent that he resisted the natives who allowed him to "discover" the sources of the rivers. "I will merely add, that the Indian, as long as he remains such, will ever be his own master and sovereign, and bear his independence proudly about him; but that as soon as he becomes civilized, he will be capable of being converted even into the vilest of slaves; that his heart is by its nature the seat of dissimulation and mischief, of inhumanity and cruelty, and that civilization will meet with powerful obstacles in the state or structure of his mind, and only with great difficulty be enabled to make him truly good."

49. Lakier, *A Russian Looks at America*, 145.

50. Alexis de Tocqueville, *Democracy in America*, trans. Francis Bowen (New York: Alfred A. Knopf, Everyman's Library, 1994), 23, 24. Martin Warnke writes about the "concept of natural giantism" in *Political Landscapes* (Cambridge: Harvard Univ. Press, 1995), 90, 93.

51. Robert E. Bieder, *Science Encounters the Indian, 1820–1880* (Norman: Univ. of Oklahoma Press), 109, 112.

52. William W. Warren, *History of the Ojibway Nation* (Minneapolis: Ross & Haines, 1957), 181, 182. Warren, the first *anishinaabe* historian, was born May 27, 1825, at La Pointe, Madeline Island, Lake Superior. He was an interpreter, elected as a member of the Minnesota Territorial Legislature. He died on June 1, 1853. His history was published by the Minnesota Historical Society in 1885. The crane totem, *ajijaak*, is also known as the "echo makers." The crane family are "numerous, and form an important element of the Ojibway tribe," he wrote more than a century ago. "They reside mostly on the south shores of Lake Superior and toward the east in the Canadas, though they have representatives scattered in every spot where the Ojibways have set foot and lighted their fires." The name "echo maker" is derived from the word *baswewe* in the language of the *anishinaabe* and pertains "to the loud, clear, and far reaching cry of the Crane. This clan are noted as possessing naturally a loud, ringing voice, and are acknowledged orators of the tribe."

53. Robert Berkhofer Jr., "The North American Frontier as Process and Context," in *The Frontier in History*, ed. Howard Lamar and Leonard Thompson (New Haven: Yale Univ. Press, 1981), 48, 49.

54. Henry F. Dobyns, *Native American Historical Demography* (Bloomington: Indiana Univ. Press, 1976), 1, 2.

55. Russell Thornton, *American Indian Holocaust and Survival* (Norman: Univ. of Oklahoma Press, 1987), 100, 101.

56. Francis Paul Prucha, *The Indians in American Society* (Berkeley: Univ. of California Press, 1985), 33, 34.

57. Dickens, *American Notes*, 217, 218.

58. Vine Deloria Jr., *Behind the Trail of Broken Treaties* (Austin: Univ. of Texas Press, 1985), 130, 131, 132.

59. W. David Baird, *Peter Pitchlynn: Chief of the Choctaws* (Norman: Univ. of Oklahoma Press, 1972) 19, 20.

60. Annie Heloise Abel, *The American Indian as Slaveholder and Secessionist* (Lincoln: Univ. of Nebraska Press, 1992), 75, 78, 79.

61. Dickens, *American Notes*, 219.

62. Roy Harvey Pearce, *Savagism and Civilization* (Berkeley: Univ. of California Press, 1988), 49, 104.

63. Dickens, *American Notes*, 302.

64. Baird, *Peter Pitchlynn*, 84. "With diminishing cotton profits and an increasing emphasis upon cattle, Peter had far too much invested in slaves in the late 1850's," notes Baird. "In fact, he never found slavery profitable unless he hired his Negroes out to others."

65. Dickens, *American Notes*, 219.

66. M. H. Dunlop, *Sixty Miles from Contentment: Traveling the Nineteenth-Century American Interior* (New York: Basic, 1995), 113.

67. Philip Kuberski, *The Persistence of Memory: Organism, Myth, Text* (Berkeley: Univ. of California Press, 1992), 131, 133. "So powerful was the break between oral cultures and literate cultures that even now we consider that history begins only when it can be found written on a scroll or graven on a wall," writes Kuberski.

68. David Glassberg, *American Historical Pageantry* (Chapel Hill: Univ. of North Carolina Press, 1990), 1, 4, 139, 140, 178, 179.

69. Sidner J. Larson, *Catch Colt* (Lincoln: Univ. of Nebraska Press, 1995), 10, 11, 158.

70. Jimmie Durham, "Those Dead Guys for a Hundred Years," in *I Tell You Now: Autobiographical Essays by Native American Writers*, ed. Brian Swann and Arnold Krupat (Lincoln: Univ. of Nebraska Press, 1987), 163.

71. Ward Churchill, *Indians Are Us? Culture and Genocide in Native North America* (Monroe ME: Common Courage Press, 1994), 89, 94, 98, 99, 287, 288, 289. He named Anna Mae Aquash, Leonard Peltier, and twelve others as *indians* with courage and integrity.

72. Jamake Highwater, "Second-Class Indians," 9.

73. Nichols and Nyholm, *A Concise Dictionary of Minnesota Ojibwe*, 47, 60. The *anishinaabe* have been named the Ojibwe, Ojibway, Chippewa, and Chippeway in English.

74. Warren, *History of the Ojibway Nation*, 72, 73. The *anishinaabe* words

gabekana and *giiwekana* appear in Nichols and Nyholm, *A Concise Dictionary of Minnesota Ojibwe.*

75. William Jones, cited in Ruth Landes, *Ojibwa Religion and the Midewiwin* (Madison: Univ. of Wisconsin Press, 1968), 190, 191. Jones also notes that "a person has as many as four souls." Some natives who sense when they are about to die may release one soul as an animal or bird.

76. Erich Fromm, *To Have or to Be?* (New York: Harper & Row, 1976), 21, 22, 81, 87, 99.

77. Henri-Jean Martin notes in *The History and Power of Writing* (Chicago: Univ. of Chicago Press, 1994), 27, that "cultures dominated by animism" were not "equipped to discriminate between the reality of the signified and the signifier. . . . Initially an instrument of power in the hands of small groups of priests, soothsayers, and scribes serving a deified monarch, writing was above all a means to domination and to the establishment of hierarchy, hence it was the expression of the ideology of a limited elite."

78. William E. Connolly, *Political Theory and Modernity* (Oxford: Basil Blackwell, 1988), 2, 3.

79. Arthur Kleinman and Joan Kleinman, "The Appeal of Experience; The Dismay of Images: Cultural Appropriations of Suffering in Our Times," *Daedalus*, special issue, "Social Suffering" (winter 1996): 2, 9, 10. "When those whose suffering is appropriated by the media cross over to places of refuge and safety, they often must submit to yet another type of arrogation," the authors note. The native is represented as the aesthetic *victime*, the persona of commodity sufferance; the arrogation of many authors.

80. Judith Lewis Herman, *Trauma and Recovery* (New York: Basic, 1992), 1, 53, 54, 177, 207. Many natives suffer "survivors guilt" over the stories and images of the massacres at Sand Creek and Wounded Knee.

81. Zygmunt Bauman, *Modernity and the Holocaust* (Ithaca: Cornell Univ. Press, 1991), 44, 45, 58.

82. Donald B. Smith, "From Sylvester Long to Buffalo Child Long Lance," introduction to *Long Lance*, by Chief Buffalo Child Long Lance (New York: Cosmopolitan Book, 1928; reprint, Jackson: Univ. Press of Mississippi, 1995), xii, xiii (page citations are to the reprint edition).

83. Donald B. Smith, *Long Lance: The True Story of an Imposter* (Lincoln: Univ. of Nebraska Press, 1982), 32, 33, 34.

84. Grey Owl, *The Men of the Last Frontier* (Toronto: Macmillan, 1931), 210, 211.

85. Smith, *Long Lance,* 170.

86. Bunny McBride, *Molly Spotted Elk: A Penobscot in Paris* (Norman: Univ. of Oklahoma Press, 1995), 103.

87. Smith, *Long Lance,* 145, 146, 147. "I am persuaded that *Hiawatha's* popularity resulted, at least in part, from the solace it provided in assuaging the American conscience," writes Michael Kammen in *Mystic Chords of*

Memory (New York: Knopf, 1991), 85. "Knowing and loving *Hiawatha* meant knowing the noble savage and perpetuating his traditions." Surely the simulations of natives are not sources of knowledge. Knowing and loving *Hiawatha* is a racialist celebration of the absence of natives, as the presence of natives has seldom been a source of knowledge.

88. Smith, *Long Lance*, 148.

89. Means, *Where White Mean Fear to Tread*, dust jacket copy.

90. Smith, *Long Lance*, 112, 148.

91. Smith, *Long Lance*, 209, 223, 228, 231.

92. Irv Letofsky, "City Man Who Said He Was Psychologist Allegedly Mis-represented Credentials," *Minneapolis Tribune*, May 16, 1974.

93. Letofsky, "City Man Who Said He Was Psychologist."

94. Gerald Vizenor, "Ralph Ware: Alleged Psychologist," editorial, *Minneapolis Tribune*, May 17, 1974. "Ralph Ware may not be a certified clinical psychologist, but as a group leader and community organizer with tribal people he is a trusted man with good humor," my editorial began. Ware, who considered the letters and documents of an investigation, told me that his academic credentials were true. He had, it seemed to me at the time, convinced himself that his pose was his actual presence. The audience that once honored that pose, however, would no longer sustain his presence. "It was tradition in some woodland tribal groups for individuals to declare their identities. If a large number of people believed it, then it was so until ridicule caused one to change." The native poses of absence are contingencies.

95. Washington Irving, "The Sketch Book of Geoffrey Crayon, Gent.," in *Washington Irving: History, Tales and Sketches* (New York: Library of America, 1983), 1002, 1005. The romance of the warrior is not unusual in literature, but here, and in other essays by Irving, the native is celebrated as a courageous individual and not yet constructed as the communal issue of sacred traditions.

96. John Joseph Mathews, *Sundown* (Norman: Univ. of Oklahoma Press, 1934), 303, 304.

97. Louis Owens, *Other Destinies* (Norman: Univ. of Oklahoma Press, 1992), 49, 50, 60.

98. Tobin Siebers, *The Ethics of Criticism* (Ithaca: Cornell Univ. Press, 1988), 139. Siebers discusses Friedrich Nietzsche's *Thus Spoke Zarathustra*.

99. Arnold Krupat, *Ethnocriticism: Ethnography, History, Literature* (Berkeley: Univ. of California Press, 1992), 216, 217.

100. Thomas McLaughlin, "Figurative Language," in *Critical Terms for Literary Study*, ed. Frank Lentricchia and Thomas McLaughlin (Chicago: Univ. of Chicago Press, 1995), 83, 84.

101. Gemma Corradi Fiumara, *The Metaphoric Process* (New York: Routledge, 1995), 11, 14.

102. White, *Tropics of Discourse*, 73.

103. Tropary is a *troper*, a book of tropes. *New Shorter Oxford English Dictionary* (1993).
104. Krupat, *Ethnocriticism*, 229, 230, 231.
105. Arnold Krupat, *The Voice in the Margin* (Berkeley: Univ. of California Press, 1989), 133, 134.
106. Mircea Eliade, *The Myth of the Eternal Return or, Cosmos and History* (Princeton: Princeton Univ. Press, 1954), xiii, 3, 46, 89, 95, 156.
107. Henry Leavitt Ellsworth, *Washington Irving on the Prairie* (New York: American Book Co., 1937), 5. This *Narrative of a Tour of the Southwest in the Year 1832* was edited by Stanley Williams and Barbara Simison. President Andrew Jackson appointed Ellsworth as one of three commissioners "to study the country, to mark the boundaries, to pacify the warring Indians, and, in general to establish order and justice" after "passage by Congress in 1830 of the Indian Removal Bill." Irving traveled with Ellsworth to Fort Gibson in 1832.
108. Washington Irving, *A Tour on the Prairies* (Norman: Univ. of Oklahoma Press, 1956), 21, 22.
109. Ellsworth, *Washington Irving on the Prairie*, 6.
110. Irving, *Tour on the Prairies*, 43, 44, 45.
111. Lee Clark Mitchell, *Witnesses to a Vanishing America* (Princeton: Princeton Univ. Press, 1981), xv, 25.
112. Glassberg, *American Historical Pageantry*, 142, 148.
113. W. S. Penn, *All My Sins Are Relatives* (Lincoln: Univ. of Nebraska Press, 1995), 53, 54, 55, 56, 57, 61. The creations, citations, and tropes of native identities are also "Indian" in his autobiographical narrative.
114. Patricia Penn Hilden, *When Nickels Were Indians: An Urban Mixed-Blood Story* (Washington: Smithsonian Institution Press, 1995), 18, 200, 201, 214.
115. Penn Hilden, *When Nickels Were Indians*, 214.
116. Terry Wilson, *The Underground Reservation: Osage Oil* (Lincoln: Univ. of Nebraska Press, 1985), 237. Wilson provided the author with a copy of the 1906 Approved Roll of Osage Indians in Oklahoma. Albert Penn, listed under the William Penn Band, received an allotment and roll number, but no date of birth or Degree of Indian Blood was entered in the certified roll of members (Department of the Interior, Office of Indian Affairs, 1921, 73).
117. Jonathan Culler, *In Pursuit of Signs: Semiotics, Literature, Deconstruction* (Ithaca: Cornell Univ. Press, 1981), 38, 39.
118. Donald M. Lowe, *History of Bourgeois Perception* (Chicago: Univ. of Chicago Press, 1982), 3, 4. The first person narrative voice is not heard in the book but is perceived as an inner voice; however, there is a romance of presence in such a narrative, and more so if the stories are native, a suggestion of oral stories.
119. Robert Smith, *Derrida and Autobiography* (Cambridge: Cambridge Univ. Press, 1995), 76, 77.

120. Forrest Carter, *The Education of Little Tree* (Albuquerque: Univ. of New Mexico Press, 1986), 5, 191, 192.
121. Forrest Carter, *Education of Little Tree*, 116.
122. Dan T. Carter, "The Transformation of a Klansman," *New York Times*, Oct. 4, 1991.
123. Felicia Lee, "Best Seller Is a Fake, Professor Asserts," *New York Times*, Oct. 4, 1991.
124. Rennard Strickland, "Sharing Little Tree," foreword to *Education of Little Tree*, by Forrest Carter, v, vi.
125. Henry Louis Gates Jr., " 'Authenticity,' or the Lesson of Little Tree," review of *The Education of Little Tree*, by Forrest Carter, *New York Times*, Nov. 24, 1991.
126. Franz Kafka, *Amerika*, trans. Willa Muir and Edwin Muir (1927; New York: Schocken Books, 1946), viii.
127. Albert Camus, "Hope and Absurdity," in *The Kafka Problem*, ed. Angel Flores (New York: Gordian Press, 1963), 267, 268. "The whole of Kafka's art consists in compelling the reader to re-read him," observes Camus. "His denouements, or their absence, suggest explanations, but explanations which are not clearly revealed and which require, in order to appear well founded, that the story be re-read from a new angle." Kafka and the absence of natives is that new angle.
128. John Urzidil, "The Oak and the Rock," in *Kafka Problem*, ed. Flores, 301.

CHAPTER 3. LITERARY ANIMALS

1. Paul Shepard, *The Others: How Animals Made Us Human* (Washington: Island Press, 1966), 90, 91.
2. Warren, *History of the Ojibway Nation*, 34, 47, 88.
3. Elias Canetti, *The Agony of Flies*, trans. H. F. Broch de Rothermann (New York: Farrar, Straus & Giroux, 1994), 47, 95. Originally published as *Die Fliegenpein* (1992).
4. Warren, *History of the Ojibway Nation*, 368, 373. See also Gerald Vizenor, *Interior Landscapes: Autobiographical Myths and Metaphors* (Minneapolis: Univ. of Minnesota Press, 1990), 4, 5, 6. The Long Knife is a name for the Americans. The name is a translation of *gichimookomaan* (*gichi*, big or great, and *mookomaan*, knife) a descriptive metaphor of the first contact with white men who carried swords.
5. Bakhtin, *Dialogic Imagination*, 237.
6. Claude Lévi-Strauss, *Totemism* (Boston: Beacon, 1963), 1, 3, 10.
7. Warren, *History of the Ojibway Nation*, 43, 44.
8. Lévi-Strauss, *Totemism*, 19, 20.
9. George Lakoff and Mark Johnson, *Metaphors We Live By* (Chicago: Univ. of Chicago Press, 1980), 3, 193, 229, 235.

10. Samuel R. Levin, *Metaphoric Worlds* (New Haven: Yale Univ. Press, 1988), 4, 5, 6.

11. Louis Owens, *Wolfsong* (Albuquerque: West End Press, 1991; reprint, Norman: Univ. of Oklahoma Press, 1994), 7 (page citations are to the reprint edition).

12. Darryl Lyman, *The Animal Things We Say* (Middle Village NY: Jonathan David Publishers, 1983), 59, 61, 63, 65, 66.

13. James Serpell, *In the Company of Animals* (Oxford: Basil Blackwell, 1986; reprint, New York: Cambridge Univ. Press, 1996), 66, 72 (page citations are to the reprint edition). See also René Girard, *Things Hidden Since the Foundation of the World* (Stanford: Stanford Univ. Press, 1987), 69.

14. Shepard, *The Others*, 64.

15. James Rachels, *Created from Animals: The Moral Implications of Darwinism* (New York: Oxford Univ. Press, 1990), 156, 164, 166, 170, 171. Darwinism would abandon "the idea of human dignity" for some other ethic. "The idea of human dignity is the moral doctrine which says that humans and other animals are in different moral categories; that the lives and interests of human beings are of supreme moral importance, while the lives and interests of other animals are relatively unimportant." This idea has been used to categorize natives as primitive, in the perverse myth of savagism and civilization, because natives were described as closer to animals than to the "human nature" of monotheistic creation. That natives created totems, and told stories of animal consciousness, confirmed the absence of a "moral doctrine" in the image of the God.

16. Shepard, *The Others*, 88.

17. John Stodart Kennedy, *The New Anthropomorphism* (New York: Cambridge Univ. Press, 1992), 9.

18. William James, "Psychology: Briefer Course," in *William James* (New York: Library of America, 1992), 432.

19. Kennedy, *New Anthropomorphism*, 15.

20. Kennedy, *New Anthropomorphism*, 24.

21. Jeffrey Moussaieff Masson and Susan McCarthy, *When Elephants Weep: The Emotional Lives of Animals* (New York: Delacorte, 1995), xiii, xxii, 219.

22. Kennedy, *New Anthropomorphism*, 158, 159.

23. Roland Barthes, *Writing Degree Zero* (New York: Hill & Wang, 1968), 10.

24. Louis Owens, *Bone Game* (Norman: Univ. of Oklahoma Press, 1994), 147. See also Louis Owens, "The Last Stand," in *Native American Literature*, ed. Gerald Vizenor (New York: HarperCollins, 1995), 190.

25. Jack London, *The Call of the Wild*, in *Jack London* (New York: Library of America, 1982), 1, 7, 55.

26. Jack London, "The Law of Life," in *Jack London*, 367.

27. Jacqueline Tavernier-Courbin, *The Call of the Wild: A Naturalist Romance* (New York: Twayne, 1994), 74, 79.

28. Mary Allen, *Animals in American Literature* (Urbana: Univ. of Illinois Press, 1983), 78, 79.

29. Margaret Marshall Saunders, *Beautiful Joe: An Autobiography* (1893; reprint, Bedford MA: Applewood Books, 1994), 7, 13, 14, 15, 304. This was the Canadian writer's first novel. *Beautiful Joe* was compared, as the ultimate anthropomorphic moral animal story, to *Black Beauty*.

30. George Lakoff, *Women, Fire, and Dangerous Things* (Chicago: Univ. of Chicago Press, 1987), 368, 586.

31. Paul Shepard, *The Tender Carnivore and the Sacred Game* (New York: Charles Scribner's Sons, 1973), 150, 154.

32. Erich Fromm, *The Anatomy of Human Destructiveness* (New York: Holt, Rinehart & Winston, 1973), 132, 133, 136.

33. Paul Shepard, *Thinking Animals: Animals and the Development of Human Intelligence* (New York: Viking, 1978), 256, 260.

34. Allen, *Animals in American Literature*, 5, 6, 7, 12, 19, 33, 34.

35. Jace Weaver, ed., *Defending Mother Earth* (Maryknoll NY: Orbis, 1996), xii, 162. Means wrote the foreword to this collection of essays.

36. N. Scott Momaday, *The Names: A Memoir* (New York: Harper & Row, 1976), 3.

37. Joseph Klaits and Barrie Klaits, *Animals and Man in Historical Perspective* (New York: Harper & Row, 1974), 1.

38. Aristotle, *Rhetoric*, vol. 2 of *The Complete Works of Aristotle*, ed. Jonathan Barnes (Princeton: Princeton Univ. Press, 1984), 1404b32–34, 1405a8- 13.

39. Frank Lentricchia and Thomas McLaughlin, ed., *Critical Terms of Literary Study* (Chicago: Univ. of Chicago Press, 1990), 83, 84.

40. John Searle, "Metaphor," in *Metaphor and Thought*, ed. Andrew Ortony (New York: Cambridge Univ. Press, 1979), 93, 105, 123. "The question, 'How do metaphors work?' is a bit like the question, 'How does one thing remind us of another thing?' There is no single answer to either question, though similarity obviously plays a major role in answering both. Two important differences between them are that metaphors are both restricted and systematic; restricted in the sense that not every way that one thing can remind us of something else will provide a basis for metaphor, and systematic in the sense that metaphors must be communicable from speaker to hearer in virtue of a shared system of principles."

41. Philip Wheelwright, *Metaphor and Reality* (Bloomington: Indiana Univ. Press, 1962), 70, 148.

42. Donald Davidson, "What Metaphors Mean," in *On Metaphor*, ed. Sheldon Sacks (Chicago: Univ. of Chicago Press, 1978), 32, 33.

43. Robert Rogers, *Metaphor: A Psychoanalytic View* (Berkeley: Univ. of California Press, 1978), 7.

44. Janet Martin Soskice, *Metaphor and Religious Language* (Oxford: Clarendon, 1985), 15, 58, 59, 60.

45. Lakoff and Johnson, *Metaphors We Live By*, 3, 4. "Primarily on the basis of linguistic evidence, we have found that most of our ordinary conceptual system is metaphorical in nature."

46. N. Scott Momaday, *The Ancient Child* (New York: Doubleday, 1989), 17. See also Louis Owens, *Other Destinies* (Norman: Univ. of Oklahoma Press, 1992), 93.

47. Paul Shepard and Barry Sanders, *The Sacred Paw: The Bear in Nature, Myth, and Literature* (New York: Viking Penguin, 1985), 130.

48. Momaday, *Ancient Child*, 303, 304.

49. Charles Woodard, *Ancestral Voices: Conversations with N. Scott Momaday* (Lincoln: Univ. of Nebraska Press, 1989), 17.

50. N. Scott Momaday, *House Made of Dawn* (New York: Harper & Row, 1968), 31, 32, 33, 64.

51. Susan Scarberry-Garcia, *Landmarks of Healing* (Albuquerque: Univ. of New Mexico Press, 1990), 52.

52. Woodard, *Ancestral Voices*, 22.

53. Oswald Ducrot and Tzvetan Todorov, *Encyclopedic Dictionary of the Sciences of Language* (Baltimore: Johns Hopkins Univ. Press, 1979), 261, 263.

54. Leslie Silko, *Ceremony* (New York: Viking Penguin, 1977), 132, 133.

55. Owens, *Other Destinies*, 184.

56. Silko, *Ceremony*, 195, 196.

57. Louise Erdrich, *Tracks* (New York: Harper & Row, 1988), 10, 37, 54, 60, 89, 168.

58. Erdrich, *Tracks*, 35, 40, 139.

59. Erdrich, *Tracks*, 18.

60. Owens, *Bone Game*, 96.

61. Louis Owens, *The Sharpest Sight* (Norman: Univ. of Oklahoma Press, 1992), 12.

62. Gordon Henry Jr., *The Light People* (Norman: Univ. of Oklahoma Press, 1994), 170, 171.

63. Georges Bataille, "The Object of Desire," in *The Accursed Share*, (New York: Zone, 1991), 2:137, 138.

CHAPTER 4. FUGITIVE POSES

1. George Steiner, *In Bluebeard's Castle* (New Haven: Yale Univ. Press, 1971), 3. "The echoes by which a society seeks to determine the reach, the logic and authority of its own voice, come from the rear. Evidently, the mechanisms at work are complex and rooted in diffuse but vital needs of continuity."

2. W. J. T. Mitchell, *Picture Theory* (Chicago: Univ. of Chicago Press, 1994), 13, 14.

3. Roland Barthes, *Image-Music-Text* (New York: Hill & Wang, 1977), 38, 39.

4. Baudrillard, *Simulations*, 2, 5, 130. "Simulation is no longer that of a territory, a referential being or a substance. It is the generation by models of a real without origin or reality. . . . To dissimulate is to feign not to have what one has. To simulate is to feign to have what one hasn't. One implies a presence, the other an absence." See also Paul Roth, "Ethnography without Tears," *Current Anthropology* 30, no. 5 (Dec. 1989): 556; Arthur Kroker, *The Possessed Individual* (New York: St. Martin's, 1992), 134.

5. William Mitchell, "When Is Seeing Believing?" *Scientific American* (Feb. 1994): 68–73.

6. Janet Maslin, "Tom Hanks as an Innocent Interloper in History," film review of *Forrest Gump*, *New York Times*, July 6, 1994.

7. Elizabeth Edwards, ed., *Anthropology and Photography 1860–1920* (New Haven: Yale Univ. Press, 1992), 8, 11, 12.

8. Gans, *Originary Thinking*, 212, 213. "Postmodernism," he points out, "may well be the era of simulation, but it is no accident that it has been so far an era dominated by theory rather than esthetic practice."

9. Baudrillard, "Simulacra and Simulations," in *Jean Baudrillard*, ed. Poster, 170, 171.

10. Mark Rosen, introduction, *Jean Baudrillard*, ed. Poster, 1, 8.

11. Jack Goody, *The Domestication of the Savage Mind* (New York: Cambridge Univ. Press, 1977), 37, 150.

12. Anthony Grafton, *New Worlds, Ancient Texts* (Cambridge: Harvard Univ. Press, 1992), 108.

13. Grafton, *New Worlds*, 108, 111. Grafton points out that "Staden's primary goal is to tell a traditional Christian moralizing tale both to edify and to inspire devotion." How ironic that a monotheistic moral tale becomes the interimage simulation of savagism.

14. William C. Sturtevant, "First Visual Images of Native America," in *First Images of America*, ed. Fredi Chiappelli (Berkeley: Univ. of California Press, 1976), 419, 420, 433.

15. Grafton, *New Worlds*, 126, 130. De Bry's illustrations based on the watercolors of John White "cleverly combines ethnographic detail about the native Virginians' way of life with details of New World flora and fauna, and attempts to provide detailed and accurate images of non-European life." De Bry was a Flemish goldsmith and engraver who established a printing house in Frankfurt am Main.

16. Grafton, *New Worlds*, 129.

17. Paul Hulton, "Images of the New World: Jacques Le Moyne de Morgues and John White," in *The Westward Enterprise*, ed. K. R. Andrews, N. P. Canny, and P. E. H. Hair (Detroit: Wayne State Univ. Press, 1979), 175.

18. Hulton, *Westward Enterprise*, 197.

19. Hulton, *Westward Enterprise*, 198.

20. Hulton, *Westward Enterprise*, 210.

21. William Cronon, "Telling Tales on Canvas: *Landscapes of Frontier Change*,"

in *Discovered Lands, Invented Pasts*, by the Yale University Art Gallery (New Haven: Yale Univ. Press, 1992), 44.

22. Iskander Mydin, "Historical Images—Changing Audiences," in *Anthropology and Photography, 1860–1920*, ed. Elizabeth Edwards (New Haven: Yale Univ. Press, 1992), 74; and Christopher Pinney, "The Parallel Histories of Anthropology and Photography," in *Anthropology and Photography*, ed. Edwards, 249.

23. Vizenor, *Manifest Manners*, 4, 5, 6, 17. "Manifest manners are the simulations of dominance; the notions and misnomers that are read as the authentic and sustained as representations of Native American Indians."

24. Patrick Smith, *Warhol: Conversations about the Artist* (Ann Arbor: UMI Research Press, 1988), 359.

25. Joan Halifax, *The Fruitful Darkness* (New York: HarperCollins, 1993), 26, 27.

26. Halifax, *Fruitful Darkness*, 98, 99.

27. Halifax, *Fruitful Darkness*, 187, 188.

28. Pierre Bourdieu, *Photography: A Middle-brow Art* (Stanford: Stanford Univ. Press, 1990), 71, 72.

29. Lowe, *History of Bourgeois Perception*, 39, 135.

30. Roland Barthes, *Camera Lucida* (New York: Hill & Wang, 1981), 6, 12, 13.

31. David Freedberg, *The Power of Images* (Chicago: Univ. of Chicago Press, 1989), 438, 439.

32. Linda Hutcheon, *The Politics of Postmodernism* (New York: Routledge, 1989), 123.

33. Roland Barthes, *Image—Music—Text* (New York: Hill & Wang, 1977), 17.

34. John Tagg, *The Burden of Representation* (Amherst: Univ. of Massachusetts Press, 1988), 63, 64.

35. Serres, "Panotic Theory," 27, 30, 31.

36. Gans, *Originary Thinking*, 46.

37. Susan Sontag, *On Photography* (New York: Farrar, Straus & Giroux, 1973), 14, 15, 97.

38. Jean-Luc Nancy, *The Birth to Presence* (Stanford: Stanford Univ. Press, 1993), 1, 2.

39. John Berger, *About Looking* (New York: Pantheon, 1980), 50, 51.

40. Nancy, *Birth to Presence*, 191, 192, 196.

41. Barthes, *Camera Lucida*, 6, 87.

42. Rennard Strickland, *The Indians of Oklahoma* (Norman: Univ. of Oklahoma Press, 1980), 46, 47.

43. Christopher Lyman, *The Vanishing Race and Other Illusions* (New York: Pantheon, Smithsonian Institution Press, 1982), 19, 20, 21. "Just as it was difficult for Curtis to see Indians for what they were through the veil of his culture at the time, so is it difficult for us to see him and his work for what *they* were through the bias of our time."

44. Mick Gidley, "Edward S. Curtis' Indian Photographs: A National

Enterprise," in *Representing Others*, ed. Mick Gidley (Exeter UK: Univ. of Exeter Press, 1994), 103, 104.

45. Herman Viola, *The Indian Legacy of Charles Bird King* (New York: Doubleday, Smithsonian Institution Press, 1976), 13.

46. Andrew J. Cosentino, *The Paintings of Charles Bird King* (Washington: Smithsonian Institution Press, National Collection of Fine Arts, 1977), 71, 74, 75. Cosentino points out that even "the untrained eye can see, for example, that many of King's Indian portraits have features that are markedly Caucasoid. This may largely be explained by the fact that many of the delegates he painted were of mixed blood, as well as by the artist's tendency to soften and round his forms." King rounded his *indians* too much into a homogeneous interimage ethnicity. Moreover, the *indian* delegates who posed for the artist were as unique in their countenance as any other human subject in his studio. King was painting *indian* portraits for the government, and the time given to fugitive poses in his studio was limited. The author seems to suggest that *indians* are a pure race, and the end of the pure *indian* is intermarriage. King, in fact, created the pure *indian*, the rounded homogeneous *indian* in his lazy portraits, as interimage simulations.

47. William Cronon, "Telling Tales on Canvas," 53, 55, 56.

48. John Napier, *Hands* (Princeton: Princeton Univ. Press, 1980; rev. ed., 1993), ed. Russell H. Tuttle, 4, 8.

49. Robert Brilliant, *Portraiture* (Cambridge: Harvard Univ. Press, 1991), 106, 107.

50. Sontag, *On Photography*, 64.

51. Dorothy and Thomas Hoobler, *Photographing the Frontier* (New York: G. P. Putnam's Sons, 1980), 117.

52. Julie Inness, *Privacy, Intimacy, and Isolation* (New York: Oxford Univ. Press, 1992), 7, 42.

53. Bakhtin, *Art and Answerability*, 126.

54. Bakhtin, *Speech Genres*, 146, 147.

55. Gisèle Freund, *Photography and Society* (Boston: David R. Godine, 1980), 4, 35, 78.

CHAPTER 5. NATIVE TRANSMOTION

1. Francis Paul Prucha, *American Indian Treaties* (Berkeley: Univ. of California Press, 1994), 196, 197.

2. Gerald Vizenor, "Ojibways Seek Right to 'Regulate' Rice on Wildlife Refuge," *Minneapolis Tribune*, Sept. 13, 1968.

3. Prucha, *American Indian Treaties*, 385, 387. "The result was a series of decisions about land claims, tribal sovereignty and jurisdiction, and hunting and fishing rights that greatly benefited Indian tribes and helped

tremendously to reestablish and revitalize Indian reservation communities. It should not be assumed, however, that all this was accomplished without controversy or that the treaty provisions were so 'clear and plain' that unanimity in the courts came as a matter of course."

4. Louis Owens, "Mapping, Naming, and the Power of Words" (paper presented at "The Art of the Wild," an environmental writing conference, Squaw Valley Community of Writers, Squaw Valley CA, July 1995).

5. Henry R. Schoolcraft, *Archives of Aboriginal Knowledge*, (Philadelphia: J. B. Lippincott, 1860), 1:333, 334. See also Bieder, *Science Encounters the Indian*. Schoolcraft, in the early years of his service, was romantic about natives, but later, compared to other "scientific" observers of his time, he viewed natives as "children" who had lost their "native energy," and considered race as inherited and a cultural category.

6. Frances Densmore, *Chippewa Music* (Minneapolis: Ross & Haines, 1973), iv, 4, 15, 107, 108.

7. Densmore, *Chippewa Music*, 24.

8. Frances Densmore, *Chippewa Customs* (Minneapolis: Ross & Haines, 1970), 174, 175.

9. Densmore, *Chippewa Customs*, 177.

10. Warren, *History of the Ojibway Nation*, 373.

11. Richard Kearney, *The Wake of Imagination* (Minneapolis: Univ. of Minnesota Press, 1988), 2, 3. "The contemporary eye is no longer innocent. What we see is almost invariably informed by prefabricated images. There is, of course, a fundamental difference between the image of today and former times: now the image *precedes* the reality it is supposed to represent."

12. Francis Paul Prucha, *Documents of United States Indian Policy* (Lincoln: Univ. of Nebraska Press, 1990), 171, 173.

13. Charles F. Wilkinson, *The Eagle Bird: Mapping a New West* (New York: Pantheon, 1992), 30.

14. Norman J. W. Thrower, *Maps and Civilization* (Chicago: Univ. of Chicago Press, 1996), 137, 138. The United States Public Land Survey "has been characterized as 'the triumph of geometry over geography.'"

15. Vizenor, *Interior Landscapes*, 16, 54. The allotment document is recorded in the General Land Office of the United States, vol. 776, p. 240. My son, Robert Vizenor, and I located the actual land issued in a patent to Alice Beaulieu on the reservation. However, the task was not easy; first we obtained several county and township survey maps, and then by car measured the distance on rural section line roads. Finally, on foot we located the original allotment. My grandmother had never seen the actual land; she would have been amused, because the area of her patent was muskeg and therefore of no value to a lumber company. My grandmother and the company that leased the land had two things in common: an

agreement of an annual fee to lease the allotment for the timber, and neither my grandmother nor the company ever saw the land.

16. Thrower, *Maps and Civilization*, 45.

17. Schoolcraft, *Archives of Aboriginal Knowledge*, 415, 416, 417.

18. Nichols and Nyholm, *A Concise Dictionary of Minnesota Ojibwe*. The word *oshkaabewis* is an animate noun; the plural is *oshkaabewisag*. Baraga, in *A Dictionary of the Otchipwe Language*, listed *oshkabewiss* as a "waiter or attendant to an Indian Chief." Seth Eastman produced illustrations for the manuscripts of Henry Rowe Schoolcraft. The connection between the totemic crane in the document and the actual *oshkaabewis* is not certain.

19. Warren, *History of the Ojibway Nation*, 318.

20. Helen Tanner, *Atlas of Great Lakes Indian History* (Norman: Univ. of Oklahoma Press, 1987), 98, 144. "The maps in the Atlas emphasize the location of Indian villages at significant dates in the history of the Great Lakes Region."

21. Schoolcraft, *Archives of Aboriginal Knowledge*, 340.

22. David Turnbull, *Maps Are Territories* (Chicago: Univ. of Chicago Press, 1989), 18, 19, 20, 26. See also Thrower, *Maps and Civilization*; Harald E. L. Prins, "Children of Gluskap: Wabanaki Indians on the Eve of the European Invasion," in *American Beginnings: Exploration, Culture, and Cartography in the Land of Norumbega*, ed. Emerson Baker et al. (Lincoln: Univ. of Nebraska Press, 1994), 95–117. For instance, "Non Chi Ning Ga's Missouri map is an American Indian map which differs from a modern map of the same area only in the details." This shows that "so-called 'primitive' maps are in fact comparable with modern Western maps in many respects."

23. Joyce M. Szabo, *Howling Wolf and the History of Ledger Art* (Albuquerque: Univ. of New Mexico Press, 1994), 23, 119.

24. Szabo, *Howling Wolf*, 21, 31, 32, 42, 168.

25. Frederick Hartt, *Art: A History of Painting, Sculpture, Architecture* (New York: Harry N. Abrams, 1976), 390, 391.

26. George Heard Hamilton, *Painting and Sculpture in Europe, 1880–1940* (New York: Penguin, 1987), 215, 216. See also Sam Hunter and John Jacobus, *Modern Art*, 3d ed. (New York: Harry N. Abrams, 1992), 120, 121.

27. Armin Zweite, *The Blue Rider in the Lenbachhaus, Munich* (Munich: Prestel-Verlag, 1989), 38, 39, 40, 61.

28. George Horse Capture, "From Museums to Indians: Native American Art in Context," in *Robes of Splendor: Native North American Painted Buffalo Hides*, Musée de l'Homme (New York: New Press, 1993), 45, 65, 67. Originally published as *Parures d'histoire*, Réunion des musée nationaux (Paris, 1993).

29. Dorothy V. Jones, *License for Empire: Colonialism by Treaty in Early America* (Chicago: Univ. of Chicago Press, 1982), xii.

30. Michael J. Kaplan, "Issues in Land Claims," in *Irredeemable America: The Indians' Estate and Land Claims*, ed. Imre Sutton (Albuquerque: Univ.

of New Mexico Press, 1985), 71, 72, 76, 82. United States courts "have recognized that certain rights flow from occupancy and use of the land for a long time, and that they flow to the occupants. They have also acknowledged that these rights may be established either by proof of actual occupancy and use or by demonstrating that the government has, at some point in the past, conceded the requisites." That "right of occupancy," however, "can be hollow. It is a right granted by the conqueror . . . and consists mainly of a right that flows in the wrong direction," writes Kaplan. "Aboriginal title may be extinguished at will by the sovereign. Such title has been viewed as permissive, temporary, and withdrawable by the government at any time."

31. David J. Elkins, *Beyond Sovereignty: Territory and Political Economy in the Twenty-First Century* (Toronto: Univ. of Toronto Press, 1995), 101, 197, 256.

32. Max Oelschlaeger, *The Idea of Wilderness* (New Haven: Yale Univ. Press, 1991), 30, 31, 32, 33.

33. William Cronon, *Changes in the Land: Indians, Colonists, and the Ecology of New England* (New York: Hill & Wang, 1983), 37, 53, 169. English colonists practiced "Indian hunting and gathering as a justification for expropriating Indian land. To European eyes, Indians appeared to squander the resources that were available to them," writes Cronon. "Colonists thus rationalized their conquest of New England: by refusing to extend the rights of property to the Indians, they both trivialized the ecology of Indian life and paved the way for destroying it."

34. N. Scott Momaday, *The Way to Rainy Mountain* (Albuquerque: Univ. of New Mexico Press, 1969), 7.

35. Momaday, *The Names*, 3.

36. Richard Slobodin, "The Study of Reincarnation in Indigenous American Cultures: Some Comments," in *Amerindian Rebirth: Reincarnation Belief Among North American Indians and Inuit*, ed. Antonia Mills and Richard Slobodin (Toronto: Univ. of Toronto Press, 1994), 293, 294.

37. Maurice Cranston, *The Noble Savage: Jean-Jacques Rousseau, 1754–1762* (Chicago: Univ. of Chicago Press, 1991), 308.

38. Judith Shklar, *Men and Citizens: A Study of Rousseau's Social Theory* (New York: Cambridge Univ. Press, 1985), 43, 168.

39. Aristotle, *Politics*, vol. 2 of *The Complete Works of Aristotle*, ed. Jonathan Barnes (Princeton: Princeton Univ. Press, 1984), 1263a37–38, 1279a28–31.

40. Warren, *History of the Ojibway Nation*, 72, 73.

41. F. H. Hinsley, *Sovereignty* (New York: Cambridge Univ. Press, 1986), 2, 16, 122, 123, 124, 125.

42. Jens Bartelson, *A Genealogy of Sovereignty* (New York: Cambridge Univ. Press, 1995), 141, 239.

43. Michael Ross Fowler and Julie Marie Bunck, *Law, Power, and the Sovereign*

State (University Park: Pennsylvania State Univ. Press, 1995), 64, 70, 140, 152.

44. Prucha, *American Indian Treaties*, 2.

45. Wilkinson, *The Eagle Bird*, 39.

46. Prucha, *Documents of United States Indian Policy*, 202.

47. Prucha, *American Indian Treaties*, 356, 357.

48. Prucha, *American Indian Treaties*, 2, 197.

49. Gidon Gottlieb, *Nation against State: A New Approach to Ethnic Conflict and the Decline of Sovereignty* (New York: Council on Foreign Relations Press, 1993), 34, 36, 37, 38.

50. Alan Dowty, *Closed Borders* (New Haven: Yale Univ. Press, 1987), 230. "Free emigration cuts to the heart of American concerns in the world. Throughout its history, the United States has defended the rights of the individual against the claims of the state. Few issues frame this concern so well as the right of free movement."

51. David Jacobson, *Rights across Borders: Immigration and the Decline of Citizenship* (Baltimore: Johns Hopkins Univ. Press, 1996), 76.

52. Fernando R. Tesón, "Changing Perceptions of Domestic Jurisdiction and Intervention," in *Beyond Sovereignty*, ed. Tom Farer (Baltimore: Johns Hopkins Univ. Press, 1996), 29, 51.

53. American Indian Lawyer Training Program, *Indian Tribes as Sovereign Governments* (Oakland CA: American Indian Resources Institute, 1988), 106.

54. Noah Webster, "A Citizen of America," Oct. 17, 1787, in part 1 of *The Debate of the Constitution*, ed. Bernard Bailyn (New York: Library of America, 1993), 145, 146.

55. Samuel H. Beer, *To Make a Nation: The Rediscovery of American Federalism* (Cambridge: Harvard Univ. Press, 1993), 251, 253.

56. Benjamin Franklin, "I Agree to This Constitution with All Its Faults," Speech at the Conclusion of the Constitutional Convention, Sept. 17, 1787, in part 1 of *Debate of the Constitution*, ed. Bailyn, 3, 4.

57. Prucha, *American Indian Treaties*, 26, 27, 37, 38.

58. James Madison, *The Federalist XLII*, in part 2 of *Debate of the Constitution*, ed. Bailyn, 67, 68.

59. Prucha, *American Indian Treaties*, 69.

60. James Madison, in part 2 of *Debate of the Constitution*, ed. Bailyn, 449.

61. Bradford Perkins, "The Creation of a Republican Empire, 1776–1865," in vol. 1 of *The Cambridge History of American Foreign Relations* (New York: Cambridge Univ. Press, 1993), 142, 143, 144, 145.

62. Jones, *License for Empire*, 147.

63. American Indian Lawyer Training Program, *Indian Tribes as Sovereign Governments*, 4, 35.

64. American Indian Lawyer Training Program, *Indian Tribes as Sovereign Governments*, 109, 110.

65. Robert Burt, *The Constitution in Conflict* (Cambridge: Harvard Univ. Press, 1992), 159, 160. "Prior presidents believed that they lacked practical capacity effectively to protect Indian tribal integrity against state-sponsored incursions and overlooked the possibility that a determined invocation of federal armed force might have helped to vindicate federal treaty obligations." Burt asserts that "Jackson rejected *Worcester* on the basis of principle, not pragmatism."

66. Linda Greenhouse, "Justices Curb Federal Power to Subject States of Lawsuits," *New York Times*, March 28, 1996.

67. Edward S. Corwin, *The Constitution*, 14th ed., revised by Harold W. Chase and Craig R. Ducat (Princeton: Princeton Univ. Press, 1978), 86.

68. Prucha, *Documents of United States Indian Policy*, 218.

69. Corwin, *The Constitution*, 1.

Index

Index

Index

Index

Index

Index

Index

Index

In the Abraham Lincoln Lecture Series

Sander L. Gilman
*Smart Jews: The Construction of the Image of Jewish
Superior Intelligence*

Gerald Vizenor
*Fugitive Poses: Native American Indian Scenes
of Absence and Presence*